Upon This Rock

Upon This Rock

*The Nature of Doctrine from
Antifoundationalist Perspective*

ROBERT L. FOSSETT

With a foreword by Joel P. Okamoto

☙PICKWICK *Publications* · Eugene, Oregon

UPON THIS ROCK
The Nature of Doctrine From Antifoundationalist Perspective

Copyright © 2013 Robert L. Fossett. All rights reserved. Except for brief quotations in critical publications or reviews, no part of this book may be reproduced in any manner without prior written permission from the publisher. Write: Permissions, Wipf and Stock Publishers, 199 W. 8th Ave., Suite 3, Eugene, OR 97401.

Pickwick Publications
An Imprint of Wipf and Stock Publishers
199 W. 8th Ave., Suite 3
Eugene, OR 97401

www.wipfandstock.com

ISBN 13: 978-1-61097-935-1

Cataloguing-in-Publication data:

Fossett, Robert L.

Upon this rock : the nature of doctrine from antifoundationalist perspective / Robert L. Fossett ; with a foreword by Joel P. Okamoto.

xvi + 184 pp. ; 23 cm. Includes bibliographical references and index.

ISBN 13: 978-1-61097-935-1

1. Postliberal theology. 2. Theology, Doctrinal. 3. Philosophical theology. 4. Truth—Religious aspects—Christianity. I. Okamoto, Joel P. II. Title.

BT75.3 .F67 2013

Manufactured in the U.S.A.

For Meg, Sawyer, Max, and Henry

Now when Jesus came into the district of Caesarea Philippi, he asked his disciples, "Who do people say that the Son of Man is?" And they said, "Some say John the Baptist, others say Elijah, and others Jeremiah or one of the prophets." He said to them, "But who do you say that I am?" Simon Peter replied, "You are the Christ, the Son of the living God." And Jesus answered him, "Blessed are you, Simon Bar-Jonah! For flesh and blood has not revealed this to you, but my Father who is in heaven.

MATTHEW 16:13–17

Contents

Foreword by Joel P. Okamoto   *ix*
Acknowledgments   *xiii*
Abbreviations   *xv*

   Introduction: The Modern Discussion on Doctrine   1
1   Foundationalism: What Is It and Where Did it Come From?   17
2   The Problem of Theory and Modern Accounts of Doctrine   41
3   The Authority of Scripture for Christian Doctrine   83
4   The Church and Her Doctrine   115
5   The Problem of Relativism and Other Lingering Questions   149

Bibliography   175
Index   181

Foreword

This book is abstract. It deals primarily with accounts of the nature and function of Christian doctrine, not with particular Christian teachings. This book is involved. It includes both a subtle critical analysis and a detailed constructive suggestion. This book is wide-ranging. It reaches into anti-formalism in literary criticism and anti-representationalism in philosophy to articulate a typology for and criticism of contemporary accounts of doctrine, and it brings together views and insights from the ancient church, the Reformation, modern philosophy, and recent thinking on the Trinity and the Word of God to develop and substantiate its own account of Christian doctrine.

But for all these things, this book is also quite simple. For all the places he goes and for all the sources he reaches, the author, Rob Fossett, has a simple objective: to show that Christian doctrine is properly and clearly understood as a thoroughly Christian work—made by Christians for Christians in faithful service to Christ the Lord.

In this way, Fossett is at odds with the theme and approach of George Lindbeck's *The Nature of Doctrine*, the most influential contemporary account of Christian doctrine. Of his own book, Lindbeck said: "The theory of religion and religious doctrine that it proposes is not specifically ecumenical, nor Christian, nor theological" (George A. Lindbeck, *The Nature of Doctrine: Religion and Theology in a Postliberal Age* [Philadelphia: Westminster, 1984] 7.) Lindbeck's account of doctrine came out of his long experience in ecumenical discussions. This experience showed him that usual accounts of doctrine were inadequate to understanding what was actually going on, and he sought an account that would be adequate. But he approached the task of developing a theory of religion and doctrine with the assumption that it "cannot be ecumenically useful unless it is nonecumenically plausible" (ibid., 8). Fossett, however, argues that not only the contents but also the nature and uses of Christian doctrine can be understood as grounded in a very particular conviction: Jesus is Lord. For him the hymn captures perfectly the sense: "The Church's One Foundation is Jesus Christ her Lord."

This hymn, moreover, alludes to the most important difference between him and Lindbeck and also Kevin Vanhoozer and Anthony Thiselton, with whose proposals on doctrine Fossett also deals. This difference lies in the ways they engage so-called "foundationalism," which is the project that seeks to guarantee our knowledge, meaning, and truth on "foundations" or grounds that are indisputable. "Foundationalism" does not refer to any reliance on a foundation, but to reliance on a special kind of foundation— one that guarantees "objectivity" or "neutrality." Lindbeck, Vanhoozer, and Thiselton acknowledge that foundationalism is a central problem for theology, including the conception of doctrine. They deal with this problem in significantly different ways (these differences explain Fossett's choice of these writers), but each makes a turn to "theory."

"Theory" in this case is a term adopted from Stanley Fish for "a 'method,' a recipe with premeasured ingredients which when ordered and combined according to absolutely explicit instructions . . . will *produce*, all by itself, the correct result" (Stanley Fish, "Anti-Foundationalism, Theory Hope, and the Teaching of Composition," in *Doing What Comes Naturally: Change, Rhetoric, and the Practice of Theory in Literary and Legal Studies* [Durham, NC: Duke University Press, 1989] 343). Theory is more than some generalizations or "rules of thumb" distilled from careful study, backed up by good results, and consistent with other concerns, interests, and positions. Theory is some kind of algorithm.

The attraction of theory for understanding the nature and function of doctrine is the same as for literary studies: it promises a way to ascertain "meaning" and "direction" that may claim to be "objective" or "neutral," and for this reason call for universal agreement. To be sure, this may work "in reverse" or "negatively": a theory may formally rule out objectivity or neutrality and therefore may promote relativism. For example, Lindbeck's rule theory of doctrine is a theory of this negative sort, formally ruling out an abiding "first-order" use. This gives him hope for agreement in doctrine without giving up on a formulation. (Vanhoozer makes a turn toward theory in the way he argues for the authority of the Scriptural canon, and Thiselton in the way he argues for the use of general hermeneutics.) But in any case, the promise of theory lies in objectivity and neutrality.

Fossett recognizes Fish (and others like Steven Knapp and Walter Benn Michaels) are right that relying on formal theory is confused. Theory

Foreword

in literary studies is not just impractical because one cannot gather data reliably enough. It is impossible, because such theories already depends on the particular and the local that they claim to transcend.

The same can be said about theory in studies about Christian doctrine. This is one reason Fossett calls for an "antifoundationalist" account of doctrine. This does not discredit everything Lindbeck, Vanhoozer, and Thiselton have done. Fossett himself appreciates much of their work and adopts some of it for his own work. But the way each depends on formal theory means that none of their accounts can be made to work with a patch or a replacement or an addition. Rebuilding is called for.

In Fossett's own account, we find that his attraction to antifoundationalism is theological. We see that he is not so much *against* foundationalism, *against* theory, or *against* hermeneutics as he is *for* confessing Jesus as Lord and in reflecting this confession in our theology. Accordingly, his own account of doctrine depends on Christological accounts of the Scriptures and the Church.

Indeed, Christology explains his interest in antifoundationalism. An antifoundationalist account of anything is one that recognizes that its foundations are debatable, open to challenge and rejection. Openness to challenge and rejection also characterize a Christological account of anything, including the Scriptures, the Church, and doctrine, because Jesus Christ himself was rejected and crucified. It stands only because God raised Jesus from the dead. A good deal of contemporary theology does not follow through on this conviction, and this fact explains a lot of the modern appeal of foundationalism among Christians. They should know better. At any rate, Rob Fossett does, and, more than anything else, this explains the consistency and persuasiveness of his account of Christian doctrine.

Joel P. Okamoto

Acknowledgments

This book was originally my doctoral dissertation (though it has been edited to read a little better) and as with any work of a book-length magnitude, there are many people worthy of thanks. First, I would like to thank my parents, Lamar and Elizabeth Fossett, who have been active supporters of my life at every step. They raised me to love Jesus and they have not failed to continually show me their love and grace. For this, I will be forever grateful.

I would also like to thank my home congregation of First Presbyterian Church in Chattanooga, Tennessee. It is through the leadership and influence of the pastors and elders of this congregation that I endeavored to enter seminary in 1998. First Presbyterian Church has funded, in some measure, all of my graduate degrees and was the biggest single contributor to my campus ministry at St. Louis University in the beginning of my pastoral ministry. Would that all students be so blessed to have as generous a home church as First Presbyterian of Chattanooga.

Trinity Church of Kirkwood, Missouri (PCA), hired me with the full knowledge that I was somewhat early in the writing process of this work. I am deeply thankful for my pastor and older brother in the faith, the Rev. Chris Polski, and the men on the session of the church for allowing me the freedom and time away to work on this project, in particular over the last months leading up to its initial completion as a dissertation. Without Rev. Polski's patience and generous offer of study leave this project would still remain unfinished and I would be without a PhD.

I owe a great deal of thanks to many of the faculty at Concordia Seminary for their kindness and patience in teaching this dullard of a Presbyterian. I am grateful for Dr. Charles Arand and Dr. Timothy Saleska and their willingness to interact with this work and give helpful feedback. I am also very grateful for the numerous conversations with Dr. Kent Burreson over the years, in particular our talks on liturgical theology. No one professor

Acknowledgments

did more to make me feel welcome among the Lutheran community than Dr. Burreson.

I have had many great teachers throughout my life, but no one greater than Dr. Joel Okamoto. This work is a testament to his grace as all of the best ideas contained in this work are his. Dr. Okamoto is the rare teacher who parts with his best material so that his students will have something useful to say. What is good in this book is a testament to his teaching; what is worthy of the fire is a testament to my own skill. I will be forever grateful for Dr. Okamoto's sharp mind, insightful questions, and never ending patience with me. I count myself blessed to call him my teacher, friend and older brother in the faith.

Though I have put years into this project there is no one who has sacrificed more for it than my wife, Meg. Without her patience and willingness to take this path with me, this project would never have happened. While I have spent years discussing and writing about formal theology, my wife has lived and taught Jesus to our two boys, Sawyer and Maxwell and soon to be third child. In my view, her theological work has far out matched mine and I am the better for it.

Abbreviations

BC   *The Book of Concord: The Confessions of the Evangelical Lutheran Church.* Robert Kolb and Timothy J. Wengert, eds. Minneapolis: Fortress, 2000.

    Ap   Apology of the Augsburg Confession

    LC   Luther's Large Catechism

    FC   Formula of Concord

    SA   Smalcald Articles

    SD   Solid Declaration of the Formula of Concord

ESV   English Standard Version of the Holy Bible (all Biblical references are ESV)

WCF   *The Westminster Confession of Faith.* 3rd ed. Atlanta, GA: The Committee for Christian Education and Publication, 1990.

Introduction

The Modern Discussion on Doctrine

THE UNIQUE ROLE DOCTRINE PLAYS FOR THE CHURCH

Let's begin with an obvious question: what is doctrine? In the beginning of his monumental history of doctrine, Jaroslav Pelikan notes that the definition of doctrine has changed over time and is often easier to describe than to define. Nevertheless, he begins his work by saying this about doctrines: "What the church of Jesus Christ believes, teaches, and confesses on the basis of the word of God: this is Christian doctrine."[1] In their simplest forms, doctrines are the confessions, teachings, or attempts at articulating or reflecting upon Christian beliefs about the Triune God as presented in Scripture. But Pelikan's definition, while accurate as far as it goes, is too broad for the purposes of discussion. Part of the confusion—and therein the difficulty in defining doctrine—occurs because distinctions are not often made between particular types of religious claims, whether they be confessional, ethical/imperative, teachings, commentary, expositions, good ideas, or personal reflections.

Borrowing from William Christian,[2] Paul Griffiths identifies three basic types of religious claims. The first kind of claim is "a claim about the setting of human life," which is most often a description "about the environment in which we find ourselves and live our lives."[3] This kind of religious claim is an attempt to classify a particular part of a setting of human life or

---

1. Pelikan, *Emergence of the Catholic Tradition*, 1.
2. Christian, *Doctrines of Religious Communities*.
3. Griffiths, *Problems of Religious Diversity*, 21.

as in the case of Christianity, the *entire* setting of human life (e.g., all of creation as God's creation or a statement like "Jesus is Lord"). The second kind of religious claim attempts to classify or define the nature of humans (or particular sets of humans) as the inhabitants of a setting. An example might be classifying all of humanity as sinful or perhaps isolating one particular people as a chosen group (e.g., Israel of the Old Testament, the Church). The third kind of religious claim is a claim "about the proper conduct of human life [which] is typically put in the subjunctive or imperative mood, and requires, recommends, or suggests some pattern of action."[4] An example of this would be the Ten Commandments or the ethical imperatives of the book of James.

A religious claim however, is not necessarily a doctrine; it could simply be a teaching, a reflection or even a good idea. For example, take two different and popular Christian claims: "Jesus was raised from the dead on the third day" and "you should read your Bible everyday." The first claim is not merely a teaching about Scripture, but is bound up with the identity of Christianity. To reject the claim "Jesus was raised from the dead on the third day" is to reject a claim that is foundational for Christianity. The second claim, however, can be rejected by a Christian and that person can still be considered not only part of a particular Church, but a person in good standing—though others may disagree (and some vehemently so).

While some Christian teachings can be accepted or rejected, doctrine is categorically different because assent to it is required for membership in the community. As Pannenberg argues, doctrines have a *legally binding* quality to them because they function as the explicit identity markers and rules of the Church.[5] "We believe in *this* Jesus, not *that* one." Taken as a whole, doctrine is one of the chief ways the Church demarcates herself from every other social group and it is unique to her identity.[6] Again, an obvious question to be asked is a simple one: why? Why does doctrine play such a central role in articulating the Church's identity and determining her membership? Why not some ritual or a sacrifice to be performed or perhaps a chant to be recited or a vow spoken in front of witnesses?

In Matthew 16, after having miraculously fed thousands of people on two occasions, healed countless numbers of ailing people, walked on water, and battled the religious leaders of his day, Jesus steps back from

---

4. Ibid., 22.
5. Pannenberg, *Systematic Theology*, 1:10.
6. Lindbeck, *Nature of Doctrine*, 74.

The Modern Discussion on Doctrine

the multitudes following him and asks his disciples to assess the crowds. Jesus asks, "Who do they say that the Son of Man is?" The disciples answer, "Some say John the Baptist, others say Elijah, and others Jeremiah or one of the prophets." Jesus then puts the question directly to the disciples, "Who do you say that I am?" Peter speaking for the group answers, "You are the Christ, the Son of the Living God." Jesus' response to Peter's simple confession is staggering:

> Blessed are you, Simon Bar-Jonah! For flesh and blood has not revealed this to you, but my Father who is in heaven. And I tell you, you are Peter, and on this rock I will build my Church, and the gates of hell shall not prevail against it. I will give you the keys of the kingdom of heaven, and whatever you bind on earth shall be bound in heaven, and whatever you loose on earth shall be loosed in heaven.

Peter's confession is arguably the highest confession a Christian can make: Jesus is the Messiah, the Son of the Living God.

But still, we may ask, what does the confession mean? Many Jews in the first century had hoped for the coming of the long-promised Messiah and, as the crowds in Matthew's account demonstrate, many linked Jesus to Yahweh by calling him a prophet. But as Peter would soon learn, to confess Jesus as Lord, to confess him as the long-promised Messiah, is to confess him as the crucified and resurrected Son of God. It is this Jesus, the crucified Messiah—as later preached by this same Peter and the apostles and handed down through subsequent generations of the Church—that we must confess and not some other Messiah. The reason for this is that confessing Jesus to be the crucified and resurrected Son of God is an issue of life and death because we are pledging our lives—*we are binding ourselves to his rule and care*—to this Messiah and not some other. As Jesus' response to Peter shows, this confession is no small thing, and we best be getting it right.

Concern for confessing Jesus correctly is related closely to what Frances Young argues about the genesis of doctrine in the early centuries of Christianity. She points out that "Christianity is the only major religion to set such store by creeds and doctrines."[7] She continues, "Other religions have scriptures, others have their characteristic ways of worship, other have their own peculiar ethics and lifestyle; other religions also have philosophical, intellectual or mystical forms as well as more popular manifestations. But

---

7. Young, *Creeds*, 1.

except in response to Christianity, they have not developed creeds, statements of standard beliefs to which the orthodox are supposed to adhere."[8] When we compare Christianity with other religions we see similarities when it comes to having particular sacred rituals, explanatory narratives or myths about the world, saints or heroes that have shaped whatever culture or geography in which a particular religion finds its home. But unlike other groups that delineate their community by particular practices, ethnicity, or geography, Christianity has been uniquely concerned with orthodoxy, with *right belief*. While the history of Christianity manifests a wide variety of practices, ethnicities, languages and locations, no matter where the Gospel has gone there still remains an emphasis on the truth of the Church's claims about the world and her God. Distinctions are made between true and false beliefs and whether a person is "in" or "out" of the Church is determined largely (if not entirely) by adherence to orthodox doctrine, in particular, doctrines about Jesus.

What makes doctrine and creeds unusual among Christians are not their existence in themselves, but how they *function* in determining group cohesion. All groups look to have some semblance of group unity or identity, but creedal statements and doctrines as markers of that community—as opposed to some sort of behavior or practice—is a Christian emphasis. Christians assumed early on that if you have the wrong belief,[9] then you would also have the wrong practices.[10] But it is deeper than this. Schmemann argues that fundamentally, the difference between Christianity and every other religion was the Church's recognition that her ontology was located in Jesus Christ:

> [The Church] is a cult which eternally transcends itself, because it is the cult of a community which eternally realizes itself, as the Body of Christ, as the Church of the Holy Spirit, as ultimately the new *aeon* of the Kingdom. It is a tradition of forms and structures, but these forms and structures are no longer those of a "cult," but those of the Church itself, of its life "in Christ." Now we can understand the real meaning of the patristic use of liturgical tradition. The formula *lex orandi est lex credendi* means nothing else than that theology is *possible* only within the Church . . . .[11]

8. Ibid.

9. By "belief" I do not mean merely a cognitive assent to a particular set of propositions. Beliefs are much deeper than this. Chapter 4 spends more time on this topic.

10. Young, *Creeds*, 103.

11. Schmemann, *Liturgy and Tradition*, 18.

The Modern Discussion on Doctrine

What sets Christianity apart from other competing religions is that the Church's doctrine and practice flow out of her relationship to and her worship of, the Triune God. Right relationship—which is predicated on being bound to the crucified and resurrected Jesus—leads to right practice, not the other way around.[12]

Contrast this with the religious heritage of Judaism out of which Christianity grew. As Young points out, "Judaism is not an orthodoxy, but an orthopraxy—its common core is 'right action' rather than 'right belief'—Judaism was not the source of Christianity's emphasis on orthodoxy and has formulated its 'beliefs' only in reaction to Christianity."[13] This is not to say that we cannot find creedal or doctrinal statements in the Old Testament—the *shema* of Deuteronomy 6:4 readily comes to mind—or that we don't find doctrinal statements about who the true God is and his claims on the world as his creation. We obviously can, but as the Decalogue and the context of the *shema* show, the emphasis is on right practice, not on right belief. Even with one of the clearest depictions of Jesus and his teaching and preaching, the Sermon on the Mount, we are hard pressed to find an emphasis on the role right belief should play in following Jesus. Similarly with the other books of the New Testament beyond the scope of the Gospels, creedal statements do not function in the way that they will come to function in the early centuries of the Church.

Take for example, 1 Corinthians 12:3, "Jesus is Lord," which is widely regarded as one of the earliest Christian creeds. As Thiselton argues, the phrase functions to signify where the Church's allegiance lies, but it also makes a claim about the way the world is, i.e., Jesus is the true Lord and God of all there is.[14] This confession, "Jesus is Lord," was first used in the context of worship (*lex orandi*) as a statement of personal commitment and only later did it become a way of delineating whether someone holds the right belief and thus is part of the true worshipping community. In other words, a shift happens—and it happens almost from the start—from asking "to whom are you loyal?" to the question, "what do you mean by the phrase, 'Jesus is Lord?'" Which Jesus do you worship, the crucified and resurrected Son of God or some other one?

---

12. This is akin to, but not the same as, what James K. A. Smith argues about the critical role that worship and liturgy plays for shaping our desires. See his *Desiring the Kingdom*.

13. Young, *Creeds*, 1.

14. Thiselton, *Hermeneutics of Doctrine*, 11–12.

Again, an obvious question is why? Why did Christianity develop in such a way that it not only emphasized right belief, sometimes over and against right practice, but also uniquely developed doctrines and creeds as tests of orthodoxy in contrast to not only Judaism, but to all other religions? While putting forth an answer to this question would be a book-length project in itself, we can say in general, that it was in the face of multiple and competing accounts of the world, humanity, and the divine—not unlike our own "postmodern" or pluralistic context in the West—that Christians felt the need to delineate their account from others.[15] At root in the process was not only the delineation of the identity of the Christian God as opposed to other gods, but the exclusive locus of salvation that he offered through his Son Jesus, as evidenced later in the fourth century with the intense debates at Nicaea over Jesus' relationship to Yahweh.

Nicaea, however, was not the beginning of this process. Already in the first century, the New Testament mentions struggles between true and false belief, let alone true and false interpretations, as evidenced in the warnings of Paul in Galatians as well as John in his epistles. In the second century, Ignatius warns various Churches to mind the authority of the bishops, as they are the true authorities over matters of doctrine and right belief.[16] In the same century, Irenaeus rigorously defends right belief in Jesus against Gnosticism and its deviation from the message preached by the apostles.[17] Though creeds and doctrines originated in the setting of worship, by the fourth century they had been adapted as tests of orthodoxy.[18]

The conflict over the right account of Jesus did not remain isolated to the Church and other competing religions, it became a conflict of Christian account vs. Christian account as the history of doctrinal debate since the fourth century illustrates. For better or worse, doctrines, creeds, and the concern for orthodoxy have done as much to unite the Church, as they have to divide her. Division within the Church is really nothing new and the modern splintering of the Church into the various Protestant denominations, Catholic orders, and the various Churches of the East, India, South America, Africa and Asia, highlights a problem that has been with the Church from the very beginning.

15. Hurtado gives a wonderful overview of the dense and highly competitive religious landscape of the early centuries of Christianity in the Western world. See his *Origins of Christian Worship*.

16. Louth, *Early Christian Writings*, 53–112.

17. St. Irenaeus, *Against the Heresies*; See also *On the Apostolic Preaching*.

18. Kelly, *Early Christian Creeds*.

The Modern Discussion on Doctrine

It is perhaps because of the fracturing of the Church—the democratization of the faith or even the anti-intellectual backlash of many Christians over the last several hundreds years—that the refrain of "doctrine divides, service (or perhaps love or spirituality) unites" or "no creed but the Bible" can be heard among various and diverse Church bodies in the West (and America in particular). But as the Church has gradually lost her privileged status in society and can no longer assume broad cultural acceptance of her claims, theologians have turned once again to doctrine. Of course, among some traditions, doctrine never went out of fashion but over the last thirty years, the topic of doctrine, in particular its nature and function for Christian communities, has seen a resurgence in interest. Names like William Christian, Paul Griffiths, George Lindbeck, Alister McGrath, Kevin Vanhoozer, and Anthony Thiselton (just to name a few) have all argued, in one form or fashion, for the critical role that doctrine plays for the Church. And rightly so: doctrine, creeds, and concern over orthodoxy are key features of the Church that can no more be done away with, than Jesus' question to his disciples: "Who do you say that I am?"

GEORGE LINDBECK AND THE MODERN CONVERSATION ON DOCTRINE

Perhaps no one is more responsible for the resurgent interest in doctrine than George Lindbeck. In 1984 Lindbeck set the agenda for the current Christian theological discussion on the nature and function of doctrine when he published his seminal work *The Nature of Doctrine: Religion and Theology in a Postliberal Age*. What made his work significant, however, was not only or even primarily his account of Christian doctrine, but rather his approach to discussing the issue. *The Nature of Doctrine* does not begin with a discussion of doctrine but with his now-famous typology of religion. His work remains significant, nearly thirty years after its initial publication, not merely for his theory of religion (which is groundbreaking), but for how he uses his theory of religion to conceptualize doctrine.[19]

Soon after the publication of *The Nature of Doctrine*, the theological world began responding to Lindbeck's proposal. In 1985, *The Thomist* offered a significant reaction to Lindbeck notably with William Placher providing a Postliberal affirmation of Lindbeck's project and David Tracy

---

19. Lindbeck, *Nature of Doctrine*, 8.

giving a Revisionist rejection of it.[20] Likewise, in 1988 an entire issue of *Modern Theology* was devoted to discussing the work. In fact, one of the most important effects of *The Nature of Doctrine* has been its ability to cause diverse theological groups to talk to one another and discuss its ideas.[21]

As an indication of just how important Lindbeck's work continues to be, nearly twenty years after *The Nature of Doctrine* was published Kevin Vanhoozer offered a direct rebuttal to Lindbeck with his work, *The Drama of Doctrine: A Canonical Linguistic Approach to Christian Doctrine*. Soon after Vanhoozer's work another significant scholar, Anthony Thiselton, also published a significant study on doctrine, *The Hermeneutics of Doctrine*. Though Thiselton's work is not a direct response to Lindbeck, he is familiar with Lindbeck's work and assumes many of the same problems and categories that Lindbeck critiques. These three works are not the only noteworthy or important publications on the topic; there are other works worth exploring that offer significant contributions to the conversation. But as I will demonstrate in chapter 2, these three works in particular, are all remarkable examples[22] of the same fundamental problem that continues to plague the discussion on doctrine and religious discourse in general. Of these three works, Lindbeck's account of doctrine is by far the most important and I consider him to be the key player in the discussion over doctrine as his work continues to set the terms of the debate. Because of this, his project is worth explaining in more detail.

SETTING THE TERMS OF THE DEBATE: GEORGE LINDBECK'S CULTURAL-LINGUISTIC THEOLOGY

The impetus for Lindbeck's work is largely ecumenical. He recounts having heard reports from various Roman Catholic, Orthodox, and Protestant theologians engaged in theological and ecumenical dialogue, that claimed on crucial doctrinal topics such as the Eucharist, justification, or even the Papacy, that these once antagonistic traditions were now in basic agreement, even though they each continued to adhere to their historic doctrinal positions. For some, this is virtually impossible to believe (me included). After all, how could a Lutheran and a Catholic come to consensus or even

---

20. Placher "Revisionist and Postliberal Theologies," 392–416; Tracy, "Lindbeck's New Program for Theology," 460–72.

21. Thiemann, "Intratextuality and Speaking of God," 377–382.

22. That is, they are all part of a typology that I will later call "antifoundationalist theory."

reconciliation over a doctrine like justification without one side capitulating their view?[23] It seems complete nonsense for one tradition to say they continue to hold to their historic articulation of a doctrine—in particular, with a historically divisive doctrine like justification—and in the very next breath claim to have reconciled with another hostile position without having changed their view. Instead of dismissing such claims as irrational or mistaken, Lindbeck sought to explain how this might actually be happening. The problem as Lindbeck sees it, is not necessarily with the ecumenical participants and their claims of reconciliation, but rather with the mental concepts for explaining the situation provided by our current theories of religion and doctrine. What was needed was a different option—what I call, an "antifoundationalist" option—to get around our inability to explain the data.

Lindbeck argues that the two usual concepts of doctrine are derived from two long-standing theories of religion: the "cognitive-propositionalist" and the "experientialist-expressivist." The cognitive-propositionalist theory of religion highlights "the cognitive aspects of religion and stresses the ways in which Church doctrines function as informative propositions or truth claims about objective realities."[24] This view sees religions as "similar to philosophy or science as these were classically conceived" and has a "preoccupation with the cognitive or informational meaningfulness of religious utterances."[25] If Lindbeck is right, then this has been the prevailing view of conservative Protestants and evangelicals for the last two hundred years or so. Conversely, the experiential-expressivist theory of religion "interprets doctrines as noninformative and nondiscursive symbols of inner feelings, attitudes, or existential orientations." This view "highlights the resemblances of religions to aesthetic enterprises" and is congenial to the "liberal theologies influenced by Continental developments that began with Schleiermacher."[26] Within these two theories of religion are found two theories of doctrine that use the same typology.

The cognitive-propositionalist theory of doctrine conceives of doctrines as truth claims that are objective and universal regardless of context. Lindbeck argues that "for a propositionalist, if a doctrine is once true,

---

23. *Joint Declaration on the Doctrine of Justification.*
24. Lindbeck, *Nature of Doctrine*, 16.
25. Ibid.
26. Ibid.

it is always true, and if it is once false, it is always false."[27] Doctrines in this view are of a piece with Descartes' "clear and distinct" ideas or the modern scientific search for unbiased facts that are verifiable by reason or some other normative standard. The expressive-experientialist theory of doctrine, on the other hand, interprets doctrines as noninformative and nondiscursive symbols of universal shared religious "feelings, attitudes, existential orientations, or practices, rather than by what happens on the level of symbolic (including doctrinal) objectifications."[28] These universal shared experiences are not particular to Christianity but are expressed in a multitude of different ways through different traditions and religions. What is universal is not the propositional, discursive or intellectual content (like with the cognitive-propositionalist), but rather the emotive, existential or attitudinal content. While the cognitive-propositionalist and experiential-expressivist theories of doctrine seem to be at odds with one another, both positions (as Lindbeck articulates them) turn on the familiar dualism of rationalist vs. romanticist and are two opposing poles of the same foundationalist mood. They may be conflicting positions, but they have both been equally shaped by foundationalism and assume it all the way down.

To give an initial definition to the term "foundationalism" what I mean is the assumption of and/or search for some universal and objective standard or norm that can be appealed to and that stands outside of, all contexts, perspectives, biases, paradigms, and agendas. Foundationalism is perhaps easiest to recognize by the dualisms it enables, dualisms like rationalism vs. romanticism, fact vs. value, fundamentalism vs. liberalism, knowledge vs. belief, or true speech vs. rhetoric, just to name a few. The epistemological premise underlying each of these dualisms is that the left hand term is a mode of knowing that is mostly, if not purely, "direct, transparent, without difficulties, unmediated, independently verifiable, unproblematic, preinterpretive, and sure; and, conversely, that the mode of knowing named by the right hand term is indirect, opaque, context dependent, unconstrained, derivative, and full of risk."[29] This underlying epistemology has real traction for us, in large part because of the *rhetorical* force of its promise of certainty. Foundationalists—when it comes to their claims—are always looking to claim the "higher" ground: "we're for fairness and you are for biased judgment; we're for merit and you are for

---

27. Ibid.
28. Ibid., 17.
29. Fish, "With the Compliments of the Author," 41.

special interests; we're for objectivity and you are playing politics; we're for free speech and you are for censorship and ideological tyranny."[30] To put it in terms typical to many debates: "my position is based on the clear facts, while your position is mere belief." Or even more relevant for theology: "my position is based on the clear, literal reading of the Biblical text, while your position is trying to force your politics and tradition into the author's mouth." There is real power in being able to claim your position is the clear, unbiased, and rational position in contrast to your opponent's position that is biased, mired in beliefs, and in essence, irrational. Each dualism is assuming and/or looking for a common *foundation* that is clear and universal to all people, but as I will argue throughout this work, no such foundation exists. It is this exposure of foundationalism as the implicit assumption and the essential problem in the discussion over doctrine that makes Lindbeck's account *groundbreaking* and sets the agenda for the discussion that has followed in his path. Let's return to his account.

With the two prevailing theories of doctrine—the cognitive-propositionalist and experientialist-expressivist—it is hard to see how either theory can account for reconciliation between two competing doctrinal positions without capitulation by either side occurring. What Lindbeck rightly understood, was that a third approach was needed and his answer was the cultural-linguistic model of religion and its concomitant regulative theory of doctrine.

In his cultural-linguistic model of religion, Lindbeck defines religions as "comprehensive interpretive schemes, usually embodied in myths or narratives and heavily ritualized, which structure human experience and understanding of the self and world."[31] They are "a kind of cultural and/or linguistic framework or medium that shapes the entirety of life and thought. It functions somewhat like a Kantian *a priori*, although in this case the *a priori* is a set of acquired skills that could be different."[32] Adherents to a particular religion and their thoughts and experiences are "shaped, molded, and in a sense constituted by linguistic forms."[33] He argues that, "[Religions are] similar to an idiom that makes possible the description of realities, the formulation of beliefs, and the experiencing of inner attitudes,

---

30. Fish, *There's No Such Thing as Free Speech*, 16.
31. Ibid., 32.
32. Ibid., 33.
33. Ibid., 34.

feelings, and sentiments."[34] As opposed to the cognitive-propositionalist theory of religion, the cultural-linguistic theory is not primarily "an array of beliefs about the true and the good," nor is it like the experiential-expressivist theory in which religions and their doctrines are symbols "expressive of basic attitudes, feelings, and sentiments."[35] For Lindbeck, to enter into a religion is to enter into a particular culture with its own particular language. Christianity then is a particular way of construing reality, but it is not the only way of doing it. The culture and language of Christianity is not universal to all people and is accessible only to those who become fluent in its language and skilled in its practices.

Religions then are very much like Wittgenstein's "language game,"[36] in which participants learn a vocabulary of discursive and nondiscursive symbols that only make sense within a particular form of life. As a culture, a religion does not merely have propositions or collections of symbolized feelings or experiences, it has both and both are tied to the particular practices and narratives of that religion. Lindbeck further explains:

> Religion cannot be pictured in the cognitivist (and voluntarist) manner as primarily a matter of deliberately choosing to believe or follow explicitly known propositions or directives. Rather, to become religious—no less than to become culturally or linguistically competent—is to interiorize a set of skills by practice and training. One learns how to feel, act, and think in conformity with a religious tradition that is, in its inner structure, far richer and more subtle than can be explicitly articulated. The primary knowledge is not *about* the religion, nor *that* the religion teaches such and such, but rather *how* to be religious in such and such ways. Sometimes explicitly formulated statements of the beliefs or behavioral norms of a religion may be helpful in the learning process, but by no means always. Ritual, prayer, and example are normally much more important. Thus—in so far as the experiential-expressive contrast between experience and knowledge is comparable to that between "knowing how" and "knowing that"—cultural-linguistic models, no less than expressive ones, emphasize the experiential or existential side of religion, though in a different way.[37]

---

34. Ibid., 33.
35. Ibid., 33.
36. Wittgenstein, *Philosophical Investigations*; *Blue and Brown Books*.
37. Lindbeck, *Nature of Doctrine*, 35.

Lindbeck offers a solution to the stalemate between cognitivists and experientialists by arguing that both are necessary components of religions. But he reverses what both cognitivists and experientialists assume: it is the form of life, the embodied practices and narratives of the religion that give doctrines their meaning—whether they be discursive (cognitivists) or non-discursive (experientialists)—not the other way around. Propositions find their meaning *within* the form of life and likewise, it is the "outer" practices of the religion that give meaning and content to "inner" experiences. For Lindbeck, "religions are not expressions of the transcendental heights and depths of human experience, but are rather patterns of ritual, myth, belief, and conduct which constitute, rather than being constituted by, that which modern people often think of as most profound in human beings, viz., their existential self-understanding."[38] All of reality, the way we see the world and everything in it (at least religiously), is *socially constructed* by whatever religion a person participates.[39]

Within his cultural-linguistic theory of religion, Lindbeck argues for a regulative or rule based theory of doctrines in which doctrines function as grammatical or linguistic communally authoritative rules for discourse, attitude, and action. A regulative view of doctrine—and this is key for Lindbeck—has "no difficulty explaining the possibility of reconciliation without capitulation. Rules, unlike propositions or expressive symbols, retain an invariant meaning under changing conditions of compatibility and conflict."[40] For Lindbeck, a regulative view of doctrine can actually explain why Lutherans and Catholics can be reconciled on the doctrine of justification, without either tradition changing their articulation of the doctrine.

Perhaps the most striking and innovative feature of Lindbeck's account is his notion that doctrines function "intrasystematically." That is, doctrines function *within* the confines of a religion's culture and practices, not *without*. Lindbeck's espousal of a regulative theory of doctrine is nothing new and he rightly points to the *regula fidei* as an example of how the early Church thought, at least in part, about the role of doctrines.[41] What is new with Lindbeck's account is that this is the *only* function doctrines have. "The novelty of rule theory . . . is that it does not locate the abiding and doctrinally significant aspect of religion in propositionally formulated

38. Ibid., 62.
39. Ibid., 63.
40. Ibid., 18.
41. Ibid.

truths, much less in inner experiences, but in the story it tells and in the grammar that informs the way the story is told and used."[42] Doctrines far from having a first-order function of making truth claims (like in the cognitive-propositionalist theory of doctrine), function only as second-order rules for demarcating what is in and out for the community's talk about God. In this view, "Doctrines regulate truth claims by excluding some and permitting others, but the logic of their communally authoritative use hinders or prevents them from specifying positively what is to be affirmed."[43] For Lindbeck, first-order truth claims, "change insofar as these arise from the application of the interpretive scheme to the shifting worlds that human beings inhabit. What is taken to be reality is in large part socially constructed and consequently alters in the course of time."[44]

With this brief overview of Lindbeck's account it is not difficult to see why he is by far the most important dialogue partner in the debate over the nature and function of doctrine and why his account of doctrine has been highly influential. In my view, his account is still the definitive account of doctrine and the best offering so far. But while I agree with much of his cultural-linguistic model of religion, his project (like the others I will critique in chapter 2) ultimately gives way to the very categories he seeks to overcome and instead of arguing *against* them he ultimately argues *within* them. Nonetheless, with his typology of doctrine, Lindbeck sets the terms and categories for the modern discussion on doctrine that are currently still in play and in my view, should be.

THE THESIS AND LAYOUT OF THE WORK

My project is neither complicated nor profound: I am arguing for an account of Christian doctrine that will bring to light the lingering entrenchment of foundationalism within the context of religious discourse and will show this entrenchment for what it is: a confusion (if not idolatry) inherited from the Enlightenment and ultimately from Plato. In its place, I offer an account of doctrine that is more explicitly Christological than any current offerings and that at the same time, moves the discussion over doctrine past the assumptions of foundationalism. No matter the twists and turns that this work will take and the diversity of topics it will address, at root

---

42. Ibid., 80.
43. Ibid., 19.
44. Ibid., 82.

The Modern Discussion on Doctrine

there is just one concern: *a properly Christian account of doctrine begins and ends with Jesus and is founded solely on him. Scripture, the Church and her doctrine need nothing else for their validity.*

Chapter 1 serves at least three purposes. My first purpose is to locate my audience: this work is for the Church living within the confines of Western religiousness in the opening decades of the twenty-first century, in particular with the English-speaking world that borders the Atlantic Ocean. If I am being honest however, this work is aimed squarely at the Church in America with a keen eye towards evangelicals. My second purpose is to introduce the problem of foundationalism and give examples of how it works. Foundationalism is a complicated thing, so I will be repeatedly describing it throughout the entirety of the work. Nevertheless, chapter 1 attempts to give a good description of the problem. My third purpose is to describe how foundationalism came to be a significant problem for theology by tracing its gestation throughout Western history. Admittedly, my treatment is brief, but my point is not to give a historical treatment of the problem, but rather to trace its trajectory.

Very few scholars hold to a full-blown foundationalism anymore. In fact, most outside of a few ardent old school positivists, would openly reject it. However, even though disavowals of foundationalism are openly made, in practice these same disavowals run (often unwittingly) right back to the very foundationalism they are claiming to reject. Chapter 2 will show just how this works by narrowing the focus to the special project of theory. When I say "theory," I don't mean a proposed explanation of events, but rather a proposed formal method that is intended to stand outside of practice and regulate it. It is this latter kind of theory that is endemic to foundationalism and has come to characterize the modern discussion on doctrine, in particular with Lindbeck et al and their supposed "postfoundationalism."

Chapter 3 moves from criticism to construction and is the first part of my account of doctrine. Any account of doctrine which claims to be Christian, must account for the role that Scripture plays for authenticating doctrine. The Church has taught from the very beginning that Scripture is the standard and source by which all of the Church's speech, doctrine, and practices are measured. But how exactly does Scripture do this? Or put another way, how (if at all) is Scripture authoritative for the Church and her doctrine? I locate Scripture within the economy of salvation and argue that to understand Scripture's authority, we must see how it *functions* as one within this framework.

Much of what I argue for in chapter 3 anticipates and compliments what I argue in chapter 4. In reality, both chapters serve as one long argument and say much of the same things. Nevertheless, chapter 4 begins by explaining what it is to think in "antifoundationalist" terms and then moves to the critical argument of the work: accounting for the nature and function of the Church within the economy of salvation. It is only after we understand the proper role of the Church in the economy of salvation that we can understand how doctrine functions.

Chapter 5 deals with the lingering questions that my account raises for foundationalists, in particular the question of relativism. But before I take up relativism, I take up the problem of conflicting scriptural and doctrinal interpretation and use the long-standing disagreement over the Lord's Supper between Lutherans and the Reformed (in particular with Presbyterians) as an example of how we can conceive of the problem apart from foundationalist assumptions. I will then take up the thorny question of relativism and show how interpreting my account as "relativistic" is not only unwarranted, it is confused at best.

In all of these chapters, my aim is not innovation. I do not offer a method to help us get a better lever on our modern context, nor do I offer a new or revolutionary view of doctrine. In fact, my view of doctrine is widely held and has been for millennia. My aim in this work is to help twenty-first century Christians living within the confines of Western religiousness to shirk off the categories of foundationalism in order to place their faith more securely on their one true foundation: Jesus, the Messiah, the Son of the Living God.

1

Foundationalism

What Is It and Where Did It Come From?

This chapter takes up the problem of foundationalism and addresses it via three simple questions. First, who is affected by foundationalism? Foundationalism (as I will describe it) is a problem unique to the West and so my audience is, broadly speaking, the Christian Church in the West. Second, what is foundationalism? Foundationalism is a complicated thing, so I will offer an initial description that I will build upon throughout this work; showing as we go along just how deep-seeded the problem is for theology and religious discourse. Third, how did foundationalism become a problem for the West in the first place? The final section of the chapter will give a genealogy—really, a narrative—of the genesis and formation of foundationalism, beginning early in the history of the West and ending with the current age.

LOCATING MY AUDIENCE

The intended audience of this work is early twenty-first century Christians born into Western religiousness. By the term "Western" I mean what James Edwards means by it: we are the people shaped and influenced by (among other things) "Homer, the Bible, Plato, Cervantes, Shakespeare, Descartes, Kant, George Eliot, Nietzsche, Whitman, and Freud, and whose political consciousness was shaped by the European wars of religion and by the French, American, Russian, and Eastern European revolutions, and whose present circumstances is one of relative peace, plenty, and leisure in some one of the North Atlantic democracies, [and who] share something of a common consciousness (and something of a common fate)."[1] Despite the events of 9/11 and that at the time of this writing, the United States is engaged in two different wars and has recently endured the severest economic downturn since the Great Depression, I still find Edward's description to be accurate, as far as a succinct description of the West is possible. The West is not a self-contained group that has been hermetically sealed off from other groups, as if other traditions and cultures have not influenced it in some way. Even so, there are features that make the West distinctive as a culture.

The term "religiousness" means a way of being religious, which in turn means giving a certain kind of account.[2] Giving an account is nothing out of the ordinary; everyone does this in multiple ways. We need only think of driving a car and how someone must be able to give an account of "the rules of the road" in order to obtain a license or how someone who wants to become a citizen must give an account of their knowledge of American history, government, or customs. "Religiousness" is a particular kind of account, an orientation to questions about who or what is divine and what relationship (if any at all) humanity and the world have to the divine and to each other. Such an account contains the assumptions that underlie and give intelligibility to religious practices and beliefs. Religiousness, however, is not the same thing as holding to a particular religion or having religious practices. Someone who holds to a religion holds to "a form of life that seems to those who inhabit it to be comprehensive, incapable of abandonment, and of central importance."[3] A person need not hold to a religion to have a particular religiousness, i.e., a particular way of accounting for the divine.

The distinction of religiousness and religion becomes clearer when we consider that the West does not have a single religion defining its religiousness, though Christianity clearly dominates. The religious practices of Judaism, Christianity, Islam and the Greek Pantheon have all played significant roles in defining and shaping the religious orientation of the West. This is true for both those who are adherents of particular religions and those who are not. For example, both atheists and Jehovah's Witnesses assume the same general things when it comes to thinking about what counts as

---

1. Edwards, *Plain Sense of Things*, 4.
2. Griffiths, "Properly Christian Response to Religious Plurality," 3–26.
3. Griffiths, *Problems of Religious Diversity*, 7.

religious practices or how they conceive of the divine, even if they believe completely different things. If we were to ask either group to broadly define the word "god," they would offer similar definitions. In other words, there is a particularly Western way of being religious (as opposed to those born into Japanese Buddhism or Indian Hinduism or some other distinctive cultural religiousness) that both those who hold to a particular religion and those who do not, naturally and unconsciously assume simply as a result of being Western. To be born in the West is to naturally and tacitly assume its religiousness. Later in the chapter, I will discuss the structures of Western religiousness in more detail, but for now, it is enough to say that this work is aimed squarely at those Christians who have been shaped by the West and its religiousness, in particular those living in America in the early decades of the twenty-first century.

The central problem (but by no means, the only problem) facing the modern discussion on doctrine is the problem of foundationalism, a problem that is woven into the fabric of the Western religiousness. In the broadest sense, "foundationalism" is when Christians look for some other foundation, standard, or ground that seems more firm or stable than the Triune God. It is in essence *idolatry,* because Christians place their faith and trust in some other foundation; be it another god, some so-called "eternal" or "universal" standard, the State or the economy, the academy, or whatever else there is. The idolatrous foundation could be just about anything. The problem is not new and it goes all the way back to Adam and Eve in the Garden when trust was transferred from the Triune God to the claims of the Serpent.

In the narrow sense of the term, foundationalism, as it manifests itself in the West, is characterized by the assumption of and/or the search for some universal and objective standard that can be appealed to and that stands outside of, all contexts, perspectives, biases, and agendas. Foundationalism is a particular "mood," a particular disposition towards questions of truth, fact, interpretation and speech (among other things) and is typified in various Western movements and practices like that of the rationalists, empiricists, and romantics of the Enlightenment or with the backlash of postmodernism and its deconstructionist malcontents against the Enlightenment. Foundationalism informs the modern Western political system of Liberalism[4] and the modern economic ideologies of capitalism and

---

4. Liberalism, as in the thought of Locke, Hume, etc. that stands as the political foundation for modern Western Democracies; not the left-leaning liberal/progressive agenda of the Democratic Party in the United States.

socialism; it is the backbone of the academy with its notion of *Wissenschaft* and is the *raison d'être* of modern scientific enterprise and its so-called objective search for truth and fact. Christianity in the West—and theology in particular—has been just as influenced by foundationalism as any other practice or system of thought and has even gone so far as to be *defined* by it at times. William Placher writes,

> Ever since the Enlightenment in the seventeenth century, many forces in our culture have taught that "being rational" meant questioning all inherited assumptions and then accepting only those beliefs which could be proven according to universally acceptable criteria. "Tradition" and "authority" were bad words. If Christians wanted to join the general conversation, it seemed that these were the rules by which they would have to play. If that meant there were some things they could not say, or some ways they could not say them, then they would have to adjust accordingly—or else find themselves in increasing intellectual isolation.[5]

Placher's statement is not provocative, it is a common critique among many contemporary theologians and it is one I share: the Church has given up its Lord for some other foundation that seemed more intellectually sound, relevant, rational, or politically expedient. In turn, that idolatrous foundation—literally, foundationalism itself—has led the Church to ways of conceiving of truth, fact, and what counts as good, right, and morally acceptable that is often foreign and antithetical to the Triune God and his Word.

Identifying my audience as modern Christians embedded within Western religiousness and dealing with foundationalism raises two important questions. First, "what exactly does foundationalism look like?" The question indicates the need for a more in-depth discussion of the problem and examples of how it works. The next section of this chapter seeks to answer this question and offers a description that will be a "first pass" on the problem that will define some key terms. Because foundationalism is nuanced, multi-faceted, and deep-seeded in our consciousness, I will be describing and re-describing it throughout this work. Chapter 2 in particular will go more in-depth on the problem and will offer key examples of how the problem is manifested in the modern discussion on doctrine.

Second, "Where exactly did foundationalism come from?" While it is commonplace to pinpoint the Enlightenment as the culprit, foundationalism

---

5. Placher, *Unapologetic Theology*, 11.

Foundationalism

has roots that are ancient and it took a long time to develop into its current form. Perhaps the more relevant question is, "how did *Western religiousness* develop so that foundationalism became its *de facto* disposition towards questions of truth, fact, interpretation and so forth?" That is, "why is foundationalism not only so attractive to the Western mind, why is it we just naturally assume it, even as so many reject it?" The final section of this chapter will answer this question. In the mean time, let's turn our attention to describing the problem of foundationalism in more detail.

FOUNDATIONALISM

Foundationalism is a complicated thing and offering up a succinct definition invites easy criticism. Nonetheless, earlier I gave this brief definition of it: *foundationalism is the assumption of and/or the search for some universal and objective standard that can be appealed to and that stands outside of, all contexts, perspectives, biases, and agendas.* But foundationalism is more than this; it is a particular "mood," a disposition towards questions of truth, facts, interpretation and speech. What I mean by "mood" is what Heidegger means by it: our "Being-attuned," as the way we manifest our "state of mind" as "Being-in-the-world."[6] It is an "attunement" (*die Stimmung*), like the way in which a musical instrument, like a piano or a guitar, is tuned. As Edwards explains, "a mood," as Heidegger uses the term, "is *an attunement to things,* a way of vibrating in relation to being struck by them, a way of sounding them out in oneself."[7] A mood is not a particular set of beliefs—theological, philosophical, or otherwise—though certain beliefs may be integral in the mood's construction. A mood is a way of *receiving* beliefs and it shows itself in "the way those beliefs are framed into one's life; it is a way of phrasing them in one's continuous self-narrative, a way of tasting them on the tongue, so to speak."[8] A mood gives our beliefs a particular *Gestalt,* a particular picture or tone. A mood in this sense, is not whimsical or given over to short-term mental or emotional states of mind as the term is popularly used. A mood is the way in which we respond to or take in *whatever there is.* It is a way of acting, the way we respond to particular kinds of questions, or the specific sense we have of inhabiting our identities that is largely unconscious on our part. A mood is not a practice in and of

---

6. Heidegger, *Being and Time,* ¶29, 172–79.
7. Edwards, *Plain Sense of Things,* 12–13.
8. Ibid., 13.

itself; rather it frames, informs, and gives our practices a particular shape. Foundationalism, as a mood, is the way people born and raised within the context of Western religiousness are attuned and disposed to questions of truth, interpretation, and how we determine what counts as facts or true speech (among other things). But it is not merely Christians or other religious traditions that have been affected by foundationalism; this mood is pervasive across Western culture and has affected disparate and conflicting communities in similar ways.

Take for example the "God Delusion Debates," (sponsored by the Fixed-Point Foundation of Birmingham, Alabama) between the outspoken atheist Richard Dawkins and the Christian apologist John Lennox over the viability of Christianity and belief in God. Both scholars, despite their radically different beliefs about God and religion, without a second thought, assumed the same disposition towards questions of truth and fact and argued accordingly. In fact, it was the shared mood of foundationalism that made the debate possible in the first place. A mood and a set of beliefs then are not the same thing, though a set of beliefs may be the product of a mood; radically conflicting groups can and do share the same mood without believing the same things.

Many scholars in diverse fields have recognized the effects and influence of foundationalism upon their practices and have been taking up the problems posed by it for a long time. In the field of philosophy, Jeffrey Stout, Michael Polanyi, Richard Rorty, Donald Davidson, Fredrick Nietzsche and Ludwig Wittgenstein are all concerned with foundationalism in one form or another. In the field of science, Thomas Kuhn has similar interests, as do Peter Berger in the field of sociology and Clifford Geertz in anthropology. In the field of literary theory, Stanley Fish, Jane Tompkins, Steven Knapp, and Walter Benn Michaels are engaged in a similar way as Ronald Dworkin is in legal studies.[9] Foundationalism is not a problem facing the modern discussion on doctrine alone (or theology and religious discourse for that matter), it has been recognized as a pervasive problem across a multitude of disciplines. This is why foundationalism is best understood as a mood: it cannot be reduced to a particular worldview, practice, or set of beliefs precisely because it attempts to frame and gives shape to a myriad of different and conflicting worldviews, practices, and sets of beliefs. As a mood, foundationalism is *intrinsic* to the Western mindset—*it is our de*

---

9. These works are all listed in the bibliography for the reader's benefit.

facto disposition towards questions of truth, fact, and interpretation—and goes largely unrecognized by most of its populace.

One way of seeing how foundationalism has affected the West is by narrowing our scope and seeing how it has affected one particular practice. Take for example, Stanley Fish and his wrestling with foundationalism in the field of literary criticism. Decades ago, Fish sought to answer a common (and heavily debated) question among literary theorists: what is the source of interpretive authority, the text or the reader? As it will become clear, the question itself and the dualism it raises—text vs. reader—is foundationalist because of the assumptions it makes about both texts and readers. Nevertheless, to those who would answer the question with "the text," there is no accounting for disagreements. If the text contains its own meaning and therefore carries within its structure, its own built-in interpretation, why do disagreements over interpretation happen? Shouldn't the meaning of a text be objective, clear and obvious to all who read it? To those who answered "the reader," the embarrassment comes when two disparate readers can agree on the meaning of a text. If a text does not contain its own inherent meaning and the reader is the final arbiter of a text, using her own experiences and thoughts as her guide, how can we explain why two readers—let alone two readers who might not share the same background, ethnicity, gender, or a host of different things—can agree about so much, let alone the interpretation of a text?

The first view—the text contains its own inherent and objective meaning regardless of who reads it—we can characterize as the "objectivist," "formalist," or "textualist" (to use a term from legal interpretation) position. The second view—the text does not contain its own meaning and therefore every reader can interpret the text however she wants—we can characterize as the "relativist" or "reader-response" position. Behind both views of interpretation is what I have been calling foundationalism. Fish offers this definition:

> By foundationalism I mean any attempt to ground inquiry and communication in something more firm and stable than mere belief or unexamined practice. The foundationalist strategy is first to identify that ground and then so to order our activities that they become anchored to it and are thereby rendered objective and principled. The ground so identified must have certain (related) characteristics: it must be invariant across contexts and even cultures; it must stand apart from political, partisan, and "subjective" concerns in relation to which it must act as a constraint; and it

must provide a reference point or checkpoint against which claims to knowledge and success can be measured and adjudicated.[10]

For the objectivist, interpretation is dichotomized between the poles of fact/value, objective/subjective, reason/faith, and principle/rhetoric. Undergirding these dualisms is the assumption of a neutral, unbiased, universal, and literal view of interpretation. Interpretation is constrained by what are taken to be fundamentally clear and obvious features of the text that remain the same (universal) from context to context irrespective of the disparities of the contexts or the communities doing the interpreting. Things like language, texts, and grammar find their meaning inherently within their own structure and that structure in turn serves as the constraining force for interpretation. The fundamental assumption of the objectivist position is that the correct interpretation of a text has nothing to do with the contexts and beliefs of the people doing the interpreting, but is, *a priori*, already meaningful apart from such things. The role of the interpreter is to *find* the meaning, the correct interpretation, the authorial intention, the literal reading, or the structure that is inherent in the text. As Supreme Court Justice Antonin Scalia once remarked in the Tanner Lectures at Princeton, "it is the law that governs, not the intent of the law giver."[11] Questions about context or even questions about the intent of the author—or in Scalia's case, Congress' intention—are irrelevant, because the text (or the law) is clear and obvious *in itself*. For Scalia and other textualists, interpretation proceeds by way of the reason of a competent reader or some standard method or theory—the most common in our day being that of the scientific method, but in literary circles the search for a similarly appropriate method or theory in which to ground interpretation is a career in itself—that is constrained by general principles that are universal, universally accessible, and unconstrained by contexts, situations, presuppositions or personal agendas. For proper interpretation to take place, we need only set aside our presuppositions, our personal biases, values, gender, culture, and beliefs and set about to seeing what the objective meaning of the text really is.

But what of the other position in Fish's question about interpretive authority? What should we make of the relativist position? The relativist position is the "contra-objectivist" position because it is the "I'm-exactly-the-opposite-of-the-objectivist" position. Both the relativist and objectivist

---

10. Fish, "Anti-Foundationalism," 342–43.
11. Scalia, *Matter of Interpretation*, 35–36.

are affected by the same foundationalist mood and both tacitly accept the objectivist account of interpretation and its talk about universals, literal reading, objectivity, and so forth. The basic difference between the two positions is that the relativist is skeptical over whether it is possible to ground interpretation in some outside norm, standard, or theory or whether such things even exist at all, but is incapable of seeing interpretation in any other way. The relativist, seeing no way out of the objectivist categories, imagines a position by which someone can identify norms and standards and not be constrained by them. The relativist believes that he is free to pick whatever position he wants and in turn believes that he has done away with the objectivist view of truth all together.

But the relativist, far from having freed himself from objectivist categories, is still firmly entrenched within them. The relativist thinks he is choosing the opposing view of the objectivist: "If you argue for literal readings, then I argue against you with deconstructive ones. If you say that the only way an interpretation is true is for it to a be a universal interpretation, then I choose the opposite and say that either there is no one right reading or all interpretations are valid." All the relativist has done, however, is pick the opposing side of the same foundationalist coin. Both views of interpretation, while opposing views, *assume the same disposition towards questions of truth, objectivity, and interpretation* and debate accordingly. The relativist position, far from being a radically different view of objectivism, assumes objectivism for its own project and *is rightly characterized as sharing the same disposition, the same mood.* It may be an opposing side, but it is still the same coin.

Fish points out that, "Formalism [or objectivism] . . . is not merely a linguistic doctrine, but a doctrine that implies, in addition to a theory of language, a theory of the self, of community, of rationality, of practice, of politics."[12] Objectivism as a linguistic theory, as a theory of interpretation, implies an entire mood that stands behind it, a mood I have been referring to as foundationalism. The foundationalist mood, of which objectivism and relativism in literary interpretation are just one instance, fundamentally conceives of humans as creatures that are unconstrained by things like contexts and beliefs. Human activity—activities like reasoning, arguing, interpreting, making claims to truth, and so on—is essentially defined by freedom from the constraints of history, beliefs, and contexts. Far from being constrained by such things, human reasoning and interpretation must—in order for them to be considered true or valid—transcend them.

12. Fish, "Going Down the Anti-Formalist Road," 6.

This is not to say that humans are completely free from constraints to do whatever they please. They are not. For a foundationalist, constraints are provided by general principles, norms, methods, theories, objectives, or standards that are regarded as universal and reasonable for all people regardless of context. In turn, these things are publically recognized as the defining force and constraints of our society. The mark of intelligence and so-called "enlightenment" in Western society—if not the chief standard for many wide-ranging and highly touted professions such as journalism, the sciences, or being a Supreme Court Justice—is that a person can completely divorce herself from her past history, religion, country, gender and whatever biases she might have and can, in turn, see situations, phenomenon, texts, and laws—in essence, just about everything there is—*as they really are*. It is my position that not only is this impossible; it is at best a confused notion.

Of course, one of the chief critiques of foundationalism, as it has been widely acknowledged, is that it is implicated in everything that it seeks to transcend. As Fish puts it, "In short, the very essentials that are in foundationalist discourse opposed to the local, the historical, the contingent, the variable, and the rhetorical, turn out to be irreducibly dependent on, and indeed to be functions of, the local, the historical, the contingent, the variable, and the rhetorical."[13] Foundationalism is a *particular* mood (not a universal one) that comes out of a *particular* time period with a *particular* attunement towards questions of truth and the framing of beliefs. As a mood, it is not universally acknowledged or shared by all people. It is one mood among many. Having said all this, I readily admit that no one really holds to a full-blown foundationalism anymore. We sit uneasily between recognizing our contingent and historical status while still deeply holding to our inherited disposition towards questions of truth, fact, and interpretation. But as George Lindbeck perceptively recognized nearly three decades ago, foundationalism's categories and assumptions are still highly influential and operative, even as open rejections of them are made.

The obvious question now facing us is "where did foundationalism come from and how did it become the *de facto* disposition for Western religiousness?" My answer to this question does not merely explain how foundationalism developed, but explains how it is both highly influential even as it is largely dismissed in our own times.

---

13. Fish, "Anti-foundationalism," 345.

Foundationalism

HOW DID WE GET HERE? JAMES EDWARDS AND THE AGES OF WESTERN RELIGIOUSNESS

Pinpointing the defining moment where the West turned to foundationalism is impossible because there is no such moment. There are too many influences and nuances to pinpoint just one instance where we can say, "there it is!"[14] The most common move is to lay the blame with Descartes as he is often considered the father of modernity and foundationalism—and rightly so—but the roots of foundationalism go deeper than Descartes. Foundationalism has been shaped and molded over the course of millennia by various cultures, philosophies, and ideologies that brought it to the form we find it today. James Edward's account of why the West is attuned to foundationalism is of a piece with my own critique of foundationalism and I find his narrative about the development of Western religiousness—and concomitantly, foundationalism—to be compelling because it complements my own thinking on the subject. Much of what follows is indebted to his thinking.

Edwards begins his genealogy by describing what it means for us, as "end-of-century Western intellectuals," to be religious. I have briefly explained what the terms "Western," and "religious," but Edwards goes deeper into what an account of being religious means for those in the West. By "religious" he has in mind three structural features that "underlie, and give a certain kind of intelligibility to, the various practices of creedal affirmation, prayer, confession, repentance, virtuous action, and so on, that have been characteristic of the great Western religions: Judaism, Christianity, and Islam."[15] He sees the same features as centrally present in early Greek religion and in some aspects of Western culture that are not distinctly thought of as religious, but should nevertheless be viewed as religious practices.

The first of the three structures is "the assumption of a fundamental and binary division of what there is, a division that ranges across the whole of things (and their relations) into one of the two basic types the division defines."[16] The binary division of *sacred* and *profane* is not so much moral as it is ontological. Whatever a thing is, either sacred or profane, it has that ontology all the way down. In the West, we have typically conceived of reality as consisting of two realms or two different worlds: "this world of need

---

14. Bruno Latour argues something similar, i.e., that there are no such things as irreversible breaks in cultures throughout history. See his *We Have Never Been Modern*.

15. Edwards, *Plain Sense of Things*, 6.

16. Ibid., 7.

and lack and change; and the other world of wholeness and haleness and permanence." This binary or dualistic view of ontology has been worked out in a multitude of ways across Western history and shows up in a variety of contrasts: gods/humans, heaven/creation, Forms/material things, ego/objects, nobles/slaves and so on. No matter if the manner of describing this binary ontology is religious or philosophical, "Western religiousness has insisted upon some binary account of what there is. For our sort of religious sensibility, there is a twofold division of things at the core of reality itself. At the most basic level, we are dualists, not monists."[17]

The second structural feature of Western religiousness is that this binary account of ontology is not an account of two equal partners: one of the "worlds" is dependent upon the other. "[The sacred] is primary and self-supporting and empowering; the [profane] is secondary and dependent."[18] An example of this is the creation narrative of Genesis where Yahweh created all things *ex nihilo*, by his very Word, and therein provides for and sustains all of creation. This is similar to the "Platonic notion of the Form as the perfect exemplar of the imperfect material thing, or the Cartesian conviction that 'clear and distinct' insights underlie all our ordinary knowledge of the world, or Kant's idea that eternal Laws of Freedom show themselves in and through concrete practical maxims of the virtuous life."[19] In every case, it is assumed that the profane depends upon the sacred both for its ontological existence and for its intelligible structure. For philosophy the assumption that the sacred grounds the profane has two different, but related parts: "The ground is that which brings forth and supports, that which produces and nourishes; and the ground is that which clarifies and makes intelligible, that which justifies and rationally explains. For Western religiousness both the order of being and the order of knowledge are binary and hierarchical, and in both the basic structure is the same: the sacred (the whole, the full, the perfect, the immediately self-present, the permanent) grounds the profane (the partial, the piecemeal, the imperfect, the absent, the alterable)."[20] I think this insight is helpful, because as we will see later, it is when the sacred ground switches from the Triune God to something else considered more foundational that a significant and *idolatrous* shift occurs.

17. Ibid., 8.
18. Ibid.
19. Ibid.
20. Ibid., 9.

Foundationalism

The third structure of Western religiousness, while based on the ontological structure of sacred and profane, is actually a form of life, a practice: "[it is] a sense that the proper and harmonious relationship of sacred and profane—a relationship in which the profane world somehow recognizes and assents to its ground in the sacred order of things—has been (or at least might be) in some way breached; and, if so, that the proper order of things must continually be reacknowledged and restored in practice."[21] For example with Adam's fall into sin in Genesis 3, the relationship between the sacred and profane (Yahweh and humanity) is ruptured and propitiation—an atoning sacrifice ultimately in the form of Jesus—must be made in order to restore the relationship. This sort of practice may be manifested in a multitude of ways like that of ritual sacrifice, the act of confession and repentance, or giving alms to the poor in order to restore (at least temporarily) the relationship between the sacred and profane.

These three structures—the ontological distinction between sacred and profane, the hierarchical relationship between the two realms, and the breach between the two realms that requires practices to bring about restoration—will be present in at least some basic level in Western religiousness. Based on this, Edwards identifies four ages or "major theoretical and practical expressions" in which these three basic structures of Western religiousness have been manifested historically: 1) the Age of the Gods, 2) the Age of the Forms (Idealism), 3) the Age of Cartesian Ego-subjectivity, and 4) the Age of Transvalued Values. Each age is distinctive in the vocabulary and institutions it develops for expressing these three basic structures[22] and yet there are times when the ages run together and blend. Nevertheless, these four ages are helpful for tracking the development of foundationalism.

The Age of the Gods

In the Age of the Gods, the sacred ground of all things is divine presence. "The fully present, logically prior realm that underlies and supports all that is—the sacred—is the holy and complete reality of the gods (or a God, if one were to be a monotheist), while everything else, and especially the human world, is partial, dependent, and lacking any secure and intrinsic order; that is, profane. The gods thus identified as the sacred ground are imagined as transcendent, willful, mysterious, commanding presences, usually personified, sometimes actually symbolized as particular human beings or

21. Ibid.
22. Ibid., 11.

animals."[23] This age understands the divine as transcendent beings that are uncontrollable, all powerful, and irresistible. Humans must bend the knee and their wills to the wills of the gods. This is easily seen in the whimsy of the Greek Pantheon's demands or in what appears to be the caprice and immoral actions of Yahweh and his command to Abraham to sacrifice his only son and promised heir, Isaac. Of course, as modern Westerners we are inclined to judge the actions of Yahweh as immoral because of the second age of Western religiousness (the Age of Forms), but for people living in the Age of the Gods, "divine presence is essentially power and the will to use it; and the mundane must, sooner or later, gladly or sorrowfully, answer to that compelling force."[24] In the Age of the Gods, gods are not primarily objects of belief like they are in our present age; people have direct access and face-to-face encounters with them. It is simply assumed that god(s) is the grounding of all things and all things make sense only in light of him (if you assume a Christian or Jewish interpretation). It is also assumed that there is a significant breach in the relationship between god and humanity and some sort of atoning sacrifice is required.

There was a time in which the Triune God (or other gods in other religions), was not only viewed as the sacred grounding of all things, but his presence and function as such did not have to be explained or justified; it was assumed without a moment's thought. But obviously things changed and in the next age the notion of the Triune God—or any god for that matter—as the sacred ground of all reality is lost. Edwards understands the shift away from the divine as the sacred ground of all things in philosophical terms, i.e., it is a problem of contingency. In my view, the problem is theological in essence and should be understood as a problem of *idolatry*. When the Triune God no longer occupies the role of the sacred ground of all things something else will occupy his place. That something else will be magnified over him and will define him according to its own terms. The move to foundationalism, as an idolatrous shift away from the Triune God as the sacred ground of all things, begins with the age of the Forms.

The Age of the Forms

The Age of the Forms overlaps significantly with the Age of the Gods. Even so, there is a distinctive shift that occurs. The Age of the Forms is characterized by a shift from "divine might makes divine right," to a situation where

23. Ibid., 14.
24. Ibid., 17.

the gods themselves must answer to something "higher," to a standard that is impersonal, eternal and perfect: justice or the good itself.[25] Again, modern Westerners have a hard time conceiving of what it would have been like to live in the Age of the Gods and much of the explanation for this lies with the advent of Idealism. "With Idealism—the second epoch of Western religiousness, and an epoch sometimes not thought of as distinctively religious at all—the sacred ground is conceived not as personified divine presence, not as compelling and uncanny divine will, but as the realm of rational, impersonal, and perfect Forms: an a priori cosmic order that confers intelligible substance on things. The sacred thus becomes understood as *the ideal*."[26] No longer does the Triune God serve as the ground of all things, nor does he make the profane intelligible. God himself must answer and be governed by some standard, ideal, Form, or some notion of justice. Plato serves as the token figure of Idealism and it is his articulation of the Forms as the impersonal, consistent, rational, abstract, eternal, and immutable as the sacred grounding of all things that defines the age. The Forms are hierarchical with the Form of the Good occupying the highest position and serving as the ontological and rational grounding for everything that comes below it. The shift from the Age of the Gods to the Age of the Forms then is basically a shift from theology to philosophy with the Triune God (or any other god for that matter) being supplanted by the Form of the Good as the sacred ground of all things.

Like with the previous age, in the Age of the Forms there is a rupture between the sacred and profane that must be mended. Plato sees the problem (Plato's allegory of the Cave serves as the chief example), in strictly cognitive terms: it is the failure, on the part the profane, to know the Good or the "Real" as opposed to being taken in by "illusions" or "shadows." Plato thinks that our will is corrupt and it has been corrupted by our illusions, primarily by the illusion that the world of ordinary experience is actually the true and only world. The ritual practices intended to repair and maintain the damaged relationship between the sacred and profane are intellectual activities such as the study and discussion of philosophy or mathematics. Far from being pleasurable or academic exercises, these pursuits are viewed as "sacramental," because it is through these sorts of practices that humanity can be restored to what is real and true. As Edwards explains, "Even in the age of Idealism, therefore, the reconciliation of the sacred to the profane

---

25. Ibid., 19.
26. Ibid., 20 (emphasis original).

comes about through a kind of sacrifice, but here it is the sacrifice of one's illusions to a higher truth rather than the sacrifice of one's will to a mightier force. In the age of the gods one willingly submitted to compulsion; with Idealism one intellectually surrenders to perfection."[27]

Foundationalism, as a general problem of idolatry is always a danger for the Church, but for the Church living within the confines of Western religiousness, the first step towards foundationalism began with the move away from the personal Triune God as the grounding of all things to the Form of the Good to which even this God must answer. It is idolatrous because it assumes there is something "higher" than God himself, which makes the Triune God *secondary and governable by this standard.* Even though the Age of the Forms is a shift from theology to philosophy, it is still largely religious in orientation simply because it erected another "god" in place of the Triune God, no matter if it is the impersonal, immutable, and rational Form of the Good.

The Age of the Forms (and the Idealism that goes with it) took deep root for Christianity with the Constantinianism shift in the fourth century,[28] continued to develop through the medieval age,[29] and remained firmly

---

27. Ibid, 23.

28. John Howard Yoder understands "Constantinianism," as it is typically defined, as a problem symbolized by Constantine in the fourth century with his embracement of Christianity (*in hoc signo vices*) that over the following generations would turn Christianity from a minority religion to not only the default religious position in the West (everyone is born a Christian whether they like it or not), but makes it the stabilizing and unifying force for the Roman Empire. In connection with this shift, Yoder argues that the Church accepts the dualism of Neo-Platonist metaphysics as its norm for truth, polity, and ethics. See Yoder's *Politics of Jesus*, 8–13; *Priestly Kingdom*, 135–47.

29. Radical Orthodoxy, a theological movement out of Cambridge, traces the problem of natural theology and the rise of foundationalism, i.e., "the surrender of theology to secular reason's account of nature," to a period between Henry of Ghent (1217–93) and his arguments concerning our knowledge of God and John Duns Scotus (1266–1308) and his arguments for univocal ontology. Henry argued that any knowledge held of any created thing by the human mind is at the exact same time knowledge of God. Henry however ultimately thought this view was untenable because he assumed a fundamental ontological distinction between God and his creation. God is indeterminable—his being is not defined or determined by any other thing than himself—while his creation is not only determinable, it is determined by God himself. Scotus took issue with this and argued that this distinction cannot hold if we are to have any knowledge of God himself. If we are to know God in himself, it does not matter what route is taken (by natural theology or by revelation), ontology (*ens*) must be uniform to both God and his creation if we are to have knowledge of him. In other words, ontology—much like the Form of the Good—is elevated to a position above both the Triune God and his creation and both

entrenched within the mindset of the Church in the West up until the 17th century with little or no arguments put to it.[30] This was largely due, not to the persuasiveness of Platonism itself, but to Christianity, which grabbed hold of it and never really let go.[31] Of course, the Age of the Forms did not remain purely Platonic (as if a pure Platonism ever existed), but its categories and assumptions about the world remained largely in place and are still influential today.[32]

The Age of Cartesian Ego-subjectivity

If the Age of the Forms dominated most of the Church's history, the Age of Cartesian Ego-subjectivity has defined it since the seventeenth century. It is in this age that foundationalism comes into full bloom. As the name implies, Descartes is the patron saint of this age, with his doubt of the reliability of our knowledge and his search for epistemological certainty.[33] His quest for certainty "is another form of the Western religious attempt to encounter, and to reconcile to, the ground of the fully present, sacred Being itself."[34] Descartes assumes that our knowledge is hierarchical (just like the

---

are held accountable to it. It is a development of Idealism that leads directly to the rise of foundationalism with Descartes. Philip Blond, "Theology Before Philosophy," 1–66; Catherine Pickstock, "Duns Scotus," 544–74.

30. Of course, a counter example would be that of Thomas Aquinas and his Aristotelianism. Rightly so, but even then, we can still find Platonism's influence with his "Necessary Being" or his basic assumption of a knowable rational universe in his arguments for the existence of God.

31. "From Augustine on, most European theologians and philosophers accepted some form of what has come be called 'the great chain of Being': a conviction that reality—or, better put, Reality—is a hierarchical structure consisting of a ground of pure and ultimately substantial Being Itself, usually defined as 'God,' from which ground logically proceed various subsidiary orders of beings, one of which is human being." Edwards, *Plain Sense of Things*, 24.

32. Radical Orthodoxy, while critical of foundationalism, still assumes Platonism as the necessary framework for theology: "The central theological framework of radical orthodoxy is 'participation' as developed by Plato and reworked by Christianity, because any alternative configuration perforce reserves a territory independent of God." Milbank et al., *Radical Orthodoxy*, 3. Philip Blond has similar concerns and asserts "that no created thing stands apart from its creator and that each and every existent creation reveals its origin in the Father through showing and revealing the phenomenology of its own given form. . .God is only seen when every being and each and every visible surrenders idolatrous self-determination to enter into the beauty and light of infinite participation." Blond, "Theology Before Philosophy," 6.

33. Descartes, *Meditations on First Philosophy*.

34. Edwards, *Plain Sense of Things*, 27.

previous age), with one belief built upon another, but he questions whether our beliefs can serve as adequate foundations for our practices. After all, a devil or an evil god may have tricked us into believing certain things to be true which means our knowledge could be completely false. To have true beliefs (and therefore true knowledge) there can be no gap, no possibility of doubting or the possibility of error between what our minds represent to us and reality itself. Certainty then becomes "the sign that the customary gap between Thought and Being, between us and the solid truth on which we depend, has been closed. In that way, certainty is the guarantee that the world has a genuine and intelligible substance; it is the warrant of an a priori Order of Things upon which we can reckon."[35]

Descartes' solution to his radical doubt is his famous *res cogitans*, the "thinking thing," that he argues is the only ground that cannot be doubted. Even if the thinking thing doubts what it knows, it is self aware of its doubt and recognizes itself as a thinking thing. For Descartes, "the identity of thinking is transparent to itself as both identity (*res*) and thinking (*cogitans*)"[36] and therefore, "The ego, the "thinking thing," becomes the being, the *only* being, whose Being—whose determinate and substantial identity—is immediately self-given; there can be no question, no uncertainty, about the Being of this being, and this being alone. The ego thus becomes the subject, the *hypokeimenon,* the fixed and identity-granting ground of all other reality. It is the original source of the world's substance. Everything else takes its determinate identity, its true Being, in relation to this ego-subject, as one of its "objects."[37] The movement from divine presence to the Form of the Good to the human ego as the ground of all things is nothing short of staggering. It is the shift from *theology* to *philosophy* to *anthropology* and it was a long time in the making. Whereas in previous ages, our knowledge was grounded and made intelligible by the gods or the Form of the Good, now it is exactly the opposite: the gods and the Forms are grounded and made intelligible against the *ego-subject*. In the Age of Cartesian Ego-subjectivity, our beliefs (and comprehensively, our knowledge) then must be measured against the ego-subjectivity and must obtain to the status of being "clear and distinct" for them to be considered true at all, including our beliefs about God.[38]

35. Ibid., 27.
36. Ibid., 29.
37. Ibid.

38 Diogenes Allen comments on Descartes are apt: "By [the mind's] own powers—by its "natural light"—we can discover truths which are absolutely certain and which form

One of the consequences of this age is that we can actually ask the question, "do you believe in God?" This is significant, because if you can question whether or not God is the sacred ground of all things, then as a matter of consequence God no longer has that function anymore. Belief in God then largely becomes a private and personal matter, as it cannot be held with complete certainty according to the criteria of the ego-subject. This is akin to what John Milbank points out as the trajectory of univocal ontology of Dun Scotus (among others) and the rise of the secular in the modern age: God is forced to the periphery and is now subject to a secular construction of the world.[39]

The Age of Transvalued Values

Like other philosophers of his age—Locke, Spinoza, and Leibniz readily come to mind—Descartes conceives of the mind as the "mirror of nature," a medium where reality is accurately *reflected*. It did not matter whether you were an empiricist (like Locke) or a rationalist (like Descartes); our

the foundations for all other fields of inquiry. These truths are not derived from sense experience but are innate to reason itself. Hence the label "rationalist," that is, one who believes that our reason has access to general principles which neither have their origin in, nor can be established by sense experience." See his *Philosophy for Understanding Theology*, 173.

39. Milbank argues the following: "If theology no longer seeks to position, qualify or criticize other discourses, then it is inevitable that these discourses will position theology: for the necessity of an ultimate organizing logic cannot be wished away. A theology 'positioned' by secular reason suffers two characteristic forms of confinement. Either it idolatrously connects knowledge of God with some particular immanent field of knowledge—'ultimate' cosmological causes, or 'ultimate' psychological and subjective needs. Or else it is confined to intimations of a sublimity beyond representation, so functioning to confirm negatively the questionable idea of an autonomous secular realm, completely transparent to rational understanding." See his *Theology and Social Theory*, 1. William McClendon offers virtually the same critique: "The church's story will not interpret the world to the world's satisfaction. Hence there is a temptation for the church to deny her "counter, original, spare, and strange" starting point in Abraham and Jesus and to give instead a self-account of theology that will seem true to the world on the world's own present terms. Surely, it will be said, the "salvation of the world must rest on some better foundation than tales about an ancient nomad and stories of a Jewish healer?" The strength of this worldly appeal lies in its claim to the universal—an appeal which faith must also make somehow. Its vice is that in its approach to universal truth it abandons the truth available to Christians, which is that the church is not the world, her story not the world's accepted story, her theology not the world's theology. If we wield this point, conspiring to conceal the difference between the church and world, we may in the short run entice the world, but we will do so only by betraying the church." See his *Systematic Theology*, 1:18.

thoughts were assumed to be exact representations of reality appearing, as it were, on the mirror of our minds. Descartes assumed that for a representation to be true, it must by definition be *sub specie aeternitatis,* i.e., universal, objective, and eternally true (like the Platonic Forms), without any reference to or dependence upon history, context, or personal will. Nietzsche and the rise of the Age of Transvalued Values calls all of this into question.

For Nietzsche, the terms by which Descartes (and others of his age) constructed his epistemology (representation, cause, mirroring) negate the possibility of verification and therein the certainty so desperately wanted by Descartes. The problem is that our minds can never directly compare any representation to the objective reality it claims to represent because there is never a time in which we can climb outside of our own minds.[40] In normal everyday life we can compare a mirror image to the reality it claims to represent, like with a driver's license photo and the real person named on the ID. But no such verification is available for Descartes' model. The problem is akin to Wittgenstein's famous statement about buying a bunch of copies of the same newspaper in order to verify the truthfulness of its front-page headlines.[41] It simply cannot obtain to the sort of veracity and certainty that it claims to have; "the epistemic gap between representation and reality remains (and must remain) unbridgeable."[42]

Kant tried to refine and defend Descartes' view of representation by arguing that our experiences are partially constituted by the structures and operations of the ego-subject self, but his account ultimately fails for the same reason: he believes our representations, in order for them to be true, must see things as *Ding-an-Sich,* "as they are in themselves." Nietzsche

---

40. Nagel, *View From Nowhere*, 11.

41. "Let us imagine a table, something like a dictionary, that exists only in our imagination. A dictionary can be used to justify the translation of a word X by a word Y. But are we also to call it a justification if such a table is to be looked up only in the imagination?—"Well, yes; then it is a subjective justification."—But justification consists in appealing to an independent authority—"But surely I can appeal from one memory to another. For example, I don't know if I have remembered the time of departure of a train correctly, and to check it I call to mind how a page of the timetable looked. Isn't this the same sort of case?" No; for this procedure must now actually call forth the *correct* memory. If the mental image of the timetable could not itself be *tested* for correctness, how could it confirm the correctness of the first memory? (As if someone were to buy several copies of today's morning paper to assure himself that what it said was true.) Looking up a table in the imagination is no more looking up a table than the image of the result of an imagined experiment is the result of an experiment." Wittgenstein, *Philosophical Investigations*, §265, 93.

42. Edwards, *Plain Sense of Things,* 33.

recognizes that if there is no way to demonstrate that our representations are true (in the way that Descartes and Kant want them to be) then the metaphor of representation necessarily collapses. The reason is simple: the sense of the metaphor, "representation," is dependent upon being able to check the representation against what is being represented. The Cartesian metaphor is dependent upon some way to access the *Ding-an-sich*, "the immutable, objective, absolutely given Order of Things" to which our minds must conform in order to produce "Truth."[43] Nietzsche shows this for what it really is, *a moral fiction*.

In the place of representation, Nietzsche conceives of the basic activity of consciousness as interpretation. By "interpretation" what is meant is "the willful imposition of structure and meaning on something—a text, a set of events, a sequence of sense-experiences—that demands it. The human being is not, as Descartes would have it, a center of passive reflection, but is reality's forceful creator and manipulator."[44] Nietzsche thinks we never stop making judgments or truth claims (or judgments about truth claims); it is simply that truth must be conceived in a non-representationalist terms. For Nietzsche, this meant that our truth claims must be understood to come from a particular form of life, not universal, innate, immutable truths. In other words, instead of "thoughts as representations," we now see that we really have "thoughts as interpretations." To say that we have a comprehensive and justified set of true beliefs about the world (i.e., that we have knowledge) is for Nietzsche only to say that we are operating within the confines of a particular form of life, a particular perspective, or with a particular interpretation.

> Insofar as the word "knowledge" has any meaning, the world is knowable; but it is *interpretable* otherwise, it has not meaning behind it, but countless meanings.
> — "Perspectivism."
> It is our needs that interpret the world; our drives and their For and Against. Every drive is a kind of lust to rule; and each one has its perspective that it would like to compel all the other drives to accept as a norm.[45]

It is often assumed that Nietzsche's shift to "thought as interpretation" necessarily entails relativism. That is, since we are all interpreters (as

43. Ibid., 35.
44. Ibid., 34.
45. Nietzsche, *Will to Power*, §481, 267.

opposed to passive receptors) we are free to interpret however we want. This is simply not the case. Nietzsche understands the act of interpretation as the concrete and fundamental social practices—our "values"—that constitute and characterize a particular form of life which form the basis for culture and society.[46] Everyone is grounded in social patterns and holds to certain values (i.e., interpretations) that are normative. Nietzsche's point is to show that the claims of Cartesian epistemology are not claims that derive from universal and absolute truth, rather they are claims that emerge from a particular form of life that is unique to the West. Cartesian/Kantian representationalism is no more and no less than a particular community's interpretation of the world, an interpretation that is neither universal nor irrefutable.

If Idealism replaced God as the sacred ground of all things and the Cartesian ego in turn, took this role away from Idealism, Nietzsche took the role away from ego-subjectivity and destroyed the notion of grounding all together. Nietzsche's shift to "thought as interpretation" not only completely undermines Cartesian foundationalism; he also causes the *collapse of metaphysics*. Philosophy no longer has anything to sustain it, because the impetus for the entire project—our attempts at "climbing out of our own minds" or "achieving transcendence"—lies in ruins. Where does this leave us? For Nietzsche the answer is nihilism.

Nietzsche understands "nihilism" as our highest values devaluating themselves. What we see as absolute truth (Truth) is really nothing more than the value of truth. That is, what we claim to be truth is really nothing more than a particular community's interpretation of the world and we now see it as such. We have become self-conscious of the fact that this is just the way we see the world and because of this our highest values have been devalued. The very idea of the sacred grounding of all things has collapsed and we are left with no belief in—or even the ability to believe in—the Holy, the Sacred, or the Divine, let alone the notion of universal Truth or the ego-subject. We have become "normal nihilists": people whose lives are constituted by self-devaluating values.[47]

As "normal nihilists" we recognize that we no longer really serve the gods, or the Forms, or see ourselves as fully present ego-subjects. "Normal nihilism is just the Western intellectual's rueful recognition and tolerance of her own historical and conceptual contingency. To be a normal nihilist is

---

46. Edwards, *Plain Sense of Things*, 37n25.
47. Ibid., 46.

just to acknowledge that, however fervent and essential one's commitment to a particular set of values, that's all one ever has; a commitment to some particular set of values."[48] To be a normal nihilist is to recognize and be *self-conscious* of the fact that our way of seeing the world is just *our way* of seeing the world. Other's don't have to share our point of view and they certainly don't have to agree with us. Our views are not the "Truth" in the sense that everyone must bow the knee to particular claims or be compelled by the same notion of rationality.

If Edwards is right in his narrative of the development of Western religiousness (and I think he is), foundationalism must be understood as a problem that has had a lengthy incubation. It certainly did not just "show up" as a modern problem with Descartes, it has been bound up with the trajectory and structures of Western culture from its earliest roots in the Ancient Near East. To summarize that development: foundationalism emerges with Descartes; is anticipated by late Scholasticism (e.g., Duns Scotus and univocal ontology); is given opportunity by the shift to Constantinianism; and is a logical development of Platonic Idealism. The failure of foundationalism (as is widely touted) is not merely the collapse of Idealism, though it certainly is that. As Nietzsche so powerfully demonstrated in the *Twilight of The Idols*, the failure of foundationalism is the end of metaphysics *and there is no going back*. In its place normal nihilism has become our everyday experience and yet, at the very same time, we are still firmly entrenched within the foundationalism inherited from the Age of Cartesian Ego-subjectivity. We live between the two ages, longing for universal standards while recognizing the contingent nature and utter failure of such hopes.

After Nietzsche, the current climate in Western religious discourse feels the tension of longing for the "true world"—as defined by foundationalism and its concomitant representationalist theory of truth—while simultaneously rejecting its existence. Nietzsche's critique of Cartesian ego-subjectivity was not merely correct; it destroyed the intellectual foundations of modern Western culture and so we are left between, what seems to be, two alternatives. Either we try and reassert foundationalism by dismissing Nietzsche and yelling "foundationalism" as loud as we can or we go in the opposite direction and run past Nietzsche's critique and hit rock bottom with relativism.

---

48. Ibid., 47.

Accepting these alternatives, many thoughtful scholars have attempted to bridge the gap between the two choices and make accommodated or moderated versions of foundationalism even as they recognize our contingent, historical, and embodied nature. Such attempts have met with no success. The next chapter will show how modern accounts of doctrine have wrestled with the problems posed by foundationalism while trying to make sense of living in the age of normal nihilism. Most have attempted to get around foundationalism by choosing a middle ground, a way between foundationalism and nihilism, but as we will see, such attempts ultimately fail because they continue to assume the very things they are trying to escape.

2

The Problem of Theory and Modern Accounts of Doctrine

The demise of foundationalism has been widely acknowledged and as a result, very few people, outside of a few ardent old school positivists, actually hold to a full-blown foundationalism. In the wake of foundationalism's collapse, there have been a number of different kinds of responses. One common response has been to embrace our embodied, dispositional, and situated status as humans and in turn, assume that we are free from all constraints: "You have your truth and I have mine and who knows who is right? What's more, who cares?" This is relativism and though it sounds like a disavowal of all things foundationalist, it is still firmly entrenched within the constraints of foundationalism; it has merely chosen the opposite of objectivism. A different response that is common among more conservative scholars is to reassert foundationalism or perhaps come up with a "lite" version of it. This response accepts humanity's contingency up to a point, but fearing the loss of truth and the unraveling of society (at the hands of the relativists) it cannot let go of foundationalism and feels the need to repackage and reassert it. Still another response has been to take the two sides of a typical foundationalist dualisms—e.g., objective reality vs. our subjective disposition to it—and try to bridge the gap between the two, usually by way of some theory or method. It tries to have it both ways and looks for a middle ground between the two poles.[1]

Such responses indicate that foundationalism—far from being dead—still wields significant influence on the way we think, see, and speak about

1. As I will demonstrate, my conversation partners in this chapter are all examples of these sorts of accommodated responses to foundationalism.

the world and our God. Because we sit uneasily between the ages of Cartesian Ego-subjectivity and Nietzschian normal nihilism, foundationalism rarely manifests itself as it did with earlier generations, but rather shows up as denials that will in one breath reject foundationalism and in the next affirm everything it holds dear. These denials begin with the affirmation of human contingency, traditions, practices, or perspectivalism, but they cannot fully embrace such things and ultimately take them all back. However, pointing this out is a difficult task because many arguments sound like they have gotten around the problems posed by foundationalism, when in reality they are reworked foundationalist accounts. This is true for modern accounts of doctrine.

The purpose of this chapter is to bring out the assumed foundationalism of supposed "antifoundationalist" or "postfoundationalist" accounts of doctrine that have claimed to get beyond the problems posed by foundationalism.[2] The accounts offered by Lindbeck, Vanhoozer, and Thiselton all recognize the problems posed by foundationalism and each in turn (at one point or another) offers a method for getting around it. In each case, the method being offered ultimately fails because it assumes the very categories it tries to transcend. In order to show how this works, I have adapted a typology first put forth by Fish: "antifoundationalist theory hope," "antifoundationalist theory fear," and "antifoundationalist theory hermeneutics." (or more simply theory hope, theory fear, and theory hermeneutics).[3] At the heart of my critique is the problem that theory poses to the accounts of doctrine offered by Lindbeck et al, so I begin by explaining what I mean by the term.

THEORY AS A SPECIAL PROJECT OF FOUNDATIONALISM

By "theory" I mean a formal method, "a recipe with premeasured ingredients which when ordered and combined according to absolutely explicit instructions . . . will *produce*, all by itself, the correct result."[4] "Theory" in

---

2. I will give a full definition of "antifoundationalism" in chapter 4. For now, it is sufficient to say that antifoundationalism should not be understood as relativism, so much as it is an attempt to move past the categories provided by foundationalism, which also includes relativism. To be sure, many so-called "antifoundationalist" accounts are actually relativist accounts, but this does not take away from the proper use of the term (*abusus usum non tollit*).

3. Fish, "Anti-Foundationalism," 342–55; Knapp and Michaels, "Against Theory," 11–30; Knapp and Michaels, *Against Theory* 2.

4. Fish, "Anti-Foundationalism," 343 (emphasis original).

this sense does not mean a proposed explanation or description of events, objects, or phenomena as it is typically used in American vernacular. "Theory" means a prescribed *method*—most commonly a general method like the scientific method—that supposedly stands outside of a particular practice in order to govern it. The pursuit of this version of theory and foundationalism go together because, as the thinking goes, if we can find the right theory, the right *method*, then we will be able to transcend the particularity of language, culture, and context so that everyone—no matter their background or assumptions—might arrive at the same result. Theory attempts to escape our limited and situated status as humans by creating space between ourselves and our practices so that we might be able to come to an unbiased, universal, and true consensus.

Nihilism, generally speaking is when "why?" has no answer. "Why do you say this is true?" Or perhaps, "why is your interpretation correct?" Nihilism cannot answer such questions because it doesn't care to answer them. For a nihilist there is no meaning or truth, so there is no point in answering such questions. In contrast with this, foundationalism is concerned—"harried" might be the more accurate term—to answer these questions. In particular, a la Descartes, "how do I know that I have true knowledge about the world?" Foundationalism takes these sorts of questions very seriously and has sought to find a way to come to universal consensus about the answers. This fits well with how Nicholas Wolterstorff understands foundationalism: "The classic theory of theorizing in the Western world is foundationalism. Simply put, the goal of scientific endeavor, according to the foundationalist, is to form a body of theories from which all prejudice, bias, and unjustified conjecture have been eliminated. To attain this, we must begin with a firm foundation for certitude and build the house of theory on it by methods of whose reliability we are equally certain."[5] Wolterstorff understands foundationalism as a theory about theorizing, as a "thesis as to how theorizing should be practiced," and is itself a "*normative* theory."[6] As a theory, foundationalism works to reign in and define our practices in order to transcend the particularities of a context or the biases of a practitioner. Foundationalism wants to judge what counts as knowledge, truth and warranted belief and therein it seeks to explicitly shape and frame our practices according to such things.

---

5. Wolterstorff, *Reason Within the Bounds of Religion*, 28.
6. Ibid., 34 (emphasis original).

Wolterstorff argues that the basic question facing foundationalists is "under what circumstances are we warranted in accepting a theory, and under what circumstances in not accepting a theory?"[7] In other words, foundationalism seeks to propose a rule that would be the normative theory for the acceptance or rejection of all other theories. Wolterstorff states the rule this way: "A person is warranted in accepting a theory at a certain time if and only if he is then warranted in believing that that theory belongs to genuine science (*scientia*)."[8] In order to understand this, we have to understand what it means for a theory to belong to genuine science: "A theory belongs to genuine science if and only if it is justified by some foundational proposition and some human being could know with certitude that it is thus justified." Further: "A proposition is foundational if and only if it is true and some human being could know noninferentially and with certitude that it is true."[9] For the foundationalist, so-called genuine science is "firmly based on a foundation of certitudes which can be known noninferentially. He urges that we accept or reject a given theory wholly on the basis of our warranted belief that the theory belongs or does not belong to genuine science. Only if we thus govern our acceptance of theories can we move towards eliminating prejudice, bias, and unjustified conjecture from the enterprise of theorizing."[10]

When Wolterstorff says "genuine science," he does not mean that this sort of thinking is relegated solely to the discipline of science. Rather, "genuine science" refers to *all knowledge*. In this light, theory is not an isolated problem for the sciences; it is endemic to the Western mindset and has affected a wide variety of disciplines, including theology and religious discourse. It is easy enough to see the role of theory in the sciences, but how exactly does it become a problem for other nonscientific fields?

AN EXAMPLE OF THEORY FROM LITERARY CRITICISM: THE PERENNIAL PROBLEM OF AUTHORIAL INTENTION VS. TEXTUAL MEANING

Literary criticism is concerned with many of the same problems as theology, in particular with the question of interpretation, i.e., "what does

---

7. Ibid., 28.
8. Ibid.
9. Ibid., 29.
10. Ibid., 29–30.

this text mean?" Knapp and Michaels wonderfully illustrate the problem of theory for literary criticism with their arguments about intention and meaning—something Biblical scholars (among others) are also deeply concerned about—with their now famous work *Against Theory*.

Knapp and Michaels define "theory" this way: "By 'theory' we mean a special project in literary criticism: the attempt to govern interpretation of particular texts by appealing to an account of interpretation in general."[11] They find that contemporary theorists usually proceed along one of two paths to make this happen.

> Some theorists have sought to ground the reading of literary texts in methods designed to guarantee the objectivity and validity of interpretations. Others, impressed by the inability of such procedures to produce agreement among interpreters, have translated that failure into an alternative mode of theory that denies the possibility of correct interpretation. Our aim here is not to choose between these two alternatives but rather to show that both rest on a single mistake, a mistake that is central to the notion of theory per se. The object of our critique is not a particular way of doing theory but the idea of doing theory at all. Theory attempts to solve—or to celebrate the impossibility of solving—a set of familiar problems: the function of authorial intention, the status of literary language, the role of interpretive assumptions, and so on. . . . In our view, the mistake on which all critical theory rests has been to imagine that these problems are real. In fact, we will claim such problems only seem real—and theory itself only seems possible or relevant—when theorists fail to recognize the fundamental inseparability of the elements involved.[12]

Knapp and Michaels illustrate their "anti-theoretical" argument by pointing to the perennial literary problem of authorial intention vs. the meaning of a text. For example, it is commonplace among both literary critics and Biblical scholars to argue that an interpretation of a text is valid only in light of authorial intention. That is, a text may be capable of many different readings or meanings, but the right meaning of the text is the one the author intended. So in order to have the right meaning of the text, we must ground our interpretation with the author's intention. But Knapp and Michaels argue that grounding meaning in authorial intention is confused, because the two terms refer to the same thing: the *meaning* of the text is

11. Knapp and Michaels, *Against Theory*, 11.
12. Ibid., 11–12.

the same thing as the author's *intention*. There is no reason to treat these as two separate things: the search for a text's meaning *is the same thing* as the search for authorial intention. This is precisely the mistake that Knapp and Michaels claim E. D. Hirsch makes when he argues that the best way to find textual meaning, i.e., a valid interpretation, is to look for and ground it in authorial intention.[13]

Hirsch argues in his classic work, *Validity in Interpretation*, that the meaning of a text can be nothing other than the author's meaning, that is, the author's intention. He even goes so far as to say "that the author's meaning, as represented by his text, is unchanging and reproducible . . . meaning is determined once and for all by the character of the speaker's intention."[14] This is good as far as it goes, but Hirsch goes a step farther. "For hermeneutic theory, the problem is to find a *principle* for judging whether various possible implications [of a text's meaning] should or should not be admitted."[15] He explains his method in fuller detail:

> Previously I defined the whole meaning of an utterance as the author's verbal intention. Does this mean that the principle for admitting or excluding implications must be to ask, "Did the author have in mind such an implication?" If that is the principle, all hope for objective interpretation must be abandoned, since in most cases it is impossible (even for the author himself) to determine precisely what he was thinking of at the time or times he composed his text. . . . The first step, then, in discovering a principle for admitting and excluding implications is to perceive the fundamental distinction between the author's verbal intention and the meanings of which he was explicitly conscious.[16]

Knapp and Michaels' critique is apt:

> What seems odd about Hirsch's formulation is the transition from definition to method. He begins by defining textual meaning as the author's intended meaning and then suggests that the best way to find textual meaning is to look for authorial intention. But if meaning and intended meaning are already the same, it's hard to see how looking for one provides an objective method—or any sort of method—for looking for the other; looking for one just is looking for the other. The recognition that what a text means and

---

13. Ibid.
14. Hirsch, *Validity in Interpretation*, 216, 219.
15. Ibid., 219 (emphasis original).
16. Ibid., 220–21.

what its author intends it to mean are identical should entail the further recognition that any appeal from one to the other is useless. And yet, as we have already begun to see, Hirsch thinks the opposite; he believes that identifying meaning with the expression of intention has the supreme theoretical usefulness of providing an objective method of choosing among alternative interpretations.[17]

In one moment, Hirsch identifies meaning and intention as the same thing and in the next he pulls them apart. Hirsch brings this out in his arguments against objectivist (formalist) critics who conceive of texts as public objects that are governed by public norms. He points out that "no mere sequence of words can represent an actual verbal meaning with reference to public norms alone. Referred to these alone, the text's meaning remains indeterminate."[18] He offers up the sentence, "My car ran out of gas," as an example of how any phrase is susceptible to any number of different interpretations. He argues that there are no public norms that will help us to decide whether the sentence is talking about my Honda that is out of fuel or "my Pullman dash[ed] from a cloud of Argon." Only after we assign intention to the sentence does the right interpretation occur. Hirsch puts it this way: "The array of possibilities only begins to become a more selective system of *probabilities* when, instead of confronting merely a word sequence, we also posit a speaker who very likely means something."[19] Knapp and Michaels think Hirsch's argument has real traction until we realize that "Hirsch is imagining a moment of interpretation before intention is present. This is the moment at which the text's meaning "remains indeterminate," before such indeterminacy is cleared up by the *addition* of authorial intention."[20] But if meaning and intention are the same thing then it makes "no sense to think of intention as an ingredient that needs to be added; it must be present from the start. The issue of determinacy or indeterminacy is irrelevant. Hirsch thinks it's relevant, because he thinks, correctly, that the movement from indeterminacy to determinacy involves the addition of information, but he also thinks, incorrectly, that adding information amounts to adding intention."[21] But if intention is already present, the only

---

17. Knapp and Michaels, *Against Theory*, 14.
18. Hirsch, *Validity*, 225.
19. Ibid.
20. Knapp and Michaels, *Against Theory*, 14.
21. Ibid.

information added in the movement from indeterminacy to determinacy "is information *about* the intention, not the intention itself."[22]

To attribute a meaning, an interpretation, a language or speech act to a set of marks on a page (or a rock or anything else) is to have attributed an author's intention *already*. No matter how little or how much information we may have about a situation, an author, or a text—we may not even know who the author is and the author may not remember the specific circumstances of his writing like Hirsch fears—"as soon as we attempt to interpret at all we are already committed to a characterization of the speaker as a speaker of language. We know, in other words, that the speaker intends to speak; otherwise we wouldn't be interpreting."[23] Likewise, we also already know that what we are interpreting is language or else we would treat it as random marks or sounds and not as language. The lack of information about an author has nothing to do with the presence or absence of intention. There simply is no difference between a text's meaning and the author's intention and attempting to create a space between the two via some method will not give us the valid interpretation of the text. We need only try to imagine a situation where there is such a thing as intentionless meaning to see just how confused this is.[24]

Imagine that you are walking along a beach and you come across a series of scratches in the sand. You take a closer look and read what appears to be a poem:

> A slumber did my spirit seal;
>   I had no human fears:
> She seemed a thing that could not feel
>   The touch of earthly years.

This would seem to give us a good example of intentionless meaning. It is easy to see the writing as writing, you understand what the words mean and maybe even recognize that the words are poetic. You did all this without any knowledge of an author or without thinking about intention. But then a wave comes crashing up onto the beach where you stand and it reveals what seems to be the second stanza of the poem:

---

22. Ibid.

23. Ibid.

24. What follows is a retelling of Knapp and Michael's famous "Wave Poem" illustration, 15–17.

> No motion has she now, no force;
>   She neither hears nor sees;
> Rolled round in earth's diurnal course,
>   With rocks, and stones, and trees.

The question of intention will cease to be irrelevant (or it will become a conscious question) and you will now try and explain the marks on the beach. Are they merely accidents caused by some combination of the impact of the ocean hitting the shore, debris in the wake, and erosion of the sand? Or is some agent at work, maybe the sea is alive or Wordsworth, since his death, has decided to haunt the shores writing out lines of his poetry? No matter how many explanations we may try and offer, it seems that we will be left with one of two categorical ways of explaining the phenomenon: we will either chalk up the existence of poetry on the beach to some mechanical process of nature or we will assume the marks were written by an agent who intends to say something.

In the first category, the mechanistic explanation, we will not actually interpret the marks as words: they will only resemble words. What you were surprised to find on the beach, what appeared to be poetry, isn't poetry at all because it isn't language. *It's an accident.* As long as we thought it was language we assumed there was an author who intended to say something, even if this assumption was unconscious on our part. It was only with the arrival of the second stanza of poetry that our assumption about an author came to the front of our mind. Most of us probably assumed someone had written the first stanza with a stick or some other object, but now that it seems impossible for this to be the case, we begin to imagine that the marks have no author. But as soon as we do this we will think of them as the accidental likeness of language. That is, the marks will *appear* to be language, like a dog that appears to be smiling. But the likeness of language and language itself are not the same thing and as soon as the marks lose their intention, they also lose their meaning and their status as language. The question of whether or not the marks counted as accidents or language was decided by whether or not there was an intentional author. No theory of meaning can answer the question of whether the marks are language or not, only the empirical judgment of whether or not an author intended to communicate can decide this.

But perhaps you have decided that the marks were an accident of nature. What would it take to change your mind? Imagine now, that you see half a mile off shore, a submarine surfacing on the water, out of which people wearing lab coats assemble on its deck with binoculars. They all start jumping up and down and you hear over the crash of the waves, "We did it! We finally did it! Success!" and so forth. It is probably safe to assume that your view would change. You will have changed your mind, not because you have a new theory of language, meaning, or interpretation, but rather because you have new evidence of an author. The question of authorship is always an empirical question that must have an empirical answer. The temptation is to believe that empirical questions, such as whether or not an author wrote something, must have a theoretical answer. In all of this, determining that the marks on the beach are language—and thus that they are the communications of an intentional author—does not help us in figuring out *how* to interpret the poem; it merely helps us in deciding *whether to interpret or not*. "Either the marks are a poem and hence a speech act, or they are not a poem and just happen to resemble a speech act. But once this empirical question is decided, no further judgments—and therefore no theoretical judgments—about the status of intention can be made."[25]

It is at this point that the epistemological elephant in the room must be acknowledged because the impetus for theory is largely (if not completely) epistemological. For example, if Knapp and Michaels are correct, how can we know if we have correctly interpreted an author's intention and therein have the right meaning of her text? How can we adjudicate between competing interpretations when we can't ask the author what she meant or if she can't even remember? It is obvious to most people that there can be multiple different readings of a text, but how do we know which one is the right one? While I intend to answer these sorts of questions in chapters 3 and 4, let me offer an initial and brief answer.

Often times, convention is enough to figure out a text's meaning. I say, "my car ran out of gas," and most Americans probably know that I mean my automobile ran out of fuel. But convention cannot explain everything, because convention can just as easily fail us. Take for example that I were driving you somewhere and you said, "turn left here." If I turn left, I will run into a sidewalk, but if I turn right, I will turn on to a different street. I say, "do you mean, turn right?" You say, "Oh yes, that is what I mean." It would seem then that what you said (the text) and what you intended (authorial intention) have come apart; that we have a situation where a "text" and "intention" are not the same thing. I would argue, however, that the phrase "turn left" really did mean, "turn right." You as the person giving directions simply made the mistake of not using what people conventionally

---

25. Ibid., 24.

say when they want to "turn right." But how can this be? Didn't you fail to mean something by not holding to convention? The failure in this case, is not a failure to mean something; it is a failure to communicate your intentions clearly. As a hearer, I assume you are intending to communicate and use evidence at hand to figure out your meaning. In any communicative situation, there is never a failure to mean, but there can be a failure to communicate the meaning.

But perhaps communication is more like scoring a touchdown in football? In order to score a touchdown, you have to cross the goal line with the ball. Intending to cross the goal line and failing to do so, is not the same thing as actually crossing the goal line. No matter how many times you intend to score a touchdown, it isn't a touchdown unless you cross the goal line. But language and texts are different than scoring a touch down. The very next time you say, "turn left," I may or may not consider the possibility that you mean, "turn right." But if you say it enough times then the meaning of the phrase when you say "turn left" will become "turn right." The failure in this case, was not a failure to mean something; the failure was making yourself understood. As Knapp and Michaels argue, "Conventions don't determine meaning, but they do provide important evidence of what the meaning is. Because conventions don't determine meaning, anything can be used to mean anything and, in the right circumstances, can be correctly interpreted to mean what it is intended to mean. But because people often do use words in ordinary ways, conventional meanings do function as evidence of what people probably mean."[26]

For now, it is sufficient to say that we often have the right interpretations, but we can just as easily have confused or wrong ones. It is also true that competing groups (even Christian group vs. Christian group) often have conflicts over interpretations and there are no objective and universal standards that can adjudicate the dispute. If we accept Knapp and Michaels' position on intention and meaning our latent foundationalism still seeks to rise above our situated status and search for a method, a *theory* that will guarantee a valid interpretation. And yet, if we take Knapp and Michaels seriously, no such methods are available to us precisely because there is no way to create one that will allow us to transcend our practices. Even to suggest such a thing is incoherent.

The same problem of theory that plagues Hirsch and literary critics can be found with modern accounts of doctrine. It is not easy to see the

26. Knapp and Michaels, *Against Theory* 2, 4.

foundationalism of many so-called "antifoundationalist" or "postfoundationalist" arguments and because of this I have adapted a typology in order to bring to light the foundationalism in these accounts: antifoundationalist "theory hope," "theory fear," and "theory hermeneutics." The typology is not neat and clean and there is overlap and similarities between the three types. Nonetheless, the typology is helpful for showing how even some of the best and brightest theologians are entrenched in foundationalism, even when they are consciously trying to move past it.

A TYPOLOGY OF ANTIFOUNDATIONALIST THEORY

The first type of antifoundationalist theory, "theory hope," begins by embracing our embodied and situated status as humans. The problem comes when it is thought that because we are now self-conscious of this, now that we see ourselves as we *really are*, that this knowledge can actually do something for us. What is being privileged is "self-consciousness" as if this kind of knowledge is more insightful than knowledge that comes without reflection. "Theory hope" mistakenly thinks that our self-conscious awareness of our beliefs allows us to create distance between our beliefs and ourselves. "Theory hope" begins by avowing that all of our knowledge, reasoning, speech and interpretations come from being situated in particular contexts, but it takes it all back by arguing that our self-conscious awareness of this provides a way for overcoming our situatedness. "Indeed, any claim in which the notion of situatedness is said to be a lever that allows us to get a better purchase on situations is finally a claim to have escaped situatedness, and is therefore nothing more or less than a reinvention of foundationalism by the very form of thought that has supposedly reduced it to ruins."[27] This is perhaps the most common version of so-called antifoundationalist arguments (not just with the modern discussion on doctrine) and is the one that often leads to relativism and the abandonment of truth claims.

If "theory hope" embraces our situated status and then mistakenly falls back to foundationalism, the second type of antifoundationalist theory, "theory fear" (as the name implies), fears the implications of the loss of objectivity and universal standards and tries to find a way to *reassert* them. "Theory fear" *fears* that with the rejection of things like universal standards, the representationalist theory of truth, or objectivist interpretive methods (all these are of a piece) we will no longer be able to tell right from wrong,

---

27. Fish, "Anti-Foundationalism," 348–49.

The Problem of Theory and Modern Accounts of Doctrine

true from false, and everyone will do what is right in his or her own eyes; a fear that is evident throughout Hirsch's work. "Theory fear" is similar to "theory hope," as its adherents will often admit to our situatedness and will even hold to the role of things like traditions, beliefs, paradigms, or interpretive communities. But adherents of "theory fear" will ultimately want to ground things like truth, interpretation, or the law in something that is outside of a particular practice. This is the same sort of fear—the fear that we must have some absolute measure for the certainty of our knowledge—that led to foundationalism in the first place.

The third type of antifoundationalist theory, "theory hermeneutics," is similar to the first two types of theory in that it attempts to get around being situated. "Theory hermeneutics" accepts that we are grounded in beliefs and dispositions, but then tries to develop a method, *a hermeneutic* for getting us beyond this in order to engage a text—or in the case of this work, doctrines—not only without our personal beliefs in place, but in a way that will allow "the other" to speak to us *on its own terms*. What is imagined by "theory hermeneutics" is a space in which we can abandon our beliefs without really believing them. It is to imagine that we can see the truth about our beliefs without actually holding on to them—to know without believing.[28] In short, "theory hermeneutics" (like "theory hope") thinks we can hold our beliefs at a distance and be critical of them at the same time.

Intrinsic to antifoundationalist theory is the view that makes a distinction between knowledge and belief or like in the case of E. D. Hirsch, between meaning and intention. As Knapp and Michaels point out, when this distinction is made, typically a person will adopt one of two epistemological positions: realism or idealism. "A realist thinks that theory allows us to stand outside our beliefs in a neutral encounter with the objects of our interpretation; an idealist thinks that theory allows us to stand outside of our beliefs in a neutral encounter with our beliefs themselves."[29] Much like objectivists and relativists, both realists and idealists assume foundationalism all the way down. The idealist position is intrinsic to "theory hope" in that it allows someone to think that being self-conscious of her beliefs in turn frees her to be in a position where she can analyze those beliefs at a distance. The realist position is intrinsic to both "theory fear" and "theory hermeneutics" because it assumes that we must shed our beliefs in order to come to an untainted encounter with whatever object or text

---

28. Knapp and Michaels, *Against Theory*, 27.
29. Ibid.

we are interpreting. A text or an object "exists independent of beliefs, and knowledge requires that we shed our beliefs in a disinterested quest for the object."[30] But how do we go about shedding our beliefs and allow the object or text to speak freely? For "theory hermeneutics" (as the name suggests) this is the role that hermeneutics seeks to fill, by providing the appropriate method or theory that will allow us to transcend our beliefs and see objects or texts as "they really are in themselves."

From my cursory description of the three types of antifoundationalist theory, it should be apparent that each type has a similar project of both affirming and trying to escape our situatedness. Even so, each type is distinctive with a different concern for and reaction to the demise of foundationalism. My analysis of the accounts of doctrine that follow is admittedly narrow and is focused on how they fit within the typology of antifoundationalist theory and thus succumb to the very foundationalism they are trying to overcome. While there are multiple issues that could be raised and many fascinating insights explored by each author, I am constrained to let many (if not most) of them go untouched.

The Nature of Doctrine and "Theory Hope"

"Theory hope" recognizes and is self-conscious of our situated status as humans and in turn thinks that this knowledge can free us from this status. It is bound up with an idealist epistemology that thinks being self-conscious of our beliefs—or in the case of Lindbeck's cultural-linguistic account of religion, our language and grammar—allows us to be in a position where we can analyze our beliefs at a distance. It is like a baseball player who believes he can take batting practice, and at *exactly the same time,* stand back and critique his swing from a disinterested point of view. This is precisely Lindbeck's "hope" and it manifests itself in what he wants his account to do, i.e., provide a theory whose proposals are "intended to be acceptable to all religious traditions that fall within its purview. They are, in other words, meant to be ecumenically and religiously neutral. They do not in themselves imply decisions either for or against the communally authoritative teachings of particular religious bodies."[31] In other words, Lindbeck wants to provide a neutral theory—a *method* that is not invested in any particular theological position and that can transcend the ecumenical landscape—for doctrinal reconciliation that could apply to any religion, but if it is helpful

30. Ibid., 28.
31. Lindbeck, *Nature of Doctrine,* 9.

for Christianity, all the better. His "theory hope," however, is clearly demonstrated in the most intriguing (and infamous) aspect of his cultural-linguistic proposal: his view that doctrines only have a second-order function.

Lindbeck argues throughout his work that doctrine, rightly construed, has only a second-order or regulative function. That is, doctrine functions as grammatical or linguistic communally authoritative rules for discourse, attitude, and action. Lindbeck believes taking this view of doctrine explains why, for example, Lutherans and Catholics can be reconciled on historically divisive doctrines like the doctrine of justification or sacramentology, without either tradition capitulating from their particular confessional positions. He gives an example of how this works with the phrases, "drive on the right" and "drive on the left" as rules for driving in America and England respectively. Both phrases are unequivocal in their meaning and are unequivocally unopposed, yet both phrases are binding depending on what country a person lives in or whether an accident has occurred and traffic is being redirected. That is, the rule is binding and unequivocal for the particular context in which the rule finds its home. "Thus oppositions between rules can in some instances be resolved, not by altering one or both of them, but by specifying when or where they apply, or by stipulating which of the competing directives takes precedence."[32] For Lindbeck, if we take a step back and get some distance from our respective traditions, we can see how and where these doctrinal rules apply, recognize them as "just our rules," and come to doctrinal reconciliation without changing the doctrines themselves.

Lindbeck is correct to point out that doctrines have a regulative (second-order) or grammatical function, but classifying doctrine as grammar does not move us past disagreement, nor can it account for reconciliation without capitulation. D. Z. Phillips agrees: "If doctrinal statements are seen as grammatical remarks, it is important to note that within the doctrinal contexts, there will be grammatical tensions as well as doctrinal agreements. In many cases, if the tensions are to be resolved, there will have to be doctrinal capitulation. Of course, the logic of this capitulation is no longer the logic of capitulation where one man sees the description of an object he has provided is incorrect. But just because the grammar of capitulation is different, it is no less capitulation."[33] If Phillips is right, merely pointing

---

32. Ibid., 18.
33. Phillips, "Lindbeck's Audience," 146.

out the grammatical nature of doctrine does not get Lindbeck around the problem of capitulation.

If we return to Lindbeck's own example of driving on the left vs. driving on the right, there is never a time in which we can achieve reconciliation between England and the United States by simply pointing out that both countries have rules for driving and agreeing to move past our respective rules. We will either drive on the left in England or we will drive on the right in America. It's not as though we simply can agree that our rules are "just our rules" and go our merry way. The rules remain binding no matter how self-conscious we are of the respective countries. If an Englishman is going to drive in America, he must capitulate to the American rules of the road (or risk serious injury). He is just as stuck in a particular practice as he was in England and his self-conscious knowledge of this does not give him a way of escaping the situation. In terms of doctrine, even if I were to concede to Lindbeck that doctrines are only second-order grammatical rules, Lindbeck is still facing the same problem of reconciliation, even if the problem is, at root, grammatical.[34]

For example, as a Presbyterian I am fully aware and self-conscious of my confessional positions when I enter into doctrinal dialogue with those from other traditions. But just because I am self-conscious of the tradition in which my doctrinal positions emerged and at the same time, recognize other traditions in which conflicting doctrines were formulated, does not enable me to both confess Presbyterian doctrine as true and at the same time act as if it is merely a rule for my community. It is simply not possible for me to confess that the Presbyterian doctrine on predestination is equally true as the Arminian doctrine on freewill. Even though I would not hesitate to call Christians from Arminian backgrounds my brother or sister, I cannot have reconciliation on this doctrinal matter without letting go of my Presbyterian tradition and its doctrine (or vice versa). No matter how self-conscious I may be of my contextualized doctrinal formulations, knowledge of this situation does not free me from the binding nature of doctrine. In other words, it is impossible to have my doctrine and my reconciliation too.

By recognizing that doctrines function like grammar, Lindbeck believes he has found a way around being situated within a particular doctrinal tradition. His "hope" is that this knowledge will allow us to create distance between us and our particular confessional traditions and in turn

---

34. Ibid., 148.

enable participants in religious and ecumenical discourse to transcend doctrinal positions and come together in reconciliation. Lindbeck's "theory hope," however, is not the end of his problems. By assuming an idealist epistemology, Lindbeck's "theory hope" puts him on a path to relativism. This becomes clearer when we dig deeper into his regulative view of doctrine.

If the positive statement of Lindbeck's account is that doctrines only have a second-order use, then the negative statement is that doctrines do not have a first-order use, i.e., doctrines do not make truth claims. Lindbeck, as a Postliberal, is reacting against both the liberal and conservative attempts at making the faith credible to modernity by grounding rationality and ontology in so-called universal standards.[35] While he is correct in denying that such attempts actually make the faith credible, he makes a critical error by articulating what he thinks is a rejection of foundationalism: *there are no such things as first-order truth claims at all*. He writes, "For a rule theory, in short, doctrines qua doctrines are not first-order propositions, but are to be construed as second-order ones: they make . . . intrasystematic rather than ontological truth claims."[36] In short, by rejecting objectivist or realist views of truth and language, Lindbeck has mistakenly assumed the opposite, i.e., relativism.

If we return to his example of the rules of the road, we can see just how this works. Lindbeck's thinking could be stated this way: "Your tradition has its sacramental rules and my tradition has a different set and that's ok. Recognizing this, we can easily see that these rules *only apply* in our respective traditions, i.e., our cultural-linguistic frameworks. When we step back from our traditions we can see that they are just one community's rules for sacramental practice among many others." This sort of thinking is similar to a "reader-response" view of literary interpretation that encourages different (sometimes hostile) readings of the same text: "You have your interpretation and I have mine and truth really doesn't have anything to do with it because *there is no right reading*." For Lindbeck, embracing a second-order view of doctrine allows an adherent of a particular tradition to see her own tradition's doctrines as just one set of rules that are only binding for her tradition and have nothing really to say to other traditions. "You have your doctrines and I have mine and we can get along because there really is no one right way to articulate Christian claims."

---

35. Lindbeck, *Nature of Doctrine*, 51.
36. Ibid, 80.

Lindbeck seems to be thinking along similar lines as Rush Rhees who argues that religious language and its grammar is of a particular kind that does not refer to objects in a first-order fashion like other types of language.[37] After all, if I wanted to say, "There is my house," we can easily investigate my claim. But this is not true when I say, "There is my God." I can't point to God like I can my house. We can point to Christian practices and find the meaning of the term "God" there (like Lindbeck argues), but we cannot refer to an ontological God like we can my ontological house. For Rhees, we can see the familiar foundationalist dualism of fact vs. value or reason vs. faith, because for him, claims about God are a matter of *faith*, whereas claims about my house are a matter of *fact*.[38] Is this what Lindbeck wants to argue? Yes and no. On the one hand, like Rhees, he denies that religions and their doctrines make first-order claims, but on the other hand, he says first-order claims are possible. His confusion on the issue is easiest to see in his famous example of the Crusader and his cry of "*Christus est Dominus.*"

As the example goes, Lindbeck argues that the Crusader's cry of "*Christus est Dominus,*" is "false when used to authorize cleaving the skull of the infidel (even though the same words in other contexts may be a true utterance)."[39] It is false for Lindbeck because the Crusader used the term in a way that violates the Church's regulative use of the phrase. Jesus, after all, did not send his people out as warriors among the Muslims, but as sheep

37. Rhees, *Without Answers*, 132.

38. Rhees, in discussing whether someone can point to an experience of God as the foundation and proof for a belief in God, argues the following: "I will say only that I think they are confused in what they make of it. They sometimes talk as though they observed God on these occasions. And this invites the question, "How do you know it was God?" Frank Buchman answers, "Well how do you know red's red"; and I suppose someone might also say "Well, how do you know it was your brother you were talking with just now?" But that will not do. I have means of identifying a man, and if anyone doubts my first assumption I can check. I know it is red because I know red when I see it; i.e., because I know what "red" means, i.e., because I have learned the word by ostensive definition and the rest of the usual method. Nothing of that sort can apply to an "experience of God."" It is one thing to say that we cannot verify a person's individual claim to have experienced God in some way. It is quite another to say that religious language does not, in fact *cannot*, refer to an ontological God. At the center of Christianity is the claim about a real, historical man Jesus who is both God and man, who was born of flesh, suffered and died and was raised on the third day and was glorified by God his Father. This is not self-referential language for a worshipping community; it is, by implication of the claim it makes, *a description of how the world is*. Rhees seems to be operating with an empirical notion of epistemological justification that no object or claim can bear the weight of, in particular religious claims. Ibid., 130–31.

39. Lindbeck, *Nature of Doctrine*, 64.

The Problem of Theory and Modern Accounts of Doctrine

among the wolves. Lindbeck explains his position this way, "A statement, in other words, cannot be ontologically true unless it is intrasystematically true, but intrasystematic truth is quite possible without ontological truth. And intrasystematically true statement is ontologically false—or, more accurately, meaningless—if it is part of a system that lacks the concepts or categories to refer to the relevant realities, but it is ontologically true if it is part of a system that is itself categorically true (adequate)."[40]

For a claim to be considered true, in the conventional sense of the word, it has to meet two criteria. First it has to be true within the system of its utterance and cohere with the rules that are already in place. So "Christ is Lord," first must cohere within the concepts, categories and beliefs of the Christian religion. This however does not mean "Christ is Lord" is necessarily an ontologically true statement. As Lindbeck points out "Denmark is the land where Hamlet lived," is intrasystematically true for Shakespeare's play *Hamlet*, but it is ontologically false because it is a play and not a historical event. In order for "Christ is Lord" to be true, the whole system in which the utterances have meaning must correspond to reality and this, Lindbeck argues, can only be shown by performance. He explains, "if the form of life and understanding of the world shaped by an authentic use of the Christian stories does in fact correspond to God's being and will, then the proper use of *Christus est Dominus* is not only intrasystematically but also ontologically true." In other words, the phrase "Christ is Lord" not only has to cohere to Christianity's grammar, Christianity in turn has to *correspond* with an actual God who is accurately conveyed by its practices.

It is not at all clear how this would work. How could you know if religious practices correspond with an ontological God, in particular if you can't point to that God? Lindbeck doesn't say, but that's not his point. His point is that truth claims cannot be divorced from a person's embodiment of them. He writes, "Paul and Luther, at any rate, quite clearly believed that Christ's Lordship is objectively real no matter what the faith or unfaith of those who hear or say the words. What they were concerned to assert is that the only way to assert this truth is to do something about it, i.e. to commit oneself to a way of life; and this concern, it would seem, is wholly congruent with the suggestion that it is only through performative use of religious utterances that they acquire propositional force."[41] But if we take Rhees' and Lindbeck's claims seriously—that religious language cannot

---

40. Ibid., 64–65.
41. Ibid., 66.

make first-order claims about an ontological God—then Lindbeck seems confused for even mentioning Christ's Lordship as "objectively real."

The phrase "propositional force" brings out the confusion. Lindbeck is not saying that these statements have actually taken on propositional *content,* as most Christians would conventionally use the phrase (like Paul and Luther), rather statements like "Christ is Lord," are "important, but not propositional." He explains that "[Christ is Lord] becomes a first-order proposition capable (so nonidealists would say) of making ontological truth claims only as it is used in the activities of adoration, proclamation, obedience, promise-hearing, and promise keeping which shape individuals and communities into conformity to the mind of Christ."[42]

In other words, it is only in the space provided by a shared practice that statements like "Christ is Lord," can take on "propositional" or "ontological" force as we are conformed to the "mind of Christ." Those who are outside of the Christian community and not skilled in its language and practices, cannot possibly make sense of what is being said or done. This is true as far as it goes: Christian doctrines are largely misunderstood if not at times incomprehensible outside of the community in which they are uttered, but this does not mean that God cannot speak to those outside of the Christian community, let alone that Christian language does not have propositional content. But Lindbeck goes well beyond this by arguing that doctrines cannot really speak to truth or falsehood at all, but only speak with this sort of force (the word "style" keeps coming to mind) within the performative practice of the community.

So if we take Lindbeck seriously, doctrine cannot speak to the ontological reality of God because doctrines only regulate our talk about God. But as we have seen, Lindbeck also seems to want to say that doctrines can speak in this way. So which is it? Can doctrines and our language make first-order claims or not? If they cannot make first-order claims then we have to seriously question whether Lindbeck's proposal can accept divine revelation. That is, if doctrine cannot make a first-order claim about God or the world, how is our talk about God, well, *not just talk about ourselves*? How is our doctrine conforming us to the mind of Christ and how would we know it if it did? But if Lindbeck admits to a first-order use of doctrine then his project is completely undermined. Lindbeck seems to be feeling the tension between the historical understanding of doctrines—that they actually speak to ontological reality and make true claims about the Triune

42. Ibid., 68.

The Problem of Theory and Modern Accounts of Doctrine

God—and what he wants his own model of doctrine to do, i.e., provide a method for doctrinal reconciliation without capitulation.

What is going unacknowledged in this discussion is Lindbeck's assumption that he must operate according to a theory of truth and language. Lindbeck is well aware of realism and representationalism as put forth by Descartes and Kant and rightly rejects it. However, as he is still thinking like a foundationalist, he assumes that if truth claims do not represent to us things *Ding-an-sich* then as a matter of consequence, there cannot be any such things as truth claims at all. Lindbeck's proposal unwittingly assumes the representationalist theory of truth and language even as he claims to move beyond it with his attempted use of Wittgenstein's notion of religions as cultures. Lindbeck's foundationalism forces him to believe that not only does he need a theory of truth and language; his only options are between realism and idealism and as realism it not a palatable option for him, he's left with idealism. Richard Rorty's "antirepresentationalist" account of language helps to demonstrate the serious problems facing Lindbeck's choice of idealism.

Rorty, borrowing from Donald Davidson's account of language,[43] argues that before Wittgenstein, language was pictured as a medium either of representation or expression. By "medium" is meant something "standing between the self and the nonhuman reality with which the self seeks to be in touch."[44] In this view of language, humans are conceived of as networks of beliefs and desires and our language then serves as the medium, the go between, by which our beliefs and desires *correspond* to reality. As we saw in chapter 1, this representationalist or realist view of language is concerned with having a "right fit" with reality in just the same way that Descartes and Kant are concerned with having knowledge of "things as they really are." This concern is born out either by conceiving of language as a medium of representation (a medium for showing the hidden truths of objective reality waiting to be discovered) or as a medium of expression (a medium for expressing the hidden reality that lies within us). A representationalist or realist thinks that reality determines our thought and language, whereas an idealist, (like Lindbeck) thinks just the opposite: our thoughts and language give rise to our reality.[45]

---

43. Davidson, "Nice Derangement of Epitaphs," 89–107.
44. Rorty, *Contingency, Irony, and Solidarity*, 10–11.
45. Rorty, *Objectivity, Relativism, and Truth*, 5

These two opposing views of language correlate with now familiar dualisms (e.g., rationalists vs. romanticists), but in particular, these views correspond with Lindbeck's own typology of religion and doctrine, *the cognitive-propositionalists vs. experiential-expressivists.* Lindbeck assumes for first-order truth claims to occur, language must be able to represent reality according to the terms set forth by Descartes and Kant. Lindbeck rightly rejects the realist view of language, but in so doing, he wrongly commits himself to idealism and as a matter of consequence, calls into question whether God has revealed himself (our language about God gives rise to his reality) and is forced to embrace relativism. Even though Lindbeck tries to make use of Wittgenstein, he doesn't choose a Wittgensteinian account of language. Instead, his proposal is a reworked version of experiential-expressivism, expanding it from an *Ich Theologie* to a *Wir Theologie*.

Rorty argues that a Wittgensteinian account of language "naturalizes mind and language by making all questions about the relation of either [mind or language] to the rest of the universe causal questions, as opposed to questions about adequacy of representation or expression."[46] In the Wittgensteinian picture of language, language loses its purpose—purpose as representing the world or the human self or having some other teleological or theological account—when we let go of a representational view of language. "To drop the idea of languages as representations, and to be thoroughly Wittgensteinian in our approach to language, would be to de-divinize the world."[47] What Rorty means by "de-divinize" is to put to death the view that the world or the self has an intrinsic nature of which our languages must represent. Rorty argues that the notion of an intrinsic nature is predicated on the idea "that the world is a divine creation, the work of someone who had something in mind, who Himself spoke some language in which He described His own project."[48]

On the one hand, Rorty is correct to argue for a "de-divinized" view of language: there is nothing intrinsic to the world that forces our language to conform to it. For example, we do not use the term "atom" because the term fits with the way atoms are in themselves (realism or representationalism). But the opposite is also true too: atoms are not what they are because of how we use the term "atom" (idealism).[49] On the other hand, Rorty goes a step

---

46. Rorty, *Contingency*, 15.
47. Ibid., 21.
48. Ibid.
49. Rorty, *Objectivity*, 5.

The Problem of Theory and Modern Accounts of Doctrine

beyond this by arguing that denying reality an "intrinsic nature" necessarily negates the possibility of creation and revelation. Like Nietzsche, Rorty correctly assumes that the "Death of God" means the death of metaphysics, but by linking metaphysics with the Triune God—a problem, as I argued in chapter 1, that plagues theology and religious discourse—Rorty cannot entertain the possibility of the Triune God both creating and speaking into our world. As we will see later in the chapter, both Vanhoozer and Thiselton believe the same thing: *if we deny a realist or representationalist view of language and truth, we deny not only the notion of truth and language, we deny that the Triune God speaks.*

For Rorty, in the place of representation, language should be thought of as tools for dealing with the world for one purpose or another. Borrowing from Davidson, he argues that there is no such thing as language, if by language we mean a representational view of language. Rorty again: "Think of the term "mind" or "language" not as the name of a medium between self and reality but simply as a flag which signals the desirability of using a certain vocabulary when trying to cope with certain kinds of organisms. To say that a given organism—or, for that matter, a given machine—has a mind is just to say that, for some purposes, it will pay to think of it as having beliefs and desires. To say that it is a language user is just to say that pairing off the marks and noises it makes with those we make will prove a useful tactic in predicting and controlling its future behavior."[50]

Rorty as an "antirepresentationalist" argues that the world is independent of us and that our language has been influenced and shaped by the world. Further, he believes in the truth and he thinks that claims about the world are either true or false, but not because they correspond to anything intrinsic to the world. Rorty simply denies the world any special status as the standard of truth by which our claims must correspond. Rorty again:

> The antirepresentationalist is quite willing to grant that our language, like our bodies, has been shaped by the environment we live in. Indeed, he or she insists on this point—the point that our minds or our language could not (as the representationalist skeptic fears) be "out of touch with reality" any more than our bodies could. What he or she denies is that it is explanatorily useful to pick and choose among the contents of our minds or our language and say that this or that item "corresponds to" or "represents" the environment in a way that some other item does not. On an antirepresentationalist view, it is one thing to say that a prehensile

50. Rorty, *Contingency*, 14.

thumb, or an ability to use the word "atom" as physicists do, is useful for coping with an environment. It is another thing to attempt to explain this utility by reference to representationalist notions, such as the notion that the reality referred to by "quark" was "determinate" before the word "quark" came along (whereas that referred to by, for example, "foundation grant" only jelled once the relevant social practice emerged).[51]

Just as Knapp and Michaels argue that we don't need a theory of interpretation to govern the practice of interpretation, Rorty's point is that we don't need a theory of language and truth to account for language and truth. He takes it for granted that some statements are true and others are false, but there isn't much to be said about it: "I would remark that since Plato the meanings of normative terms like *good*, *just*, and *true* have been problems only for philosophers. Everybody else knows how to use them and does not need an explanation of what they mean. I am perfectly ready to admit that one cannot identify the concept of truth with the concept of justification or with any other. But that is not a sufficient reason to conclude that the nature of truth is an important or interesting question."[52] Rorty doesn't think we need to concern ourselves any longer with questions like "what is the nature of truth?" because it is a question based on false assumptions, assumptions that begin with Plato and continue in our own day with foundationalism.

Lindbeck sees it otherwise (as do all the other accounts of doctrine in this chapter) and as a foundationalist, thinks he must have a theory of language and truth. Finding the realist or representationalist view of language and truth unacceptable, he assumes the idealist position, which leads him to his "theory hope." Coupling his rejection of realism with his "hope" for doctrinal reconciliation, Lindbeck embraces relativism by rejecting the first-order function of doctrine. His "hope" is to transcend the constraints of foundationalism and find a way to explain and encourage ecumenical reconciliation without losing the distinctives of the particular confessional bodies.

Lindbeck's account begins with so much promise by rightly asserting with his cultural-linguistic model that competing groups see the world in particular and different ways. Christianity is one such way and the language, practices, and the sacred text of the religion all work to provide

---

51. Rorty, *Objectivity*, 5.
52. Rorty and Engel, *What's the Use of Truth?* 45.

conceptual models for making sense of the world. Correctly, Lindbeck highlights that becoming competent in Christianity is akin to learning a skill, practice or language. This is good as far as it goes, but Lindbeck's account ultimately fails when it assumes the very foundationalism it is trying to transcend. Instead of moving the current state of religious discourse past long entrenched foundationalist dualisms, he has merely reworked the experiential-expressivist position and pushed it head long into relativism.

The Drama of Doctrine and Theory Fear

If Lindbeck's work is the one I find most important and influential in the current discussion on doctrine, Vanhoozer's account is the one of which I am the most sympathetic. His approach to theology and doctrine is both expansive and detailed and I am in agreement with much of what he *exhorts*. In particular, I find much of his pastoral critiques aimed at conservative evangelicalism to be useful and needed.

In place of Lindbeck's cultural-linguistic model for doctrine, Vanhoozer offers his canonical-linguistic model that is in large-part a reaction to what he perceives as the loss of biblical authority in Lindbeck's account. Vanhoozer is right to point out the lack of discussion on proper Christian foundations—in particular with the Bible—as a deficiency in Lindbeck's work, though Lindbeck does hold to the authority of the Bible for not only doctrinal formation, but also as an important authority (if not the ultimate authority) in the Christian Church.[53] To be fair to Lindbeck, his account purposefully lends itself to non-theological studies of religion, which explains the shallow discussion about Christian authorities and the role they play with the Christian community. An implication of this however, is that Lindbeck's account isn't necessarily Christian.

Nevertheless, Vanhoozer thinks that in the place of the authority of Scripture, Lindbeck's account privileges the authority of the community and its use of Scripture. On the one hand, this is a good fear to have: I think Vanhoozer rightly calls into question whether Lindbeck's account can actually allow for God not only to speak through his written Word, but to be active in the world. But on the other hand, recognition of this causes Vanhoozer to frame the debate in what should now be familiar literary terms. His reaction to Lindbeck is like how a formalist might react to someone from the reader-response camp, the central question being "who or what

---

53. See Lindbeck's understanding of the Bible's authority in *Nature of Doctrine*, 117–19.

is authoritative in interpretation, the text or the reader?" Vanhoozer says "text," Lindbeck says "reader." In contrasting his model with Lindbeck's model of doctrine (as well as Reinhard Hütter's account of the Church, doctrine, and practice[54]) Vanhoozer frames his central problem in these terms:

> To state the core problem: how can the biblical text exercise authority *over* the church if its meaning depends on its use *in* and *by* the church? Or better: Whose use of biblical language is normative for Christian doctrine? The text's? The interpretive community's? The Spirit's? Lindbeck and Hütter privilege the ecclesial and pneumatological dimensions, respectively. While not at all despising these contributions, the canonical-linguistic model accords primacy to Scripture as a species of divine discourse. With Lindbeck, we may say that Scripture makes sense on its own terms; with Hütter, we should say that the basis of doctrinal authority must be the Spirit's work. The way forward, I believe, is to see the Scriptures themselves as "spirited practices."[55]

In Vanhoozer's view, the cultural-linguistic turn to church practice, which is indicative of both Postliberal theology and much of what counts as so-called "postmodern" theology and its turn to the community,[56] comes at the expense of biblical authority. He's right. Vanhoozer is not against the turn to Church practices per se, in fact he commends a particular kind of practice that sees *sola scriptura* not as an abstract principle, but as a "concrete theological practice: a performance practice, namely, the practice of corresponding in one's speech and action to the word of God."[57] If Lindbeck put forward a method for Church practice that is reader oriented (the

---

54. Hütter, building upon the accounts of Oswald Bayer and Lindbeck, argues that theology should be understood not merely as ecclesiological practices with no reference to the Triune God (a significant problem in Lindbeck's account), but should understand the Church as the "soteriological locus of God's actions, as a space constituted by specific core practices and church doctrine." See his *Suffering Divine Things*, 26–27

55. Vanhoozer, *Drama of Doctrine*, 98–99.

56. As even Vanhoozer will argue, the turn to the community and its practices is not all bad and much of it is needed. Okamoto in describing the postmodern "Emerging Church," a church movement that has intentionally turned to the community and its practices, writes, "an emerging church is a group that, on the one hand, seeks to be faithful to the Gospel and, on the other hand, is conscious and concerned about the Gospel's practical embodiment in the individual and corporate lives of Christians." The concern is to truly embody belief in Jesus Christ and to bridge the gap between theory and practice. This is Vanhoozer's concern too. See Okamoto, "Emerging Church and the Postmodern World."

57. Vanhoozer, *Drama of Doctrine*, 16.

cultural-linguistic model of doctrine) then Vanhoozer is pursuing a similar project by prescribing a method that is textually oriented (the *canonical-linguistic* approach to Christian theology). To this end, Vanhoozer is not giving us as an account of doctrine—a description of how doctrine functions in the community—so much as he is exhorting the Church to make Scripture her primary authority and to conform her thoughts, words, and actions to it. To be sure, Vanhoozer does offer a description of how doctrine functions, but his description is always at the service of his method and his method bears a striking resemblance to formalism. This is clearly seen in both his rejection and espousal of foundationalism.

Vanhoozer is adamant throughout *The Drama of Doctrine* that he rejects any notion of foundationalism as I have described it. He argues that the lone foundation for his theology is Jesus Christ and further argues against foundationalist epistemology and its assumptions about knowledge as a view from nowhere.[58] But he can't quite fully embrace this and articulates a supposed "postfoundationalist" position: "The *postfoundationalist* seeks to "hold onto the ideals of truth, objectivity, and rationality, while at the same time acknowledging the provisional, contextual, and fallible nature of human reason." Knowledge on this view is neither immediate nor indubitable; it is rather mediated via interpretive frameworks. No set of data is ever foundational because the data is always framework-filtered and theory laden. Nevertheless, thanks to aperspectival realism, we may say that some filters allow true knowledge to get through. The postfoundationalist thus enables the epistemological lion to lie down with the hermeneutical lamb."[59]

It is simply confused to hold on to the "ideals of truth, objectivity and rationality," while admitting to the "provisional, contextual, and fallible nature of human reason." How can a contexualized person transcend his context and obtain to some objective norm that stands outside of the context? If you reject foundationalism, why even bother saying this? Claims are either true or false and the notion of "objective" is irrelevant to the discussion because no such thing exists. We can hear his confusion on the matter when he says "no set of data is ever foundational because the data is always framework-filtered and theory laden." What he fails to recognize is that the reason we perceive data as data is because of our frameworks; in fact *our frameworks are the content of our knowledge*. The frameworks don't allow true knowledge to get through; they are what determine what is true or

---

58. Ibid., 265–305.
59. Ibid., (emphasis original).

false for us in the first place.[60] Vanhoozer is on the right track by claiming Jesus alone is the sole foundation for theology (something he repeatedly mentions), but he doesn't seem to understand the implications of denying foundationalism and its claims on what counts as true, rational, objective, and so forth.

Vanhoozer assumes he needs a theory of truth and language and just like Lindbeck, his foundationalism constrains him to choose between two opposing options: the realist vs. the idealist. Vanhoozer chooses realism, which is evidenced by his consequent choice of the textualist position in the question of interpretive authority. Vanhoozer in one breath rejects foundationalism as a view from nowhere, but in the next, he openly embraces the realist theory of truth and language and by consequence a realist view of textual interpretation. This becomes clearer if we consider Vanhoozer's project as an example of "theory fear."

If you will recall, "theory fear" fears the implications of the loss of objectivity and universal standards and tries to find a way to *reassert* them. Without such things, "theory fear" believes we will no longer be able to tell right from wrong, true from false, and everyone will do what is right in his or her own eyes. Even though Vanhoozer rejects foundationalism, he *fears* the loss of objectivity, in particular with the loss of the Bible as the objective authority for the Church. He is, of course, right to want to preserve the authority of Scripture and I am in complete agreement with him on the supremacy of Scripture as the *norma normans*—the norm that norms all of the Church's speech, worship, doctrines, and practices.[61] But Vanhoozer's "theory fear"—with his so-called "postfoundationalism"—forces him to the opposite side of the debate with Lindbeck and leads him to assert a realist (and thus foundationalist) view of the Biblical text in his attempt to reassert the authority of the Bible for Christian doctrine.

We can make better sense of Vanhoozer's "theory fear" if we consider briefly one of his previous works, *Is There A Meaning in This Text?* This work, like *The Drama of Doctrine*, is a direct response to a scholar he radically disagrees with; in this case, Stanley Fish and his work, *Is There a Text in This Class?* Vanhoozer's reading of Fish and other so-called "postmodern" literary theorists is essentially the same as his reading of Lindbeck: "Fish's approach to hermeneutics effectively removes authority from the

---

60. In my view, "frameworks" are another word for "beliefs," which I discuss in chapter 4.

61. I will provide my own account of the authority of Scripture in chapter 3.

Bible or, for that matter, from any text. Interpretation ultimately takes its cue not from the text, but from the reader's identity. It is not the canon but the community that governs the reader's interpretive experience. The contemporary literary critic increasingly tends not simply to describe the reader's response, but to *prescribe* it. The text, again, becomes only a mirror or an echo chamber in which we see ourselves and hear our own voices."[62]

As Vanhoozer sees it, the question of interpretive authority boils down to two options: either the text is authoritative or the reading community is. Both *The Drama of Doctrine* and *Is There a Text in This Class?* assume this dichotomy all the way down and choose the formalist position: the text carries within its structure, its own inherent meaning that can be known by those who endeavor in the sometimes-hard struggle to interpret it. This becomes evident when we look at how he defines interpretation: "The term "interpretation" appears in the present work with two very different senses. The more positive sense (call it *realist*) treats interpretation as a mode of knowledge. The more negative sense (call it *nonrealist*) views interpretation as an excuse in human ingenuity and invention and fails to carry the connotation of knowledge."[63]

These two interpretive strategies of "realist" and "nonrealist" both assume a realist vs. idealist theory of truth and language, but also trade on the text (realist) vs. reader (nonrealist) dichotomy. The "nonrealist" is someone who reads the text in whatever fashion he desires, reading from a self-consciously partisan or even hostile position with no concern for the text and its meaning. The "nonrealist" isn't concerned with reading the text in itself; he is concerned with creativity and devising his own innovative reading. The "realist" however, reads in submission to the text and seeks to learn from it. The "realist" puts himself and his own reading of the text—he is open to correction—to the only independent standard there is: "determinate textual meaning."[64] Vanhoozer calls this method of interpretation, "critical hermeneutic knowledge," and explains his view further:

> In the final analysis, the ideal of the single correct interpretation must remain an eschatological goal; in this life, we cannot always know. Stated more positively, *meaning is a regulative idea, one that orients and governs interpretive practice.* While we cannot assume that the history of biblical interpretation is progressing, we can at

62. Vanhoozer, *Is There a Meaning in This Text?* 24.
63. Ibid., 11n1.
64 Ibid., 300.

least insist that the ideal of meaning should regulate the conflict of interpretations, provided that interpreters adhere to the mission of redeeming the text and recovering meaning: "The only way to go beyond the struggle, or at least to make it productive, is to constitute a community of interpreters sharing a primary concern for the book's verbal meaning." What exactly is this regulative ideal of "verbal meaning"? Towards what kind of norm are our interpretations striving? I suggest that the regulative ideal of literary interpretation is none other than the literal sense.[65]

Vanhoozer recognizes the difficulty in interpretation and knows all too well how many conflicting Christian interpretations of the Bible there are. But if we are to move past the current morass of Biblical interpretation, what is needed is a method for regulating our interpretive practices. Vanhoozer's method should sound familiar: "If the author's intention is embodied in the text, then the ultimate criterion for right or wrong interpretation will be the text itself, considered as a literary act."[66] His project is virtually the same as E. D. Hirsch's—in order to find a text's meaning, we must ground interpretation in authorial intention—and like Hirsch, he is confused right from the beginning.

Vanhoozer thinks in order for proper interpretation to occur, we must assume the formalist view of the text and interpretation: the "ideal of meaning should regulate the conflict of interpretations, provided that interpreters adhere to the mission of redeeming the text and recovering meaning."[67] For Vanhoozer, only those who assume the formalist view are actually concerned about the text and its meaning. Otherwise, we become "nonrealists" and are putting our own words into the author's mouth. Put into Christian terms, only those who assume a realist or formalist position will submit to the Bible and its authority, allowing the Triune God to speak through it and in turn, shape us.

Vanhoozer is simply incapable of seeing the issue in any other terms than text vs. reader and he is thus held captive by a picture, a theory of interpretation (and truth and language for that matter) that forces him to mistakenly interpret Fish as a relativist (something that Fish rightly and adamantly denies). When we boil things down, for Vanhoozer we are either realists or nonrealists which, by implication, means we either believe truth

---

65. Ibid., 303.
66. Ibid.
67. Ibid.

The Problem of Theory and Modern Accounts of Doctrine

is objective or we believe everything is relative. For a foundationalist, even a thoughtful one like Vanhoozer, who tries to articulate varying degrees between the two poles of objective vs. relative, at bottom these are the only two options available to us and he can't see it any other way. It is this same realist or formalist view of the text that stands behind Vanhoozer's account of doctrine.

For Vanhoozer, doctrine points us to the *dramatis personae*, the Triune God, and his on-going redemptive action and in turn, it helps us to conform our lives to the Bible and perform it according to what it directs. This is good as far as it goes, but how do we make sense of this when there is no firm agreement on exactly what the determinate meaning of any given text of the Bible is? Among Protestantism alone, there are over twenty-six thousand denominations that are only somewhat in agreement. This is not taking into account Catholicism, the Churches of the East, South America, Africa, and India. How do we account for them too? How can we account for when two spiritually led Christians, who are operating not as rogue individualists or textual innovators, but as thoughtful practitioners in two different traditions, disagree over the proper "fit" of particular doctrines or the reading of a particular passage of Scripture? How do we adjudicate between the two positions?[68] As we have already seen, Vanhoozer would say the literal meaning of the text (at least, the regulative "ideal" of such a thing) must determine who is right. But what happens when the rift is significant and divisive like over Christology and the Lord's Supper with Lutherans and the Reformed? Neither tradition is being purposefully innovative in the way that Vanhoozer describes nonrealists. In fact, both are actively and humbly looking for and claiming to have, *the literal sense of the text.*[69] How can Vanhoozer's account of doctrine, (let alone his theory of interpretation) explain how two Christian traditions, both led by the same Holy Spirit and both appealing to the same passage of the Bible while using up-to-date exegetical and historical methods, can radically disagree over the literal meaning of the text?

There is no doubt in my mind that Vanhoozer's project, which repeatedly argues that the Church must be shaped and directed by the authoritative script through the work of Spirit, is a good *prescription* for the Church. Of course, Christians must be shaped by Scripture. But in my view, he

---

68. Christian Smith makes a withering attack against biblicism on just this point. See his *Bible Made Impossible*.

69. By "literal sense" I simply mean what the author intended.

cannot make sense of why the Church does not interpret the Biblical text in the same way. If the text carries its own inherent meaning and God is still speaking through it in the power of the Holy Spirit, why do disagreements ever arise? In his account of interpretation, Vanhoozer points out that all interpreters are fallible and marred by sin: "It may be that interpretive disagreement arises not because of some defect in the text, but rather because of a defect in us—all of us. What else is the doctrine of original sin but a statement of the universality of cognitive malfunction, a confession that our design plan has been flawed through illicit tampering? Not only do our cognitive functions not always function as they ought, but we interpret in an environment strewn with cognitive and moral pollution. Cognitive malfunction can be corporate as well as individual."[70] Of course, being sinful does account for some of the conflicts of interpretation, but can this really do full justice to the problem? He acknowledges in his account of doctrine that the Church is fractured and full of division and his chapter 12 attempts to deal with the issue, but it really only amounts to a gloss. "The Holy Spirit has not, as far as we know, ratified any one confession of faith or settled on any one denomination. The Spirit is more "catholic" than that."[71] Ok, fair enough, but how does this help us make sense of disagreements? He goes on to talk of regional differences (particular regional confessions of the Reformation would be an example of this), improvisations, and different groups highlighting different aspects of the same Gospel. Again, fair enough, but there is a categorical distinction between a difference of emphasis and disagreement over the literal meaning of a text. It is one thing for Christians in Japan to highlight Jesus as suffering servant[72] or Lindbeck's medieval crusader emphasizing Jesus as *Christus Victor*. It is quite another when two different traditions disagree not only over the literal meaning of an ecumenical creed, but over what the literal reading of a passage of Scripture is.[73] Can we really claim that those Christians who are committed to the "ideal" of rationality, objectivity, and the "determinate meaning of the text," through the leading of the Holy Spirit, are the ones taking Scripture seriously and are more likely to be conformed to it and perform it as intended? Which Christians, exactly, are doing this?

70. Vanhoozer, *Is There a Meaning in This Text?* 299.

71. Vanhoozer, *Drama of Doctrine*, 423.

72. See Shusako Endo's wonderful novel *Silence* as an example of this.

73. Again, I have in mind, the Lutheran and Reformed debates over Chalcedon and what it means for Jesus to be both God and man. I will actually take up this specific example in chapter 5.

The Problem of Theory and Modern Accounts of Doctrine

Vanhoozer's method cannot account, in any depth, for the complexities of the Church as the context for doctrine, let alone the difficulties she faces in interpreting Scripture, particularly among competing claims amongst her members. To be fair, Vanhoozer does go into lengthy detail regarding the relationship of Scripture to tradition, the *regula fidei*, and our contextualized nature as creatures. He readily argues that Scripture and traditions go together, that people read the text from within traditions and yet, because he cannot conceive of the issue in anything other than foundationalist terms coupled with his fear of the loss of Biblical authority for the Church and her doctrine, he mistakenly assumes a formalist—and thus thoroughly foundationalist—view of the text.

Vanhoozer's account, for all of its wonderful exhortations for the Church to conform her worship, life, and practices to Scripture, to embody it and perform what it says; is ultimately undermined by its realist views of the text and cannot shake free of the foundationalism it is trying to move past. Instead of helping the Church conceive afresh its role in the modern age, as performers and participants in the Triune God's on-going drama of redemption, Vanhoozer's account keeps us squarely stuck within the assumptions that led to the problems he decries with modern approaches to doctrine in the first place.

The Hermeneutics of Doctrine and "Theory Hermeneutics"

If Lindbeck and Vanhoozer were self-consciously trying to move past foundationalism, the newest player in the debate, Anthony Thiselton and his *The Hermeneutics of Doctrine*, is not. With the first two accounts, my point was to show how so-called antifoundationalist accounts were really just reworked foundationalist ones. Not so with Thiselton. Not only does he not give up on foundationalism (though as we will see, he advocates a moderated version of it), he assumes it is a necessary and intrinsic component to the hermeneutic enterprise.

If you will recall "theory hermeneutics," the third type in my typology, gladly accepts that we are situated in beliefs and traditions, but then turns around and tries to develop a method, *a hermeneutic* for getting us beyond such things and seeing a text—or in the case of this work, doctrines—not only without our personal beliefs in place, but in a way that will allow "the other" (whether it be a text or doctrines or whatever) to speak to us *on its own terms*. This is precisely what Thiselton's project wants to do. My critique of Thiselton will perhaps be the most straightforward (and shortest) of the three accounts, because there is nothing to prove. Thiselton just is a foundationalist in his approach to doctrine. In fact, to be engaged in hermeneutics as it has typically been practiced for the last century is to be engaged in foundationalist theory, full stop.

Thiselton's project obviously, as his title suggests, makes a connection between doctrine and hermeneutics because, as he sees it, both involve communal understanding, transmitted traditions, wisdom, commitment, and action. Like Karl Rahner, Thiselton thinks doctrinal engagement really ought to be thought of as the art of "understanding," "listening," embodying "truth" and "love,"[74] which are the same sort of characteristics valued in hermeneutics.[75] For Thiselton, hermeneutics is both an art and a practice—it is formative (*Bildung*)—because it seeks to transform an interpreter into the kind of reader that is open and attentive to what is "other."[76] On the one hand, we must admit, if not embrace and celebrate, our contingency, our situatedness that finds its home in traditions and communal understandings.[77] But on the other hand, we also must embrace "the otherness" of the text—or in this particular case, doctrine—and allow it to stand apart from us on its own terms. While we are all situated within beliefs and traditions, nonetheless we must allow "the other" to remain "the other" and speak to us on its own terms, without imposing our preconceived notions, categories, presuppositions or beliefs onto it.[78] This is perhaps best understood as *dialectic*, in which a finely tuned balance is sought between the ontology of the interpreter and the ontology of "the other," allowing for true understanding and communication to occur.[79] Thiselton articulates this dialectic in terms of two horizons.

The first horizon "concerns the formulation of initial *preunderstandings* (or a readiness to understand). It relates to the attempt to identify *points of engagement* between the interpreter and the subject matter."[80] This

---

74. Karl Rahner, *Theological Investigations*, 1:4.

75. Thiselton, *Hermeneutics of Doctrine*, xvii. Take for example, Gadamer's comments: "Hermeneutics is above all a practice, the art of understanding. . . . In it what one has to exercise above all is the ear, the sensitivity for perceiving prior determinations, anticipations, and imprints that reside in concepts." See his, "Reflections on My Philosophical Journey," 17.

76. Thiselton, *Hermeneutics*, xvii

77. Ibid., xvii.

78. Ibid.

79. Ibid., 134–44.

80. Ibid., xx (emphasis in original).

The Problem of Theory and Modern Accounts of Doctrine

horizon looks for preunderstandings (*Vorverständnis*) "that will allow the *prior or existing horizons* of people to find *a point of overlap or engagement* with *that which has yet to be understood.*"[81] The second horizon is different. "It seeks to identify *what the "otherness" of the doctrinal subject matter demands* as a horizon within which its claims will be heard *without distortion* and without the interpreter's *imposing alien questions, concepts, and conceptual worlds upon it.*"[82] In other words, the first horizon involves the interpreter looking for bridges or points of contact between the interpreter and her own tradition and the doctrinal matter to be interpreted. The second horizon is a very different kind of understanding because it seeks to allow the doctrinal matter to speak on its own terms, without the interpreter asserting her own beliefs and context onto it and thus distorting the doctrine.

Take for example, the doctrine of the cross as it is currently being debated between essentially the Lutheran reading of Paul (this applies to more than just Lutherans) and the "New Perspective on Paul."[83] The "New Perspective" raises the question of whether the Lutheran tradition that begins with the problem of human sin, alienation and bondage and then works towards the cross as the solution to that problem is actually being true to Paul's writing. A different interpretive strategy (presumably a different Christian tradition) might not even have this debate because it is approaching the theology of the cross through the concept of "human solidarity" which could apply equally to "being in Adam" and "in Christ" without reference to questions of order, i.e., who was our federal head first, Adam or Jesus? Perhaps an even simpler preunderstanding would be the notion that "someone else has done something for us that we are incapable of doing for ourselves." This is a common experience in life and may help to make contact with the doctrine. Liberation theology offers yet another interpretive strategy because it has exposed something deeply significant in human life: liberation from oppression. Approaching the theology of the cross from the perspective of liberation may "open doors of understanding that readily lead on to perceptions of the meaning of redemption and salvation." These different interpretive strategies provide examples of the way the first horizon works: we take our own language, grammar, context, and tradition (e.g., Lutheran views on justification, second temple Judaism,

---

81. Ibid., 310–11 (emphasis in original).
82. Ibid., xx, cf. 310–11 (emphasis in original).
83. The following is a summary of his example on 311–20.

liberation theology) and use them to try and make contact with the doctrinal matter, i.e., the doctrine of the cross.

In the second horizon of understanding, the interpreter must assume the doctrine's context in order to not impose her own tradition upon it and in turn, allow the doctrine to retain its ontology as "other." Returning to the doctrine of the cross, Thiselton argues that the New Testament writers locate their discussion of the work of Christ "within the horizons of understanding drawn from the Old Testament." Because of this, we cannot entertain questions about whether or not Jesus' death should be interpreted as a sacrifice without first recognizing how deep and important the notion of sacrifice is in the Old Testament. For the New Testament text to truly be "other," we must first assume its Old Testament context. Further, we cannot rightly let the text speak on its own terms without also assuming the context of divine grace within it, particularly in light of such doctrines as expiation, propitiation, substitutionary atonement and so forth. The problem that people have with these sorts of doctrines in our modern age "rests less on any lack of forcefulness in the traditional terms than on the fact that those who are competent to interpret them do not explain their context with sufficient forcefulness or clarity." In other words, "We need to retain a frame of reference that not only keeps in view the currency of such terms as representation, substitution, and participation within their proper historical and logical-conceptual contexts by respecting their logical or conceptual grammar within ongoing traditions. We also need to respect and identify the decisive importance of their relation to a doctrine of divine grace and to the pattern of narrative history, covenant, and eschatological promise to which they also belong."[84]

Thiselton sees his project as a way of rediscovering and making doctrine relevant again for the Church through his well-worn hermeneutical method. If we return to the literary question I have been using as an example of foundationalist theory—text vs. reader—Thiselton does not choose one side or the other, he seeks to split the horns. If Lindbeck's chooses "reader" and Vanhoozer chooses "text," Thiselton chooses "both" and argues that both the text (second horizon) and the reader (first horizon) speak in mutual dialogue. This is what he calls hermeneutics and it is confused right from the beginning.

Thiselton's first horizon is true as far as it goes. It is true that interpreters bring their beliefs and traditions to the interpretive task. As a confessing

---

84. Ibid., 312.

The Problem of Theory and Modern Accounts of Doctrine

Presbyterian, I read Scripture and understand the doctrine of the cross from the Reformed perspective. This is something I naturally do as someone gripped by the Westminster Confession of Faith (among other things). So for Thiselton to recommend that I make contact with the doctrine of the cross from my already-in-place Reformed tradition (my first horizon) is confused. This is what I already do when I interpret and I can't help but do it, so why recommend that I do it? Making me self-consciously aware that this is what I am doing when I interpret the doctrine of the cross or the relevant Biblical texts doesn't give me a handle for better understanding what I am doing and it certainly doesn't allow me to shed those beliefs and allow the doctrine or the text to speak to me on its own terms as "other." The Reformed tradition thinks its doctrinal statements concerning the cross (let alone its reading of the Bible) are *already correct as they are*. When I read the Bible or articulate the doctrine of the cross, I am articulating what I believe is the meaning the author intended and therein the right articulation of the doctrine.

In the same way, Liberation theology thinks its interpretation of the cross as "liberation from oppression" is what the Bible *literally* means. The Lutheran tradition is no different, and as any knowledge of the tradition will show, Lutheran's argue that their articulation of the doctrine of the cross comes from careful exegesis (which includes knowledge of the context of both Old and New Testaments), consultation of the Fathers, historical investigation, and is in line with orthodox theology as originated with Jesus and preached by the apostles.[85] There is no need to commend using our particular traditions as an interpretive practice: *it is already just what we do*.

Thiselton recommends this as an interpretive strategy because he assumes, just like Vanhoozer, that as interpreters, we can somehow let go of our first horizon of understanding (our traditions, communities, etc) and let the Bible speak to us on its own terms (the second horizon), *without our traditions distorting it*. This is simply confused. While I am not against exegetical, narrative, grammatical, or historiographical methods for analysis of Scripture—hermeneutical tools designed to move us past our perspectives—use of such methods does not allow Scripture (or any text) to speak to us on its own terms. *It allows the text to speak from the perspective of whatever method or tool we are putting to it*. Historiography and

---

85. Payton agues that not only did Lutheran Reformers use careful exegesis of the Biblical texts in their original languages, they did so with the hope of letting the texts speak on their own terms. See his *Getting the Reformation Wrong*, 132–59.

exegesis are important tools, but they are not "objective" in the sense that Thiselton seems to imply in his method. It is not apparent to me how the use of historical investigation (among other tools) somehow frees us from our own context. We will still be reading the historical context of the text from our own twenty-first century context. Again, I am not denying the use of exegetical or historical tools for Christian interpretation; I am denying that they allow us to gain distance from our own traditions and beliefs in order to look "objectively" at a text as "other." I am also not denying that we cannot learn another context or be intimately familiar with some other time period or culture, but we will not think their thoughts as they do; we will think them according to our own context. This is just what it is to be creaturely, human, and finite.

When we look again at the second horizon, it seems to me that what Thiselton should be doing is advocating we read the text or approach doctrinal claims *as Christians*. If we are to assume divine grace as the proper context of the Biblical text as he says the text demands, then we must read it as Christians, not as those who have somehow shirked our beliefs. As Christians we bring to the text the right disposition or perspective that the author of the text actually requires, i.e., we read it in light of *Jesus Christ and him crucified*. I am not saying that Scripture, through the power of the Holy Spirit, is unable to change our views or even change our preconceived notions of the text (like my Presbyterianism). Scripture certainly can and does do this, but this does not take away from the particular "hermeneutical method" that has been advocated throughout the Church's history: the assumption that Jesus Christ (and his narrative) is the correct context for reading Scripture *on its own terms*. Unless we assume this *before* reading, we will not allow the text to be "other." To be sure, advocating we read Scripture or understand doctrinal material from a Christological perspective does not guarantee correct reading and it certainly does not solve all the hard problems of interpretation or resolve serious disagreements between conflicting traditions. But as Jesus showed his disciples on the road to Emmaus (Luke 24:13–34) and similarly as Philip taught the Ethiopian (Acts 8:26–34), assuming Jesus as the right context and interpretive strategy for reading is not only allowing the Triune God to speak through Scripture on its own terms, it is coming to the text with the right hermeneutic *already in place*.

At root, Thiselton simply is a foundationalist and his hermeneutical approach to doctrine is a symptom of this. The deeper problem he faces is that his foundationalism forces him to conceive of the Triune God and humanity according to these same foundationalist assumptions:

> If the capacity to deploy reason in the sense of cognitive judgment and wisdom is one implicate (among others) of bearing the image of God as creaturely human beings, a hermeneutical horizon of understanding for interpreting humanness comes into focus. Human rationality does not relate to "cleverness" in deploying information, but to a responsible reasonableness that transcends the merely instrumental reason postulated by David Hume *and today by a radically postmodern contextual relativism*. Theories that make "rationality" depend wholly on gender, class, education, and social situation devalue the reasonableness that belongs to the very givenness of *being human*. Even Wittgenstein, for all his valid recognition of plurality in life, believed that *being human* provided certain shared foundations for judgment that transcend a radical contextual relativism.[86]

For Thiselton, being a reasonable human is synonymous with being a foundationalist and to that end, I have no doubt that my arguments will fail to persuade him of the wrong headedness of his hermeneutics. This bears itself out in Thiselton's broader discussions on rationality and truth.

As the block quote above indicates, Thiselton outright rejects the contemporary insistence that there are no universal standards or norms by which to judge claims—what he calls "radically postmodern contextual relativism." Instead he agrees with Pannenberg's coherence view of truth and the *scientific* pursuit of theology and notes that "Pannenberg repeats his conviction that the question of the truth of Christianity cannot be raised as a scientific concern *without inquiry into "the truth of all areas of human experience."* The importance of *coherence* as a major criterion of truth and the *universality* of a hermeneutical framework of understanding provide strong reasons for maintaining this conclusion." [87]

Thiselton distinguishes between a "hard" or "classical" foundationalism, characterized by Descartes and logical positivists, and a "soft" or "moderate" foundationalism, characterized by contemporary philosophers who simultaneously hold to human contingency and some measures of reasonableness and scientific ideals.[88] He holds to the latter with "some

---

86. Thiselton, *Hermeneutics of Doctrine*, 228 (emphasis in original).
87. Ibid., 159 (emphasis in original).
88. Ibid., 126–34.

modest confidence in transcontextual reasonableness."[89] It is virtually the same view held by Vanhoozer in which we hold to the ideals of objectivity, rationality, and "determinate textual meaning" though we approach such things from situated positions.

But as I argued with Vanhoozer, if this is true then there is no accounting for disagreement. It is not enough to say that some people are rational and others irrational, particular when well-educated and thoughtful people who are filled with the Holy Spirit cannot agree on the right interpretation of a text, let alone on what counts as "transcontextual reasonableness." I do not deny that Christian doctrines and their truth claims describe the way things are, nor do I deny that a text can mean anything other that what its author intends. These things just go without saying and are, in my view, obvious. I simply think Thiselton's "modest confidence" in the notion that there is some transcontinental standard of reason by which to judge claims is wrong.

Thiselton's continued adherence to foundationalism seems to be predicated, like Vanhoozer, on the fear that once we give up on foundationalist (the "softer, moderated" version) assumptions about truth, rationality, and so forth then we give up on the Triune God as a transcendent being who is not only "other," but who has and continues to reveal himself through his Word. By implication, if we give up on foundationalism we also give up on the transformative power of grace and the eschatological movement of redemption.[90] I don't see how this follows.

Foundationalism is so deeply bound up with the West's understanding of theology, language, truth, and interpretation that both Rorty and Thiselton are agreed: if we reject foundationalism and its concomitant representationalist or realist theory of truth and language, we are rejecting the Triune God himself. Thiselton is captivated by foundationalism and believes that if we reject it (as I do) all we are left with is relativism and we make God out to be whatever we want. To be sure, there are those who gladly embrace relativism, but rejection of foundationalism does not force us to this. The reason Thiselton misunderstands thinkers like Fish and Rorty is because he reads their work with foundationalist assumptions and cannot transcend his own interpretive strategy (first horizon). This of course undermines his whole argument because he is not able to allow these so-called "radical postmodern contextual relativists" and their texts

---

89. Ibid., 172.
90. Thiselton, "Two Types of Postmodernity," 581–606.

to be truly "other" and must define them according to his already-in-place foundationalist assumptions. Affirming a contextually dependent rationality and a contextually dependent interpretive strategy does not preclude the Triune God from speaking. Rather it shows how radical our Lord's grace is and how far he is willing to condescend in order to rescue his people; the greatest example of this being the Incarnation of the Son of God. With the Incarnation God does not remain "other," *he becomes one of us.*

When I deny foundationalism, I am not denying rationality or the *Imago Dei* as Thiselton alleges. Rationality is bound up with being human, but rationality has always been context dependent. Denying foundationalism does not force us to affirm the incommensurability between cultures, traditions, languages, though there are some things that are clearly incommensurable. Things like language, rationality, emotions, and volition are all intrinsic to being human, but it does not follow that these things serve as evidence for some version of transcontextual rationality.

SUMMARY

Foundationalism conceives of humans in a particular way. As a mood, it shapes how we make contact with the world and it gives shape to our practices, practices like theological reflection and interpretation. So deeply has it touched the Western Church that many of its best and brightest scholars cannot help but interpret the Triune God, humanity, theology, the Church, and her practices by anything other than foundationalist categories. Lindbeck assumes relativism, while both Vanhoozer and Thiselton assume objectivism. All three equally assume foundationalism and cannot break free from a picture of truth and interpretation that should have been rejected a long time ago.

Hopefully it is becoming clear, that foundationalism far from being a problem of centuries past, still wields incredible influence on the way we think, see, and speak about our world and our God. The accounts offered by Lindbeck, Vanhoozer, and Thiselton all recognize the problems posed by foundationalism and each in turn (at one point or another) offers a theory, a prescribed method, for getting around it. In each case, the theory or proposal being offered ultimately fails because the theory itself is foundationalist and assumes the very categories it tries to transcend. In other words, they were confused from the start.

But now comes the difficult part, the move from criticism to construction. William Placher's words are fitting:

> Now comes the hard part. It is easy to criticize appeals to some universal standard of rationality, appeals that seem to assume the Enlightenment dream survives intact. It is easy to criticize various forms of radical relativism—the Wittgensteinian fideists' image of cultures as self-contained worlds that cannot interact, Foucault's self-destructive refusal to admit to taking a moral stand, Rorty's appeals to "what we can take seriously" as the standard of sanity. It is more difficult to describe a middle ground—in part because defense always comes harder than criticism, in part because the middle ground needs to be unsystematic, ad hoc, a work of *bricolage*, and any quick summary risks turning in spite of itself into a general theory.[91]

Placher is right: it is far easier to criticize foundationalism (and those who continue to assume it) than it is to describe a way past it. With the next two chapters we come in full to the primary burden of this essay: my claim to be able to move the modern discussion on doctrine past foundationalism. Chapter 3 is my account of the doctrine of Scripture as the authoritative standard by which all of the Church's doctrine must be judged. In this chapter, I will attempt to account for the authority of Scripture and its interpretation apart from foundationalist assumptions. Much of what I will argue in chapter 3 assumes and is clarified by chapter 4. Chapter 4 then, attempts not only to clarify arguments made in chapter 3, but also to account for the Church and her doctrine apart from foundationalist assumptions. The two chapters function as two parts to one long argument. To this end, not only do both chapters assume and imply the other, they both say similar, if not the same sorts of things.

---

91. Placher, *Unapologetic Theology*, 105.

3

The Authority of Scripture for Christian Doctrine

In the Introduction, I briefly mentioned William Christian's work that recognizes two kinds of doctrines. The first kind of doctrine he calls "primary doctrines." These are doctrines that make claims about the setting of human life and the conduct of life in that setting.[1] The second kind of doctrine Christian calls "governing doctrines." These are doctrines that provide the principles and rules that govern the formation and development of other doctrines. They are doctrines about doctrines, i.e., they are doctrines that regulate other doctrines. I begin my own account of doctrine, with an account of *the governing doctrine for doctrine in the Church*, the doctrine that claims that the rule and measure that regulates the Church's worship, practice, preaching, and teaching is Scripture.

An initial question to ask is, why take up this doctrine? Christian writes, "When members of a community reflect on deriving its doctrines from its sources, questions of the following sorts would be directly relevant."[2]

1. What are the authentic sources of the community's doctrines?
2. Are some of the sources more important than others for this purpose?
3. How is it to be decided whether the sources warrant a decision that what is said in some sentence is an authentic doctrine of the community?

---

1. Christian, *Doctrines of Religious Communities*, 2.
2. Ibid., 87.

When accounting for the Church's doctrine, taking up the question of Scripture is not merely taking up "a" governing doctrine, as if it is just one doctrine among many; the doctrine of Scripture is "the" governing doctrine for doctrine. Why? This passage from the Westminster Confession of Faith serves as a fairly representative answer:

> The whole counsel of God concerning all things necessary for His own glory, man's salvation, faith and life, is either expressly set down in Scripture, or by good and necessary consequence may be deduced from Scripture: unto which nothing at any time is to be added, whether by new revelations of the Spirit or traditions of men. Nevertheless, we acknowledge the inward illumination of the Spirit of God to be necessary for the saving understanding of such things as are revealed in the Word: and that are some circumstances concerning the worship of God, and government of the Church, common to human actions and societies, which are to be ordered by the light of nature, and Christian prudence, according to the general rules of the Word, which are always to be observed.[3]

The WCF teaches, from its very first chapter, that Scripture is *the* authoritative source and measure for all other Christian doctrine. Everything that follows in the WCF finds its source and measure in Scripture. This is similar to what David Kelsey argues. Commenting on a diversity of Protestant theologians through the twentieth century, he writes, "Virtually every contemporary Protestant theologian along the entire spectrum of opinion from the "neo-evangelicals" through Karl Barth, Emil Brunner, to Anders Nygren, Rudolf Bultmann, Paul Tillich and Fritz Buri, has acknowledged that any Christian theology worthy of the name "Christian" must, in *some* sense of the phrase, be done "in accord with scripture.""[4] The doctrine of Scripture as the rule and norm for the Church's doctrine, worship, speech, and practice is the central, if not pivotal, concern for any account of doctrine because every other doctrine finds its source, authenticity, and measure with Scripture.

For example, Christian finds this same doctrine at work early in the Church's history with Irenaeus and his arguments against the gnostics in *Against Heresies*. Christian notices that Irenaeus makes claims of the primary doctrine kind: claims about the setting of human life, the creation of the world, the history of redemption, and how Christians should conduct

---

3. WCF, 1.6.
4. Kelsey, *Proving Doctrine*, 1.

their lives in this setting.[5] But Irenaeus is not content to merely put forth these sorts of claims, "he wants to argue that certain doctrines taught by various gnostics are not authentically Christian."[6] Irenaeus can't simply say the gnostics are wrong; he has to demonstrate how they fail to be authentically Christian by appealing to a particular Christian standard that is recognized as the authoritative source and measure for all other doctrines. "So he needs a framework for arguments on questions of the form: Is s a Christian doctrine? These questions cannot be argued unless there is some non-arbitrary way of dealing with them. They call for principles and rules to guide arguments and judgments."[7] Christian argues that Irenaeus develops the following framework for dealing with such questions:

1. s is not a Christian doctrine unless it is in accord with the Scriptures.
2. Passages in the Scriptures, like passages in Homer, ought to be interpreted in their contexts.
3. Apostolic tradition confirms and amplifies what the Scriptures say.
4. Bishops can be relied on to preserve apostolic tradition.[8]

Christian further elaborates: "Now in *Against Heresies* it is clear that Irenaeus means to speak not just for himself but for his community. So he must be putting forward these principles and rules as Christian doctrines. And, since their function in the situation in which he speaks is to guide judgments as to whether something is a Christian doctrine or not, we might say of the framework as a whole that it is being proposed as a Christian doctrine about Christian doctrines."[9] For Irenaeus, the standard or framework by which we determine whether or not a something is a Christian doctrine (Is s a doctrine of R?) is Scripture. It is by the standard of Scripture that all claims, doctrines, and practices must be measured to determine if they are *authentically* Christian or not. It is not enough to simply claim something is a Christian doctrine; it must *measure up* to the standard of Scripture.

The doctrine that teaches that Scripture is the standard for Christian preaching and teaching is nothing new. Scripture has been regarded as the

---

5. Christian, *Doctrines of Religious Communities*, 12.
6. Ibid.
7. Ibid.
8. Ibid.
9. Ibid.

measure and standard for not only doctrine, but for all of the Church's worship and practices since the very beginning of the Church. In fact, this is one of the primary reasons for Scripture's existence: to function as the rule and norm for the people of God. For most of Christian history it has been assumed that Scripture is authoritative for the Church's doctrine and yet, in the modern age this is disputed. As Vanhoozer feels deeply (and rightly so), Scripture has lost its privileged status as the standard and source by which the Church measures and authenticates all of her claims.

It is not a coincidence that Scripture's loss of authority mirrors the rise of foundationalism. John Behr, writing about the advent of the New Testament and its relationship to apostolic tradition and the canon argues the following:

> If we are to understand the particular contours of this debate and its resolution, we must avoid reading its terms in the manner set by the polemics of the Reformation and Counter-Reformation, in which Scripture is opposed to tradition, as two distinct sources of authority. Separating Scripture and tradition in this way introduces an inevitable quandary: if the locus of authority is fixed solely in Scripture, and "canon" is understood exclusively in the sense of a "list" of authoritative books, then accounting for the list becomes problematic; if, on the other hand, Scripture is subsumed under tradition, on the grounds that the Church predates the writing of the New Testament (conveniently forgetting, in a Marcionite fashion, the existence of Scripture—the Law, the Psalms and the Prophets), then again a problem arises from the lack of a criterion or canon, this time for differentiating, as is often done, between "Tradition" and "traditions"—all traditions are venerable, though some more so than others, yet the basis for this distinction is never clarified.[10]

As Behr sees it (and I think he's right), the discussion over the authority of Scripture in the modern age has been framed by the assumption that Scripture and the Church are two distinct and opposing authorities. To assume this dichotomy, is to assume our now familiar foundationalist dualism of text vs. reader; a dualism which cannot adequately account both for how Scripture is authoritative for the Church and how the Church goes about reading and interpreting Scripture. Assuming this dualism forces us to understand both Scripture (text) and the Church (reader) as two *independent* entities, each with their own distinct ontology and autonomy.

10. Behr, *Way To Nicaea*, 12–13.

The Authority of Scripture for Christian Doctrine

The question of interpretive authority, of text vs. reader, is a question that I keep revisiting. Admittedly, I like the question and have used it as almost the defining question of the essay because it simply and deeply illustrates the dichotomies brought out by foundationalism. But more than this, the question touches upon many issues that are central concerns for the Church and theology, not least of these would be concerns over the place and role of Scripture and its interpretation, as well as the role that Scripture plays in the formulation of doctrine. With Behr, I contend that the way Scriptural authority has typically been framed—i.e., *sola scriptura* (the text as a stand alone authority over the Church) vs. Church tradition (the Church that stands in authority over Scripture)—is confused.

Coupled with questions brought out by the text vs. reader dualism is the question of whether or not Scripture is even authoritative in the first place. This question, perhaps more than any other question in the twentieth century, has dogged conservative evangelicals as the most dire and important question facing the Church mainly because of the onslaught of attacks against Scripture, calling into question its authority and validity as the Word of God.[11]

In light of all the difficulties facing the doctrine of Scripture as the authoritative source and measure for the Church and her doctrine, we cannot be content to merely assert the doctrine and move along, no matter how true it is. The modern age has called far too much into question for the Church to assert the doctrine of Scripture without some sort of explanation and justification for the claim. Further compounding the problem, foundationalism has led to confusion about the role of Scripture (text) and the Church's role in interpreting it (readers). How do we make sense of all these questions? How can we account for Scripture as the governing doctrine of the Church, both in its ontology (i.e., it is the Word of God) and in its function as the rule and norm for Christian doctrine and practice? Similarly, how can we account for the Church's role as the rightful interpreter of the text?

The purpose for this chapter is to bring clarity to these questions by accounting for the authority of Scripture, as the rule and norm for the Church and her doctrine, apart from foundationalist assumptions. My argument

---

11. Recently novelists like Dan Brown and scholars like Elaine Pagels and Bart Ehrman have made harsh attacks against the Bible, casting serious doubt—in a fairly public fashion—over its veracity, though questions and serious attacks are nothing new and have been made for the last three hundred years or so. See Brown, *DaVinci Code*; Pagels, *Gnostic Gospels*; Ehrman, *Lost Christianities*.

will first take up the topic of how and why Christians claim Scripture is Scripture. I will then turn to the question of how Scripture functions as an authority for the Church and then in the last section, I will briefly take up the question of how the Church goes about interpreting Scripture. The temptation of course is to write far more than space allows on this subject (indeed, this can easily be a book length project). Because of this, my treatment of the subject is admittedly brief and many important questions go unmentioned (and thus unanswered). Because of this, I would direct readers to Peter Nafzger's forthcoming book on this topic: *These Are Written: Towards a Cruciform Theology of Scripture*. Much of what I have to say is indebted to his work.

DO WE HAVE SCRIPTURE HERE?

In evangelical circles, the question, "Do you think Scripture is authoritative for the Church as the inspired and inerrant Word of God?" often serves as a litmus test for orthodoxy.[12] Of course, Christians should hold to the authority of Scripture, but the fact that the above question functions as a test of orthodoxy shows just how far the Bible has fallen as an authority over the last several centuries. As I affirmed in chapter 2 with my discussion of Vanhoozer, Scripture is the *norma normans*—the norm that norms all of the Church's speech, doctrines, and practices. But why do Christians claim this? Is it because this is just what Christians believe? Is it because God himself came down and wrote the text with his own finger? How do I know this book, this set of texts is the authoritative Word of God? How can I prove it?

The history of the debate over the authority of Scripture—"the modern battle for the Bible" as it is known—has been cast largely in terms of whether or not we can prove Scripture itself is true and thus authoritative. Typical arguments for the authority of Scripture (usually made by conservative Protestants) have focused on the inspiration and inerrancy of Scripture, but have also appealed to disciplines like archaeology, historiography,

---

12. For example, membership into the Evangelical Theological Society requires submission to these two doctrines: "The Bible alone, and the Bible in its entirety, is the Word of God written and is therefore inerrant in the autographs. God is a Trinity, Father, Son, and Holy Spirit, each an uncreated person, equal in power and glory." So in essence, to be a member of this professional society a person has to confess the Chicago Statement on Inerrancy and the Nicene Creed, in that order.

The Authority of Scripture for Christian Doctrine

and literary studies to bolster its arguments. The logic of typical defenses of the authority of Scripture goes something like this:

1. The Scriptures are authoritative because they are inspired by the Holy Spirit.
2. Because they are inspired they are historically true.
3. Their authority, therefore, stands or falls with their historical truthfulness.

Harold Lindsell is a good example of just this sort of logic: "The authority of the Bible is viable only if the Bible itself is true. Destroy the trustworthiness of the Bible, and its authority goes with it. Accept its trustworthiness and authority becomes normative. . . . Infallibility and authority stand or fall together."[13]

Arguments for the authority of Scripture have focused on the formal properties of the text—its truthfulness and perfection as a divine object[14]—and the arguments, both for and against Scripture, have been grounded in foundationalist assumptions that define the authority of Scripture in *ontological* terms. This is why, for example, the debate between text and readers comes so easily to us: we have, as Westerners, naturally framed the debate in terms of opposing ontological identities, as Thiselton illustrates with his notion of two opposing horizons. Scripture then has been mistakenly understood as having authority *as its own independent being*.

When it comes to the doctrine of inspiration, we of course want to preserve the notion of the inspiration of Scripture; the notion that it is *theopneustos*, "God breathed" (2 Tim 3:16) and that it truly is God's Word. This is good as far as it goes, but the doctrine of inspiration can hardly be used as a defense for the truthfulness of Scripture. The doctrine, no matter how good, useful, and *scriptural* it is, cannot bear the weight of what is being demanded of it by modern defenders of the Bible. Paul never intended his statement in 2 Timothy to function as the validation and defense of Scripture as truth.[15]

---

13. Lindsell, *Battle for the Bible*, 39.
14. Nafzger, "These Are Written," 35.
15. Modern defenders of the Bible have typically used *theopneustos* in fideistic terms, i.e., "God breathed it, it's true." This is hardly a useful argument because it fails to demonstrate any sort of proof for its claim. As we will see, the Bible itself doesn't defend its veracity in these terms and neither should the Church. Besides, Paul's point of mentioning *theopneustos* was for highlighting the Bible's purpose: it is "profitable for teaching, for reproof, for correction, and for training in righteousness, that the man of God may be

The Constitutive and Definitive Christian Event

The authority of the Bible—its claims to not only be true, but to be the authoritative Word of God—rests ultimately not with the doctrines of inspiration, inerrancy, or the formal features of text, but with Jesus, the one who was crucified and resurrected. Paul's words in 1 Corinthians 15:12–28 form a good basis for thinking about this:

> Now if Christ is proclaimed as raised from the dead, how can some of you say that there is no resurrection of the dead? But if there is no resurrection of the dead, then not even Christ has been raised. And if Christ has not been raised, then our preaching is in vain and your faith is in vain. We are even found to be misrepresenting God, because we testified about God that he raised Christ, whom he did not raise if it is true that the dead are not raised. For if the dead are not raised, not even Christ has been raised. And if Christ has not been raised, your faith is futile and you are still in your sins. Then those also who have fallen asleep in Christ have perished. If in Christ we have hope in this life only, we are of all people most to be pitied. But in fact Christ has been raised from the dead, the firstfruits of those who have fallen asleep. For as by a man came death, by a man has come also the resurrection of the dead. For as in Adam all die, so also in Christ shall all be made alive. But each in his own order: Christ the firstfruits, then at his coming those who belong to Christ. Then comes the end, when he delivers the kingdom to God the Father after destroying every rule and every authority and power. For he must reign until he has put all his enemies under his feet. The last enemy to be destroyed is death. For "God has put all things in subjection under his feet." But when it says, "all things are put in subjection," it is plain that he is excepted who put all things in subjection under him. When all things are subjected to him, then the Son himself will also be subjected to him who put all things in subjection under him, that God may be all in all.

For Paul, Christianity rises or falls on whether or not Jesus was crucified and raised from the dead. If he was not raised, then "we are of all people most to be pitied," because we have believed a lie and are still dead in our sins. But if Jesus was raised from the dead then a great many things were

---

competent, equipped for every good work." In other words, *theopneustos* is not discussed in the context of "defense" or "veracity," but in the context of function and use, i.e., discipleship and sanctification.

validated, chief among them being Jesus' identity as the Son of God and the salvation he purchased for his people through his death on the cross.

The central concern of the New Testament, and by implication the standard for whether it is true and authoritative, is the death and resurrection of Jesus and can be summarized in Paul's impetus for preaching: "For I decided to know nothing among you except Jesus Christ and him crucified," (1 Cor 2:1–2). All four Gospels likewise focus their accounts of Jesus on his passion as does the preaching found in the book of Acts and the remaining apostolic writings of the New Testament. Paul claims twice in the first part of 1 Corinthians 15 that Jesus was crucified, died and was resurrected in accordance with *Scripture*, i.e., the Old Testament, in essence laying out in shorthand that the Old Testament was looking forward to and is also now defined by this event.

The crucifixion and resurrection of Jesus Christ is the *definitive and constitutive Christian event*. As I will argue in more detail in chapter 4, this event is the basis for the existence of Church, her theology, and her doctrine. Likewise, the authority of Scripture, its truthfulness and validity as an authority, is *derivative* from this same defining event. It is Jesus alone, the crucified and resurrected one that makes Scripture authoritative. This is not a revolutionary or innovative claim; this is something that Scripture itself points out. For example, Matthew 28:18 claims that, in light of his crucifixion and resurrection, all authority in heaven and earth has been given to Jesus. Likewise, Hebrews 1 makes a similar claim:

> Long ago, at many times and in many ways, God spoke to our fathers by the prophets, but in these last days he has spoken to us by his Son, whom he appointed the heir of all things, through whom also he created the world. He is the radiance of the glory of God and the exact imprint of his nature, and he upholds the universe by the Word of his power. After making purification for sins, he sat down at the right hand of the Majesty on high, having become as much superior to angels as the name he has inherited is more excellent than theirs.

Jesus himself is *the definitive Word of God* (cf., John 1:1–18) and he claims that his word is the authoritative first and last word of and about God (cf., John 14:6–14).

The question of whether or not Scripture is authoritative cannot then be reduced to formal features of the text. That is, arguments for the authority of Scripture cannot rest on inspiration, inerrancy, or whether the text is historically accurate or literarily cohesive or the assumption that the text is an independent authority (as is so often understood by the use of the term *sola scriptura*), but rather depends on whether or not Jesus was raised from the dead. If he was not raised from the dead then questions of authority, inspiration and inerrancy (among other things) are irrelevant. In other words, the doctrines of inspiration and inerrancy are dependent upon Jesus for their proper articulation and understanding, not the ontology of the text itself.

As I read them, most of the modern defenses of the Bible have hung their hat on the truth of the Bible as a safeguard for Jesus. That is, if the Bible is true, then by implication, its claims about Jesus are true. Of course, the Church is right to claim that Scripture is the true account about the Triune God and the world, but Scripture can only be validated as such, *if Jesus really was raised from the dead*. The truth of Scripture, its claims to being *theopneustos* and the true account about the Triune God depend on Jesus alone.[16]

Of course, the resurrection of Jesus is a debatable claim and there is no definitive proof that will silence all skeptics and their arguments. Even with the evidence of an empty tomb and credible witnesses, the disciples failed to believe until they encountered the resurrected Lord in person (cf., Luke 24:1–43), most famously with Thomas who claimed he could not believe until he was allowed to examine Jesus' wounds (John 20:24–25). In the early part of the book of Acts, the Sanhedrin recognized Peter's preaching as remarkable, recognized that he was one of Jesus' disciples, and even recognized and could not explain what they accepted to be a miraculous healing by Peter of a man who had been born without the use of his legs and who was now walking and even leaping. Even so, the apostles' preaching of Jesus and his resurrection did not convince the Sanhedrin.

However, this does not mean then that we are reduced to fideism, i.e., that we believe the claims of Jesus' resurrection (and therein Scripture) just because we do. We have good reasons for believing Jesus was raised from the dead—chief among them being the apostles' testimony about the event—it is simply that these reasons can be contested and debated and there is no

---

16. Of course, I am giving a particular answer to the question, "who is Jesus?" As I indicated in the Introduction, my answer is the crucified and resurrected Jesus that was preached by the apostles, which is the orthodox answer to the question. This answer is by no means universal as there have been different answers to the question and rival accounts of Jesus offered throughout history. See for example, Olav Hammer, *Alternative Christs*.

definitive evidence that will silence all doubters. In fact, it is ultimately the Triune God speaking through his Word in the power of his Holy Spirit that convinces us and binds us to Jesus and his authority. Foundationalists however, want the sort of proof or arguments that will silence all debate, but no such proofs or arguments are available to us; at least not until the second coming of Christ when all debate will be settled over his identity as the true King of all creation (cf., Isa 45:22–25; Rom 14:11; Rev 20:11–15).

Recasting the Debate

If we cannot appeal to formal properties of the text as a means of proving its authority then the discussion on the authority of Scripture must be recast in relational or functional terms. Stephen Fowl argues, "To call Scripture authoritative . . . establishes a particular relationship between the text and those people and communities who treat it as authoritative."[17] Kelsey agrees: "Authoritative is part of the meaning of "scripture"; it is not a *contingent* judgment made about "scripture" on other grounds, such as their age, authorship, miraculous inspiration, etc. . . . To call certain texts "scripture" is, in part, to say that they ought to be *used* in the common life of the church in normative ways such that they decisively rule its form of life and forms of speech. Thus part of what it means to call certain texts "scripture" is that they are authoritative for the common life of the church. It is say to them that they ought to be used in certain ways to certain ends in that life."[18] To name certain texts as "Scripture" is already to have ascribed to them a position of authority, a relationship in which Scripture is authoritative for the Church. This is good as far as it goes, but *why* is it authoritative? Nafzger points out that for Kelsey (and for much of the postmodern turn to community), the reason Scripture is authoritative is based solely on its function in the Church. "For Kelsey, the authority of the Scriptures is an issue of the *church's* use of these particular writings rather than God's use of them."[19] This sort of practice is evident, for example, with Lindbeck's intratextual method of reading Scripture that tends to speak of Scripture only in terms of its use by the community.[20] Kelsey is right: the authority of Scripture

17. Fowl, *Engaging Scripture*, 6.
18. Kelsey, *Proving Doctrine*, 97, 98.
19. Nafzger, "These Are Written," 200.
20. Lindbeck, *Nature of Doctrine*, 116–24. Webster argues something similar with his take on "post-critical" (postliberal) theologians who have made a turn to the Church: "In such proposals, definition of the character, purpose and interpretation of Scripture

should be defined relationally and these texts should be authoritative for the Church and her practices, but the primary relationship for Scripture's authority is vertical, not horizontal: *the authority of Scripture depends on the risen Lord and his use of the text, not the Church's use of it.*

Webster, commenting on the act of canonization makes a similar vertical argument about Scripture: "The church's act with respect to the canon is an act of faithful *assent* rather than a self-derived judgement [sic]. The language of discipleship is not incidental here: affirming the canon is a matter of the church 'obediently embracing' what comes from God, or of the sheep hearing the shepherd's voice; that is, it is an act of humble affirmation of and orientation towards what is already indisputably the case in the sphere of salvation and its communication in human speech."[21] Of course, mentioning the issue of canonization (which texts are Scripture?) raises many questions that I do not intend to answer here, but Webster's point is appropriate for the overall discussion on the authority of Scripture. It is not as though the Church just chose whatever books it found useful for its project and decided they were normative. Rather the Church's judgment is "an act of confession of that which precedes and imposes itself on the church (that is, the *viva vox Jesu Christi* mediated through the apostolic testimony) and which evokes a Spirit-guided assent."[22] As Calvin noted, "Thus, while the church receives and gives its seal of approval to the Scriptures, it does not thereby render authentic what is otherwise doubtful or controversial. But because the church recognizes Scripture to be the truth of its own God, as a pious duty it unhesitatingly venerates Scripture."[23] What makes Scripture, Scripture is not the Church's affirmation of it (though this is important), it is the Triune God's use of Scripture, in particular with Jesus and his use of it.

Scripture's authority comes from Jesus' authoritative use of Scripture as the crucified, resurrected and thus validated Son of God. We know to accept the Old Testament as Scripture and the New Testament accounts

---

is regarded as inseparable from the place occupied by Scripture in the life and practices of the Christian community. Scripture is thus neither a purely formal authority to be invoked in theological deliberation, nor a collection of clues to help us reconstruct its religious and cultural background, nor a symbolic deposit of experience; it is the book of the church, a community text best understood out of its churchly determinacy." Webster, *Holy Scripture*, 43

21. Webster, *Holy Scripture*, 62.
22. Ibid.
23. Calvin, *Institutes*, 1:76.

about Jesus, because of Jesus and what he taught. It was Jesus who taught that the Scriptures speak and are about him and it was Jesus who taught his disciples how to read these Scriptures in light of him (cf., Luke 24:13–27). It is because of Jesus that we can read the Messianic passages of Isaiah, the Psalms, or the promises made to Eve, Abraham, Isaac, Jacob, and David and point to Jesus as being the fulfillment of those prophecies and promises. It is because of Jesus and his affirmation as the Son of the Living God through his resurrection from the dead, that the apostles were given the authority to be his official witnesses (Matt 28:18). These men became Jesus' deputized authorities, speaking in his name and with his authority, just as the prophets before them spoke with the same authority in Yahweh's name.[24] Their status as deputized authorities made their preaching about Jesus definitive and their interpretation and use of the Old Testament the official interpretation for the Church. This is why the Church received their written accounts about Jesus as Scripture along side the Old Testament and has taught for millennia that Jesus is the unity between the two testaments and the interpretive key for reading them.

Scripture's authority then is *derivative* and has no authority on its own apart from the Triune God's usage of it. Scripture itself says as much by continually pointing to God's authority, not its own. Wright agrees: "Scripture itself points—authoritatively, if it does indeed possess authority!—away from itself and to the fact that final and true authority belongs to God himself; now delegated to Jesus Christ. It is Jesus, according to John 8:39–40, who speaks the truth which he has heard from God."[25] In fact, to talk about the authority of Scripture only makes sense if it is shorthand for "the authority of the triune God, exercised somehow *through* scripture."[26] In short, Scripture is authoritative only because God exercises his authority through it.

My purpose to this point has been to shift the conversation away from foundationalist assumptions about why the text is authoritative, i.e., because of formal properties in the text and its own independent ontology, and towards the particular foundation of Jesus. To answer the question, "why is Scripture authoritative?" we need look no further than to the authority of Jesus, the crucified and resurrected Son of God. However, answering *why*

---

24. See Wolterstorff's discussion of deputized and appropriated discourse, *Divine Discourse*, 42–57.

25. Wright, *Last Word*, 24.

26. Ibid., 23.

Scripture is authoritative only gets us so far. It is not enough to simply say *why* Scripture is authoritative; we need to look at *how* it is authoritative, i.e., *how it functions as an authority for the Church*. To understand this correctly, Scripture must be understood within the economy of salvation, i.e., within the Triune God's on-going redemptive work.

HOW SCRIPTURE FUNCTIONS AUTHORITATIVELY

The question that actually gets to the heart of the problem is not whether or not Scripture is authoritative for the Church and her doctrine, but rather *how* Scripture functions as an authority. The shift from understanding Scripture's authority in terms of ontology (Scripture as a stand alone authority) to functionality can be summarized with an even simpler question: *how is Scripture used?* For many, this question immediately implies how Scripture is used by *readers*, i.e., how does the Church use Scripture? This is an important question that I will take up later in the chapter, but to assume the sole user of Scripture is the Church (or readers in general) is the same sort of ontological problem committed with treating Scripture as an independent authority in the text vs. reader dichotomy. *Scripture's primary user is the Triune God.* It is the Triune God's use of Scripture; his on-going speaking—definitively through Jesus—as mediated *through* Scripture, that defines both how Scripture is authoritative and how the Church should go about using it.

When we say that the Triune God is the primary user of Scripture we are at the same time speaking of God's authority. But what does it mean to speak of God's authority? Perhaps the simplest way of defining his authority is in terms of his sovereign rule over all things. God is both the creator of all things (Gen 1) and he is the ruler of all things (Zech 14:9) and his authority is manifested with his creating, sustaining and ruling all things. His creating and sustaining (providence) are easy enough to see, his rule however, is more difficult. God's rule is both "already" and "not yet" and we find throughout Scripture the tension of both the confession that God has always been ruling over his creation and that his Kingdom—his putting all things under his rule through his Son in the power of his Spirit—is slowly breaking into the world. Another way of describing this in-breaking of the Kingdom of God is with the term "redemption": God's remaking of all creation into something new (cf., Isa 65:17; Rev 21:5), in particular and definitively through his Son Jesus.

Wright argues that the Kingdom of God should be understood as this redemptive rule of God, first demonstrated with the grace shown to Adam and Eve, continuing with the promises made to Abraham and brought to fruition with the nation of Israel, definitively arriving with Jesus and continuing forward with the Church unto the consummation of all things.[27] God's purpose is not only to save humans (as important as this is); it is to redeem all of creation (Rom 8:18–22). Scripture then finds its proper use in this on-going redemptive work of the Triune God.

But how does God make use of Scripture in this work of redemption? Okamoto offers this succinct explanation: "God uses the Scriptures to tell his story, a story about him and his dealings with creation, particularly, definitively, in and through Jesus Christ. That is what they are about, and they are for leading people to turn from false ways, acknowledging Jesus as his Son and as the Lord, and look forward to life with God and his people through Christ and in the Spirit. If we were to ask about Jesus further, we would see that he regards himself as the fulfillment of the Old Testament, and we can see at least the beginnings of how the New Testament canon would come to be."[28] In other words, the Triune God speaks *through* these texts, originally with the Old Testament, but now definitively through his Son and therein with the New Testament as a means of redeeming his people and therein all of creation.

The Old Testament

But how, exactly did the Triune God use the written text of the Old Testament in order to accomplish this activity? Wright describes the Old Testament's role this way:

> When full allowance is made for the striking differences of genre and emphasis within scripture, we may propose that Israel's sacred writings were the place where, and the means by which, Israel discovered again and again who the true God was, and how his Kingdom-purposes were being taken forward. Reciting the scriptures was central to worship, not least in rehearsing God's Kingdom-revealing deeds and thus evoking praise and hope. . . . Again and again the point of scripture was that it addressed a fresh, prophetic word *to* Israel in the midst of its often very ambiguous "experience," breaking into Israel's own world of muddle

---

27. Wright, *Last Word*, 28–29; see also Wright's, *Jesus and the Victory of God*.
28. Okamoto, "Scriptures and their Uses."

and mistakes—doing, in fact, in verbal form what God himself was doing in breaking into the world, and into Israel's life, in judgment and mercy.[29]

God spoke *through* Scripture to remind Israel of his on-going work of redemption and to remind them of who he is and what he had done for them. We see in various places in the Old Testament (e.g., Deuteronomy; Psalm 78, 105, 135, 136; Nehemiah 9) the call for the people to remember the history of God's gracious actions on their behalf, *the story of their redemption*, and to be faithful to their suzerain, their covenant Lord. Israel was a *hearing* people and she was constituted by the Triune God's speech-act. In fact, her identity and purpose were found by *listening* to her Lord's voice: "Hear O Israel, the Lord our God, the Lord is one!" (Deut 6:4).

It is through God's saving action that he bound this people to himself and redeemed them and it is through his continued speaking, primarily though Scripture (but not isolated to it), that he *equipped* his people to serve him in his on-going work of redemption. Scripture was used by God to shape and mold every aspect of Israel's life for the purpose of equipping them for his redemptive purposes. But we also find throughout the Old Testament "the elusive, but powerful idea of God's "word," not as a synonym for the written scriptures, but as a strange personal presence, creating, judging, healing and recreating."[30] Consider just a few passages that highlight the breadth of God's action and presence through his speaking:

> In the beginning, God created the heavens and the earth. The earth was without form and void, and darkness was over the face of the deep. And the Spirit of God was hovering over the face of the waters. And God said, "Let there be light," and there was light. And God saw that the light was good. And God separated the light from the darkness. God called the light Day, and the darkness he called Night. And there was evening and there was morning, the first day. (Gen 1:1–5)

> By the word of the Lord the heavens were made, and by the breath of his mouth all their host. (Ps 33:6)

> But the word is very near you. It is in your mouth and in your heart, so that you can do it. (Deut 30:14)

---

29. Wright, *Last Word*, 37.
30. Ibid., 38.

> A voice says, "Cry!" And I said, "What shall I cry?" All flesh is grass,—and all its beauty is like the flower of the field. The grass withers, the flower fades—when the breath of the Lord blows on it;—surely the people are grass. The grass withers, the flower fades,—but the word of our God will stand forever. (Isa 40:6-8)

> For as the rain and the snow come down from heaven—and do not return there but water the earth,—making it bring forth and sprout,—giving seed to the sower and bread to the eater, so shall my word be that goes out from my mouth;—it shall not return to me empty,—but it shall accomplish that which I purpose,—and shall succeed in the thing for which I sent it." (Isa 55:10-11)

> The hand of the Lord was upon me, and he brought me out in the Spirit of the Lord and set me down in the middle of the valley; it was full of bones. And he led me around among them, and behold, there were very many on the surface of the valley, and behold, they were very dry. And he said to me, "Son of man, can these bones live?" And I answered, "O Lord God, you know." Then he said to me, "Prophesy over these bones, and say to them, O dry bones, hear the word of the Lord. Thus says the Lord God to these bones: Behold, I will cause breath to enter you, and you shall live. And I will lay sinews upon you, and will cause flesh to come upon you, and cover you with skin, and put breath in you, and you shall live, and you shall know that I am the Lord." (Ezek 37:1-6)

The Triune God creates, breaks down, vivifies, sanctifies, kills, sustains and judges (among other things) through his speaking. God's speaking is not limited to the text of Scripture, but he uses these writings in particular to speak powerfully to his people in order to redeem them, sanctify them, and equip them for his purposes. Scripture was used for the Old Testament people as a *formative* tool for their redemption and therein the redemption of the cosmos. The role Scripture played in the economy of salvation for Israel can be summarized as the Triune God's redemptive rule in, through, to and for Israel by means of both his spoken and written Word.[31]

The New Testament

How then should we understand God's use of Scripture with *New Israel*, the Church and the advent of the New Testament? Earlier I said that the definitive Christian event is the death and resurrection of Jesus, the Son of God, Messiah. It is with this event that the Triune God's redemptive activity

---

31. Ibid., 40.

comes to its climax and sees its completion. Jesus was and is the definitive fulfillment of what the Old Testament and Israel had been looking forward to and working to accomplish: *the Kingdom of God arrived in power with Jesus*. The apostle John in his Gospel rightly calls Jesus the *logos*, the Word of God incarnate, because Jesus is the living embodiment, literally the "enfleshment" of God's speaking. In short, *Jesus is the definitive speech-act of the Triune God*.

When we look at the early Church we see that the Old Testament was accepted as authoritative and useful as the Word of God, because of Jesus and his definitive completion of the story of redemption as hoped for and prophesied by the Old Testament. But at the same time, because of the definitive work of Jesus, the Old Testament does not have the same role for the Church as it previously did with the people of Israel. This means that certain parts of the Old Testament, while still testifying to and being part of the overall story of redemption (e.g., some of the ceremonial and civil laws), are no longer in play for the people of God. Okamoto argues that, "a good use of the Scriptures," i.e., the way that Jesus and his apostles used them, "will be consistent with a certain basic story of God and his dealings with creation, especially in and through Jesus Christ."[32] This does not exclude the Old Testament from the canon as clearly Jesus and the apostles regarded it as authoritative, but it does put the Old Testament in a certain place and it gives the story of Israel a certain interpretation, an interpretation that is grounded in the narrative of Jesus.[33] The issue is more complicated than I am describing here, but even so, the Church recognized (and continues to do so) that with Jesus, a decisive event occurred that necessitated the reinterpretation of the role of the Old Testament in light of him.

Long before there was a New Testament canon there was the conviction in the Church that "the word of God,"—what Paul called, "the word," "the word of truth," or simply "the gospel" (e.g., Col 1:5; 1 Thess 2:13)—to which the apostles committed themselves, was central to the church's mission and life.[34] This "word" was the story of Jesus and his death and resurrection, told as the climax of the true on-going redemptive story of God and his dealings with Israel and thus, the world. Paul, along with the other apostles and the early Church, believed this word—this story of God's redemption that climaxes with Jesus—carried power; power to change the

---

32. Okamoto, "Scriptures and Their Uses," 7.
33. Ibid.
34. Wright, *Last Word*, 48.

hearts and minds of people.³⁵ Paul says as much in Romans 1:16, "For I am not ashamed of the gospel, for it is the power of God for salvation to everyone who believes, to the Jew first and also to the Greek."

The Triune God exercises authority *through* and *by* this new Word about Jesus. He reconstitutes Israel around the *logos*, the New Adam, who is their new federal head (cf., Rom 5:12–21) and it is through the message of the apostles, the proclamation of this Jesus as Lord, that God brings his redemption to the entire world. Wright again: "The apostolic writings, like the "word" which they now wrote down, were not simply *about* the coming of God's Kingdom into all the world; they were, and were designed to be, part of the *means whereby that happened*, and whereby those through whom it happened could themselves be transformed into Christ's likeness."³⁶ In short, this new definitive Word of God, Jesus, in particular now through God's speaking of him as mediated by the Old and New Testaments, is the chief way in which the Triune God brings about his Kingdom, redeeming and transforming his people into his likeness.

Jesus' Authoritative Use of Scripture in His Church

We have seen how Scripture, as the Old and New Testaments, functions generally as the authority for the Church, but we can go deeper still by asking how God *specifically* uses Scripture as the authority for the Church's speech and doctrine. A helpful way for beginning to understand how this works is by taking a step back and locating Scripture within the broader category of the Word of God of which, Scripture is just one instance. Nafzger, in conversation with Barth and Luther (among others), does this very thing and offers a revised version of Barth's three-fold form of the Word of God which is a helpful stepping off point for our discussion.³⁷

The first form of the Word of God is the "eternal Word of God," the *logos* of John's Gospel, the second member of the Trinity "that became a human being in the person of Jesus of Nazareth by the power of the Holy Spirit. He is the personal, Spirit-anointed Word who speaks the Father's commands and fulfills the Father's promises of forgiveness, life and salvation."³⁸ The Triune God is a *speaking* God and he has spoken definitively through his personal Word, Jesus.

---

35. Ibid., 49.
36. Ibid., 50 (emphasis in the original).
37. Barth, *Church Dogmatics* 1/1, 88–124.
38. Nafzger, "These Are Written," 166.

The second form of the Word of God is the "spoken Word of God." Borrowing from Wolterstorff,[39] Nafzger argues that God often speaks through someone other than himself. Under the old covenant, the Triune God often "deputized" prophets to speak his Word in his name and with his authority in the Spirit of Christ, the eternal Word of God (1 Peter 1:10–11). Under the new covenant, Jesus "deputized" his apostles to speak his Word in his name and with his authority as guided by the Holy Spirit. It is "deputized" speech in the sense that God speaks *through* his appointed representatives. Much like a spokesperson speaking on behalf of a head of state, the prophet or apostle speaks on behalf of God in God's name with God's authority. The Word of the apostle then is rightly seen as the Word of God. The Church continues this practice, by preaching this same Word of the prophets and apostles in every age and every place, because this Word is a word of power that is living and active (Heb 4:12).

The third form of the Word of God is the "written Word of God," commonly known as Scripture. Scripture is the definitive version of the prophets and apostles' spoken Word, i.e., their deputized and thus, authoritative teaching and preaching. "As the written form of the Word, the same conclusions can be made about the Scriptures that were made about prophetic and apostolic proclamations of the Word. Like the spoken Word of the prophets and apostles, the Scriptures are also living and active and God works through the Scriptures to kill those who disobey his commands and to forgive and make alive those who believe in Jesus. . . . Jesus affirmed the truth of the Old Testament (John 10:35) and he promised the Spirit of truth to those who would eventually produce the New Testament (John 16:13)."[40]

In short, the three-fold form of the Word of God begins with the personal word of God, Jesus the *logos* (first form). It is through Jesus that the Triune God has always been speaking and continues to speak. But the Triune God also gave authority to his official witnesses and deputies (apostles and prophets) to speak on his behalf (second form). As authoritative deputies, the definitive written versions of their teaching and preaching also took on the status of the Word of God (third form). Just as we must say that the crucifixion and resurrection of Jesus is the definitive and constitutive Christian event, so we must also say that our understanding of the Word of God begins and ends with Jesus. Because of this, any discussion about how Scripture is used by God in the Church is really a discussion about Jesus'

---

39. Wolterstorff, *Divine Discourse*, 42–57.
40. Nafzger, "These Are Written," 168.

authoritative use of Scripture. But how does Jesus use Scripture or more precisely, how does Jesus use Scripture in his Church *right now*?

In the Gospel accounts we see that Jesus exercised and demonstrated at least two kinds of authority. First, when he forgave sins, (cf., Matt 9:6), raised people from the dead (cf., John 11:1–44), healed the sick (cf., Luke 6:6–11) and cast out demons (cf., Matt 8:28–34), Jesus was demonstrating definitively that he had (and continues to have) the "authority to save." Second, all throughout the Gospels we find Jesus speaking with his own authority as he taught and proclaimed the Kingdom of God and the crowds took notice of it (e.g., Matt. 7:28–29). We can say then that Jesus also exercised and demonstrated his "authority to teach." "By acting with these two kinds of authority—authority to save and authority to teach—the personal Word of God accomplished the will of his Father in the power of the Spirit."[41] Nafzger makes an interesting connection between these two kinds of authority—the authority to save and teach—with Luther's own view of the two forms of the Word of God.

Luther's first form is the "spoken Word of God" which is the proclaimed or preached Word. It is the Word through which God works to forgive sins and redeem his people unto eternal life.[42] Luther says as much in the Smalcald Articles: "We ought and must constantly maintain that God does not wish to deal with us otherwise than through the spoken word and the sacraments, and that whatever without the word and sacraments, is extolled as spirit is the devil himself."[43] Scripture itself points to the spoken word as a necessity for bringing people unto salvation:

> So faith comes from hearing, and hearing through the word of Christ. (Rom 10:17)

> Then he said to them, "These are my words that I spoke to you while I was still with you, that everything written about me in the Law of Moses and the Prophets and the Psalms must be fulfilled." Then he opened their minds to understand the Scriptures, and said to them, "Thus it is written, that the Christ should suffer and on the third day rise from the dead, and that repentance and forgiveness of sins should be proclaimed in his name to all nations, beginning from Jerusalem. You are witnesses of these things. And behold, I am sending the promise of my Father upon you. But stay

---

41. Ibid., 207.
42. Ibid., 208.
43. SA III, VIII: 10–11.

in the city until you are clothed with power from on high." (Luke 24:44–49)

The proclamation of the Kingdom of God—as it has arrived in power with the person and rule of Jesus—is a "means-of-grace-word" and it is the first and most important mark of the Church. For Luther, the Church is not a "pen-house," a house of writing; it is a "mouth-house," a house of speaking and proclamation. God does not forgive sins, justify, bring people to salvation, or give his Holy Spirit through the private reading of the written word; he does it through the *proclamation* of the word of God through the Church. This is not to say that the Triune God cannot or does not work faith through the private reading of the written text, clearly this happens. It is rather that the primary means for bringing people to faith is through the *spoken* word of God.

These two forms of the word of God, the spoken and written forms, must be distinguished, but they work together and both are authoritative. On the one hand, the written word of God is the highest norm and standard for faith, life, and teaching. Scripture is the "revelation-word," the definitive versions of the word that the prophets and apostles preached. On the other hand, the spoken word, the word that is still preached by the Church to the world, is a "means-of-grace-word," that is *bound by Scripture*. As Saarnivaara describes it, "The proclamation of the word and the administration of the sacraments are inseparably connected with the Scriptures. Only a scriptural teaching, preaching, and consolation leads men to the knowledge of Christ and salvation in Him."[44]

Nafzger argues that Jesus' two kinds of authority as found in the Gospels are of a piece with Luther's two forms of the Word of God. Jesus' "authority to save" corresponds with Luther's "spoken word of God," because Jesus gave the "authority to save" to his disciples as he sent them out in his name and he exercises this kind of authority now *through his Church* as they *proclaim* "the means-of-grace-word" throughout the world, in every age, and every tongue about Jesus.[45] Likewise, Jesus' "authority to teach" corresponds with Luther's "written word of God," because Jesus gave the "authority to teach" to his disciples in order for them to teach everything that he had commanded them to do, in turn sending them forth with the Spirit to guide them to all truth. Jesus himself exercises his "authority to teach" through the writings of his deputized authorities and these writings

44. Saarnivaara, "Written and Spoken Word," 169.
45. Nafzger, "These Are Written," 209.

The Authority of Scripture for Christian Doctrine

then serve as the final rule and norm for the Church's speech about God, which would obviously include her doctrine too.[46]

It is within this framework that the Reformation's insistence on *sola scriptura* actually makes sense: the primary function of the written Word of God is to provide the rule and norm for the Church's preaching and teaching. This is what it means to say that Scripture has the "authority to teach."[47] The Church is not free to preach and teach whatever she likes or to create her own new narratives about the Triune God. The Church, as created and founded by Jesus is bound to "teach and preach in conformity with the definitive versions of the word proclaimed by the apostles."[48] Using Scripture in this way is a practice that goes all the way back to the Bereans who judged Paul's spoken Word against the written Word of the prophets to see if what he preached and taught was true (Acts 17:10–15).

The Triune God is a speaking God and he speaks his Word in three distinct forms: 1) the personal Word as located in the Son of God, Jesus; 2) the spoken Word of his deputized authorities, the prophets and apostles and now the Church; 3) the definitive versions of the teaching and preaching of the prophets and apostles put into written form as Scripture. When it comes to Scripture, God exercises his authority through it by redeeming his people and equipping them for ministry. But it goes deeper than this. To specifically see how the Triune God uses Scripture, we must look to Jesus—the personal Word of God—and the exercising of his "authority to save" and his "authority to teach" through these texts, by using them as the norm and standard for faith and life in the Church, in particular with preaching and teaching. Everything that the Church says and does, including the formation and articulation of doctrine, must be bound to Scripture. But even so, Scripture is not an independent object; it finds its identity and use with the Triune God's redemptive activity as manifested definitively through the *logos*, the Word of God, Jesus.

THE CHURCH'S INTERPRETATION OF SCRIPTURE

In the first section of this chapter, I addressed the issue of why Scripture is authoritative and then moved to address in the next section how it functions as an authority. Looking at these two questions of Scriptural authority

---

46. Ibid., 210.
47. Ibid.
48. Ibid.

answers both why and how the Church and its worship, doctrines, and practices are to be ruled and governed by Scripture. Along the way, I have been attempting to recast our understanding of the Biblical text in non-foundationalist terms, avoiding and moving past the dualism of text vs. reader, by locating the text's ontology and authority with Jesus alone. To this end, I haven't said anything that the early Church didn't say. I have been arguing that the Church's speech about God, its doctrines, practices, and teachings are derivative from Jesus, the crucified and resurrected one, the *logos*, the personal Word of God, as measured and ruled by his authoritative written Word, Scripture. The authority of Scripture, both its existence and function as an authority, derive from Jesus alone.

This final section of the chapter, while assuming everything that has been argued above, serves as a bridge between the authority of Scripture and the Church, who in her formulation of doctrine, must submit to Scripture even as she seeks to read Scripture faithfully. As I will argue in more detail in the next chapter, the Church, like Scripture is not an independent ontological object. She is not separate from the Triune God; rather her ontology, identity, mission, teaching, and preaching all derive from the Triune God, in particular with Jesus. The standard for such activities is of course Scripture, but Scripture was written for the purpose of reading and inherent in reading is *interpretation*. Stephen Fowl summarizes the problem facing us in this final section of the chapter: "Accepting that scripture is the standard for their faith, practice, and worship does not get Christians out of the hard tasks of scriptural interpretation."[49] The answer to the problem of interpretation, as I have been suggesting all throughout this chapter, is bound up with Jesus, the crucified and resurrected one. John Behr's account of Irenaeus and the early Church's struggle for a normative Christianity is a helpful starting point for discussing Scripture and the Church's interpretation of it.

The Canon of Scripture

Behr argues that the notion of "an originally pure orthodoxy, manifest in exemplary communities from which various heresies developed and split off, " is a difficult picture to maintain, in particular when with the Pauline writings we already see people falling away from the Gospel that was delivered.[50] The question of Jesus' identity ("is it this Jesus or some other?")

49. Fowl, *Engaging Scripture*, 2.
50. Behr, *Way to Nicaea*, 13–14.

looms large from the very beginning of Christianity and continues unabated to this day. And yet the Gospel was delivered in the midst of intense debates, not only over the right interpretation of the Gospel, but which books should be included as Scripture. It is no coincidence that the formation of a Christian orthodoxy and creedal formation runs concomitantly with the formation and inclusion of the apostolic writings as authoritative Scriptural accounts to be placed side by side with the Old Testament. The rise of the New Testament is in part driven by the same concerns to confess Jesus correctly. As Behr notes about the early Church, "Not only was there a commitment to a body of Scripture, but there was also the affirmation that there is a correct reading of this Scripture, or more exactly, that there is a correct canon for reading Scripture, a canon expressing the hypothesis of Scripture itself."[51]

By the term "canon," Behr has in mind, not the listing or grouping of books as it has typically come to be used in modern exegetical studies, but what he argues was the original intent of the word as "rule" or "model" or as it came to be known in antiquity as the *regula fidei* or "the criteria for truth."[52] Borrowing from Irenaeus, Behr argues that "The point of the canon of truth is not so much to give fixed, and abstract, statements of Christian doctrine. Nor does it provide a narrative description of Christian belief, the literary hypothesis of Scripture. Rather, the canon of truth expresses the correct hypothesis of Scripture itself, that by which one can see in Scripture the picture of a king, Christ, rather than a dog or fox. It is ultimately the presupposition of the apostolic Christ himself, the one who is "according to the Scripture" and, in reverse, the subject of Scripture throughout, being spoken of by the Spirit through the prophets, so revealing the one God and Father." [53] Ultimately then, the canon is the presupposition, the assumption that must already be in place for reading scripture on its own terms—it is the canon of truth, where as Scripture is the body of truth.[54] By the end of the second century, orthodox Christianity "is committed to understanding Christ by engaging with Scripture on the basis of the canon of truth and in the context of tradition."[55]

---

51. Ibid., 14.
52. Ibid., 13n4; 33.
53. Ibid., 35–37.
54. Ibid., 15.
55. Ibid.

We can discern at least two things at work in the early Church. First, there was already from the beginning, the belief that Scripture (which at this point, meant the Old Testament) was both the body of truth and that as the body of truth it contains and speaks of Jesus Christ on its own terms. Scripture then, was considered the authoritative account about Jesus. Second, to confess that Scripture speaks of Jesus on its own terms is not to say that the text is clear and obvious to whomever reads it, as the arguments made by Irenaeus against the gnostics and their misreading of Scripture attest: they had the wrong canon, the wrong hypothesis for reading Scripture. In order to be able to read Scripture on its own terms, we must have the right criteria of truth, the right canon, *the right hermeneutic*, already in place. It is Jesus alone, the Son of the Living God, the Messiah, the crucified and resurrected one who is the proper criteria of truth for interpreting Scripture. In other words, there is no *sola scriptura* without there simultaneously being *sola fidei*. For the Church and her interpretation of Scripture, the two work together.

Frances Young finds a similar notion at work in the arguments of Athanasius in the fourth century. In her case study of Athanasius she finds that, "discerning the unitive 'mind' (*dianoia*) of scripture was seen as essential to reaching a proper interpretation."[56] She characterizes the debates between Athanasius and his Arian opponents as essentially exegetical and the debates themselves as attempts at making the meaning of Scripture explicit.[57] For example, in Athanasius' defense of the use of non-scriptural terms like *ex ousias* and *homoousious* by the Council of Nicaea, "Athanasius distinguishes between the 'wording' and the 'sense' (*dianoia*), urging those who hesitate about the Council's formula to do likewise. If they agree the sense, they should subscribe to the wording. Athanasius insists that, even if the expressions used are not, in so many words, in the scriptures, yet they contain the mind of the scriptures and so convey it to those willing to respond. If they continue to claim that it is not scriptural, that very complaint shows the disorder of their minds."[58] To put a modern spin on it, there is no such thing as a "literal reading" of the Biblical text for Athanasius apart from having the right "sense" or right "mind" of Scripture already in place. Young further comments on Athanasius' deductive arguments concerning the terms "Son" and "Word" as applied to the divine in his *De decretis*:

56. Young, *Biblical Exegesis*, 29.
57. Ibid., 30; 34.
58. Ibid., 34.

Clearly Athanasius is again valuing the mind of scripture more highly than the verbal expressions of particular texts, and that is why he can regard his watchwords as scriptural and prefer them to proof-texts. In a sense he knows that one proof-text can always be met by another. Indeed, one-third of the first oration and the whole of the second are devoted to providing orthodox exegesis of Arian proof-texts. So the basis of Athanasius' confidence that he knows what constitutes proper piety must correspond to his grounds for giving priority to what we might call the 'elevated face-value' meaning of his catena of texts, and seeing their amalgamation as expressive of the mind of scripture.[59]

When comparing Athanasius' exegesis to his opponents' exegesis it does appear that he has a serious case of exegetical contortionism as his own work is often far more complicated. But as Young explains, "fundamentally it is his sense of the overarching plot, a sense inherited from the past and ingrained in the tradition of the Church, which allows [him] to be innovative in exegetical detail and confident of providing the correct and 'pious' reading." Like with Irenaeus, Athanasius held that "The 'Canon of Truth' or 'Rule of Faith' expresses the mind of scripture, and an exegesis that damages the coherence of that plot, that *hypothesis*, that coherence, that *skopos*, cannot be right."[60] Therein, "undergirding Athanasius' exegesis is the unitive story or plot which is the mind of scripture expressed in its many words and images, and of which the one 'Son' is the subject."[61] Athanasius is confident of his exegesis because he "has received insight into the 'mind' of scripture through the Canon of Truth received from his predecessors. Paradoxically, interpretations of particular texts may be novel and recent if they cohere better with the teaching that elucidates the unity of the Bible through discerning the overarching narrative from creation through incarnation to the eschaton."[62]

The early Church would not have understood the modern notion of reading Scripture on its own terms, let alone any notion of "determinate textual meaning" without first having the proper canon, rule, *dianoia*, or hypothesis (all these terms refer to the same thing) already in place for reading it. Far from being a hindrance to exegesis or imposing an improper disposition on the text, the notion of canon or *dianoia*, allowed for creative

59. Ibid., 42.
60. Ibid., 43.
61. Ibid., 44.
62. Ibid., 44–45.

and fruitful interactions with Scripture. Without the canon as the criterion for reading Scripture, interpretation ceased to be *Christian* and became something else all together. The early Church's use of the canon and *dianoia* has several implications for our own similar pluralist modern American setting.

Implications of the Canon of Scripture for Modern Readers

First, far from being at loggerheads, Scripture and the Church compliment one another. Does the Bible have authority over the Church? Yes, it norms the Church's preaching and teaching. But at the same time, without the appropriate rule in place for reading Scripture—the redemptive narrative of Jesus as passed down through the apostles' preaching and contained in the canon of truth—the proper reading of Scripture is impossible. To borrow from Thiselton's language, if we are to allow Scripture to speak "on its own terms," for it truly to be "other," then we must assume that its core meaning and unity is bound up with the story of Jesus, or we fail to be Christian and turn the text into our own devising. Far from disavowing ourselves from our Christian beliefs and dispositions, it is only by way of this redemptive narrative that we can read Scripture as it was intended.

James Voelz argues along similar lines: "A valid interpreter of a text, then, is that person, that man or that woman, who assumes the role "required," as it were, by a given text—who becomes the reader "implied" or called for by that very text. And such a one is formed to assume that role by a community, a community which has assumed that role itself." [63] For Voelz, a reader never interprets texts in isolation; she always does so within a community. That community is made up of "other readers, with other receptors, with those who are her contemporaries, and with those who have gone before."[64] A person only becomes an implied reader, "only as she is trained to be that implied reader, within a context where the implied reader of a text is appreciated and understood."[65] Scripture then *requires* a particular disposition of its readers and requires that the redemptive narrative of Jesus must be *assumed* in order to read it properly. This means that the only "proper" or "right" reading of Scripture is with the community that has the proper disposition and the proper story already in place, i.e., the Church founded by Jesus.

63. Voelz, *What Does This Mean?* 220.
64. Ibid.
65. Ibid.

The Authority of Scripture for Christian Doctrine

This however, is not the common view of many Christians in America. Hauerwas argues that, "North American Christians are trained to believe that they are capable of reading the Bible without spiritual and moral transformation. They read the Bible not as Christians, not as people set apart, but as democratic citizens who think their 'common sense' is sufficient for 'understanding' the Scripture."[66] Scripture was intended to be read in the Church and cannot be understood as it was attended apart from it. This means then that there is no such thing as an interpretive method or theory that applies equally to Shakespeare and to St. Paul. There is no such thing as a "determinate textual meaning" or a "literal sense" without first assuming the on-going redemptive story of Jesus as the criterion, the rule by which all interpretations of Scripture must be judged. By implication this means that not all interpretations are equal or valid and not just any community's interpretation will do. "That community which has produced, received, and preserved a given set of documents—or, better put, that community whose personal formation includes the production, reception, and preservation of a given set of documents—is likely to teach its members to read those documents in a way "congenial" to them—that is, in such a way as to find in them what reasonably may be found (=what intended meaning there may be) and to allow further meanings to arise, meanings which are congruent with what intended meanings there might be."[67]

In light of this, a second implication of the canon and *dianoia* for our own pluralist setting is that being a member of this community, the Church, implies that the reader is a *believer*. Belief in Jesus implies personal commitment to Jesus as God and Lord. Belief, i.e., *faith*, is a gift from God through the Holy Spirit, which means that the Holy Spirit plays an active role in the act of interpretation. What exactly does this mean? Voelz argues the following:[68]

- We assume that the Holy Spirit inspired the writers of the Old and New Testaments and he desires for their message to be heard, understood and believed.

---

66. Hauerwas, *Unleashing the Scripture*, 15.

67. Voelz, *What Does This Mean?* 220. This of course, is an argument for reading Scripture in a particular way. I am fully aware that people do debate (vigorously) the nature of the community that produced the documents, the purpose of them, and so forth. It is not my intention to take up such issues here.

68. Ibid., 223–24.

- The Holy Spirit enables believers to read and understand the text, but not by giving them "quantum leaps of understanding," i.e., instant knowledge of history and culture or total linguistic competence allowing readers to forego hard study and to interpret the text without difficulty. Rather, the Holy Spirit gives readers/hearers "congeniality" with the text—"utter openness to and acceptance of it," i.e., faith.
- In giving the believer the faith to read, the Holy Spirit enables a reader to fully become the implied reader required by Scripture.
- The true implied reader must be a believer, that is, a *Christian*.
- A Christian is not automatically a fully implied reader as if the Holy Spirit functions as a "trump card" making up for the lack of knowledge and skills in Biblical competency. Just because someone is a Christian does not mean that he or she has ultimate insights into the meaning of the texts. If this were so, not only would all Christians be excellent interpreters, there would be no debates over interpretations between various Christian traditions.

A third implication of the canon is that recognition of the redemptive narrative of Jesus as the right rule for reading does not remove all debate or clear up all the difficult passages of Scripture, but it does put interpretive debates within the proper hermeneutical framework. As Nafzger argues, "When the biblical interpreter recognizes the centrality of the personal Word in the written Word, the cruciform nature of biblical interpretation becomes clear."[69] Nevertheless, recognition of the proper interpretive Christological framework does not cause debate to dissipate, though it does provide the parameters and rules for debate to occur (more on this in chapter 5).

Fourth, understanding that Scripture (the body of truth) speaks about Jesus and that Jesus is the proper key to understanding it (the canon of truth) as well as recognizing the requirement of the reader to be personally committed to Jesus through the power of the Holy Spirit, does not necessarily negate modern studies of Scripture. I am not suggesting that we try and return to the early centuries of the Church and pretend that we aren't modern people. Clearly this is impossible, but in the same vein, Christological assumptions about what counts as Scripture and how to rightly interpret it allows for the Church to use historical, literary, grammatical, or sociological studies in order to bring out previously unseen nuances.

69. Nafzger, "These Are Written," 224.

Assuming the proper Christological disposition towards Scripture, as well as the right redemptive story puts these tools in their proper place.

Finally, interpretation of Scripture requires a disposition of humility on the part of the reader. These texts are the definitive versions of the prophets and apostles' teaching and preaching and these men, inspired by the Holy Spirit wrote as God's deputized representatives. They spoke and wrote in his name and with his authority. Further, we recognize that these texts, as the Word of God, exist to equip us and shape us (cf., John 20: 30–31; 2 Timothy 3:16–17). Like Vanhoozer and Thiselton, John Webster argues that faithful reading of Scripture is "not the work of masters but of pupils in the school of Christ."[70] He puts it this way, "One of the chief fruits of the Spirit's conversion of the reader is *teachableness*, a teachableness which extends into the disposition with which Scripture is read." "To read Scripture," (with this teachable disposition in place), "as one caught up by the reconciling work of God is to abandon mastery of the text, and, instead, to be schooled into docility."[71] The reader of Scripture sits in submission to the text, struggling with it, and seeking to understand its meaning. To have a humble disposition, to be teachable and to abandon mastery of the text is to seek to have the Triune God speak anew into our lives, changing us and molding us into his image, equipping us for ministry, and redeeming us for his Kingdom. Scripture is unlike any other book or piece of literature and we dare not treat it as such. The Church must not only approach Scripture with reverence and all honor, but must readily submit all her claims, doctrines, teachings, and speech to the authority and scrutiny of Scripture.

SUMMARY

This chapter has been concerned with accounting for the authority of Scripture, that is, how it functions as an authority for the Church and her doctrine, apart from foundationalist assumptions. Scripture is authoritative, not because of its own formal properties, but because of Jesus and his authority and therein, the Triune God's use of Scripture in the economy of salvation. Far from having its own authority as an independent object, Scripture's authority is *derivative* and has no authority apart from Jesus and his use of it. It is for these reasons that we can say that Scripture is

---

70. Webster, *Holy Scripture*, 101.
71. Ibid. (emphasis in original).

the governing doctrine for all of the Church's doctrines, i.e., it is the measure and standard by which the Church must measure all her claims and practices.

This however, does not get the Church around the difficult practice of interpretation. The key to interpreting Scripture is the same constitutive and definitive event that gives Scripture its authority: Jesus, the crucified and resurrected one. Scripture cannot be read correctly, on its own terms, without there first being the right canon, the right unitive story already in place. This is just what it is to read the text as Christians.

4

The Church and Her Doctrine

Chapter 3 offered an account of Scripture and how it functions authoritatively as the measure and standard for the Church and her doctrine. As I argued, Scripture is the standard and source for the Church and her articulation and formulation of doctrine, but Scripture does not exist as its own independent authority; its authority is *derivative* from the Triune God and his authority. Scripture is authoritative because of God's use of it in the economy of salvation, not because the text carries its own independent ontology.

As we saw, claiming Scripture is the authoritative standard for the Church and even demonstrating how it functions as such does not get us around the difficult task of interpretation. Even though the Church submits to Scripture, it still has to read and interpret it. Because of this the Church, in order to read Scripture as it was intended to be read—to be the implied reader that the text requires—must not only have the proper disposition towards the text as believers, it must assume the unitive story of Jesus *before* it begins to read. In ages past this was known as the "canon of truth" or the *regula fidei* (Irenaeus) or the *dianoia* or the "mind" of Scripture (Athanasius). There is no "literal" sense of the text apart from this story and the text cannot be properly understood without it. This means that the Church does not need to appeal to any notion of some universal interpretive method or to the so-called ideal of "determinate textual meaning" as if such things can function as constraints for interpretation. We of course, assume that the Bible speaks, that its authors were intending to communicate something that can be rightly interpreted and understood by readers. But no general method of interpretation (like E. D. Hirsch) or the insistence that there is a meaning in the text (like Vanhoozer) can bring us to the correct interpretation. Only if we begin with the right rule for reading Scripture (the narrative of Jesus and his on-ongoing redemption) can we enter the role required by the text and its authors.

In a similar fashion to the previous chapter, my purpose is to offer an account of the Church and her doctrine apart from foundationalist categories. I use the term "account" here purposefully. By "account" I mean a description of the structure, operations, and context in and by which doctrines function. I am defining it this way because I am intentionally distancing myself from what Lindbeck, Vanhoozer, and Thiselton offered in their works. Lindbeck et al all offered *methods*—really, prescriptions—for how we should do theology. This chapter offers a *description* of the Church and how doctrine functions apart from foundationalist assumptions. My account makes no claim to help us get a better handle on doing particular Christian practices—practices like interpreting Scripture or attuning ourselves to our own Christian language—and I am certainly not proposing a method for how we should be doing theology. *To interpret this chapter as a method or proposal for doing theology is to fundamentally misunderstand this work.*

A second purpose for this chapter is to hopefully clarify some of the arguments made in chapter 3. Both chapters assume all the same things, so many of the arguments in this chapter will sound similar. One important assumption that undergirded chapter 3 (and the entirety of the work) that I have yet to adequately explain is "antifoundationalism." In fact, this essay could be called an "antifoundationalist" account of doctrine, though this is misleading in some respects. Allow me then to backtrack a bit and explain the alternative mood of "antifoundationalism" that has been operating quietly in the background throughout this work. Doing so will set the terms for what follows in my account.

TOWARDS A DEFINITION OF ANTIFOUNDATIONALISM

How are we to get beyond the problem of foundationalism? If, as we have seen, modern accounts of doctrine have tried and failed to get around the problems posed by foundationalism, is there any hope of a way forward? As Lindbeck rightly perceived, what is needed is a different way of seeing, a paradigm shift in which foundationalism and its assumptions dissolve. Antifoundationalism is just such a shift.

The Church and Her Doctrine

In chapter 1, I argued that foundationalism is a mood that fundamentally conceives of humans as creatures that are unconstrained by things like contexts and beliefs. Human activity—in particular the human activities of reasoning and interpreting—is defined by freedom from the constraints of history, beliefs, and contexts. Far from being constrained by such things, human reasoning and interpretation must—in order for them to be considered true or valid—*transcend them*. This is not to say that humans are free to do whatever they want (the hope of relativism), they are not. For a foundationalist, constraints are provided by general principles, norms, methods, theories, objectives, or standards (all these terms are synonyms) that are universal and reasonable for all people regardless of context. In turn, these so-called universal constraints are publically recognized as the parameters and constraints for Western culture (and all those who would consider themselves "enlightened" or "civilized").

Like foundationalism, antifoundationalism is also a mood. Antifoundationalism however, conceives of humanity as bound by constraints and foundations that are *local* and *particular,* as opposed to general and neutral, and it argues that things like truth claims and interpretations have their home *within* the space provided by these constraints, not outside of them. The conflict between foundationalism and antifoundationalism is fundamentally over where foundations reside and what counts as one, not over whether there are such things as foundations or not.

Antifoundationalism, however, does not stand as the exact opposite of foundationalism. For example, just because foundationalism argues that only particular kinds of claims count as true ones (objectivism), does not mean that antifoundationalism rejects the notion of truth claims all together (relativism). This is a familiar, if not confused, critique of antifoundationalism and is more accurate for the distinction of modernism vs. postmodernism. If modernism—a term that is a synonym for foundationalism—stands for an all-encompassing single metanarrative that explains everything, then postmodernity stands for its exact opposite, i.e., nothing.

Hyman describes the distinctions between modernism and postmodernism this way, "Postmodernism is . . . a negative and parasitic term that depends on the negation of something else for its self-definition."[1] It is a reaction to modernism that is characterized "as the desire for an all-encompassing mastery of reality by rational and/or scientific means."[2] For Hyman,

---

1 Hyman, *Predicament of Postmodern Theology,* 11.
2. Ibid.

postmodernism is like a younger brother who willfully pokes holes, points out paradoxes, questions, and even disrupts its older modernist brother. But they are still brothers and assume *all the same things*. I highlight this distinction between modernism and postmodernism in order to show that a similar comparison is not available for foundationalism and antifoundationalism. Despite its name, antifoundationalism is not dependent upon foundationalism for its existence, though it is obviously critical of it.

So then, what exactly do I mean by antifoundationalism? Fish offers this succinct description:

> Antifoundationalism teaches that questions of fact, truth, correctness, validity, and clarity can neither be posed nor answered in reference to some extracontextual, ahistorical, nonsituational reality, or rule, or law, or value; rather antifoundationalism asserts, all of these matters are intelligible and debatable only within the precincts of the contexts or situations or paradigms or communities that give them their local and changeable shape. It is not just that antifoundationalism replaces the components of the foundationalist world-picture with other components; instead, it denies to those components the stability and independence and even the identity that is so necessary if they are to be thought of as grounds or anchors. Entities like the world, language, and the self can still be named; and value judgments having to do with validity, factuality, accuracy, and propriety can still be made; but in every case these entities and values, along with the procedures by which they are identified and marshaled, will be inextricable from the social and historical circumstances in which they do their work.[3]

Antifoundationalism argues that there is simply no such thing as truth, meaning, or interpretation that is free from the constraints of beliefs and contexts. It denies the notion that an object can be understood as *Ding-an-sich*, as a "thing in itself," transcending our limited position as humans and seeing an object without perspective or presuppositions. Antifoundationalism argues that truth is not something to be discovered outside of a person's context, situation, history, or belief structure—truth isn't just "out there"—*truth emerges from, and indeed makes sense only within such things and functions within their constraints*. Our reasoning, interpretations, judgments, claims of factuality and truth cannot be separated from or transcend our already-in-place beliefs and contexts. In fact, these sorts of practices (reasoning, interpreting, judging) are made possible by the constraints

---

3. Fish, "Anti-Foundationalism," 344–45.

The Church and Her Doctrine

provided by our beliefs and contexts. Antifoundationalism disputes any notion of a foundation that is outside of a context (i.e., with general universal principles) and that disregards the already-in-place nature of beliefs, contexts, traditions and so forth.

Fish brings this out with his explanation of the role beliefs play in how we makes sense of the world:

> Beliefs are not what you think *about* but what you think *with*, and it is within the space provided by their articulations that mental activity—including the activity of theorizing—goes on. Theories are something you can have—you can wield them and hold them at a distance; beliefs have *you*, in the sense that there can be no distance between them and the acts they enable. In order to make even the simplest of assertions or perform the most elementary action, I must already be proceeding in the context of innumerable beliefs which cannot be the object of my attention because they are the content of my attention: beliefs on the order of the identity of persons, the existence of animate and inanimate entities, the stability of objects, in addition to the countless beliefs that underwrite the possibility and intelligibility of events in my local culture—beliefs that give me, without reflection, a world populated by streets, sidewalks, telephone poles, restaurants, figures of authority and figures of fun, worthy and unworthy tasks, achievable and unachievable goals, and so on.[4]

For Fish, beliefs are what structure our thinking and give shape and content to our practices, whether those practices are academic, legal, theological, ecclesial or whatever else there is.[5] Beliefs are the constraints that enable us to make contact with the world, to interact with it, and to talk about and describe it. Beliefs are "action oriented, situation-related, and embedded in the particularities and contingencies of everyday living."[6] Beliefs are not optional things that we can pick and choose at will as if we are shoppers in a mall. Nor are they merely cognitive or mental activities. Beliefs cannot be separated from our knowledge because our beliefs are the *content* of our knowledge and we are always and already in the grip of them.[7] There is no

---

4. Fish, "Consequences," 326–27.

5. Ibid., 324.

6. Thisleton, *Hermeneutics of Doctrine*, 21.

7. Polanyi argues along similar lines: "We must now recognize belief once more as the source of all knowledge. Tacit assent and intellectual passions, the sharing of an idiom and of a cultural heritage, affiliation to a like-minded community: such are the impulses

space between our beliefs and the actions they enable; they have a hold on us and we see and interpret texts, events, and the world according to them. Beliefs are *foundational* to our identity because they are the foundational and often unconscious assumptions, the *a priori*, that enable us to interact with the world. Everyone has beliefs that they hold to be true—whether they are conscious of them or can even articulate them is irrelevant—and as everyday experience shows, not everyone holds the same beliefs in common.

I find Fish's articulation of antifoundationalism—his view of beliefs, contexts, interpretation and so on—to be particularly helpful because of the clarity of his thought and his grasp of the issues (this is why I unapologetically use him so often). This however does not mean that I find Fish to be an innovator (in the pejorative sense of the word) or that his thought comes out of left field. His view actually derives from Immanuel Kant and his notion of *a priori*.

Kant in the preface to his second edition of *Critique of Pure Reason* makes this groundbreaking statement, "Reason must approach nature with the view, indeed, of receiving information from it, not however, in the character of a pupil, who listens to all that his master chooses to tell him, but in that of a judge, who compels the witnesses to reply to those questions which he himself thinks fit to propose. To this single idea must the revolution be ascribed, by which, after groping in the dark for so many centuries, natural science was at length conducted into the path of certain progress."[8] Kant's view overturned long-standing scientific and metaphysical dogma: the belief that our minds, and therein our thinking, conform to the objects of their attention. Kant turns this on its head and argues that we will be more successful "if we assume that the objects must conform to our cognition."[9] We interpret objects; we reason and observe them, not from a blank slate, but rather from a mediated position that is always and already in place, what he calls our *a priori* cognition. He likens his view to what Copernicus did in overturning centuries' worth of scientific thinking, by showing that the Earth revolves around the sun, not the other way around.

---

which shape our vision of the nature of things on which we rely for our mastery of things. No intelligence, however critical or original, can operate outside of such a fiduciary framework." Polanyi, *Personal Knowledge*, 266

8. Kant, *Critique of Pure Reason*, 13.

9. Ibid., 14.

The Church and Her Doctrine

Kant's basic argument is two-fold. First, he argues that our experience of the world is mediated by our senses and minds that are *a priori*, that are already in place before we even begin to observe an object. This is unavoidable because we cannot transcend our limited position as observers and our mental apparatus that is already in place. Second, Kant is trying to show the *limits* of our minds and their ability to reason. He argues that his position "serves to warn us against venturing, with speculative reason, beyond the limits of experience. This is, in fact [his argument's] primary use."[10] In other words, our reasoning is bound; it is limited to the sphere of our experience. It cannot transcend these boundaries, but must reason within their constraints.

In the generation following Kant, Schopenhauer found Kant's notion of *a priori* groundbreaking too, but at the same time sought to correct and fix much of what Kant argued.[11] Though Fish's antifoundationalism rejects much of what Kant argues, like Schopenhauer, he still finds the notion of *a priori* to be revolutionary and is rightly understood as being part of the tradition that begins with Kant, even if he diverges widely from Kant's original thought. Fish is not alone in his articulation of beliefs as the *a priori* that allow us to make contact with the world. He is part of a trajectory that includes scholars in diverse fields. For example, T. S. Kuhn, the philosopher of science, employs the concept of "paradigms" in a similar way to Fish in order to describe not only how scientific thinking actually works, but also to show how scientific assumptions change over time.[12] Clifford Geertz, in the field of anthropology, employs similar arguments with his notion of "thick description," and the description of cultures.[13] Peter Berger, in the field of sociology, puts forth similar ideas with his notion of "plausibility structures."[14] In the field of philosophy names like Rorty, Dewey, Peirce, James, Davidson, Wittgenstein, MacIntyre, Stout, and Polanyi are all concerned with similar projects.

By arguing for a different account of where foundations are located and applied (the local and particular), antifoundationalism is, by implication, arguing for a different account of epistemology. If foundationalism argues for an epistemology that is grounded in principles and norms that

---

10. Ibid., 16.
11. Schopenhaeur, *World as Will and Representation*.
12. Kuhn, *Structure of Scientific Revolutions*; *Essential Tension*.
13. Geertz, *Interpretation of Cultures*.
14. Berger and Luckmann, *Social Construction of Reality*; Berger, *Sacred Canopy*.

transcend our context (e.g., Rorty's description of an "intrinsic nature," Vanhoozer's "determinate textual meaning," or Thiselton's "transcontextual reasonableness"), antifoundationalism argues for an epistemology that emerges from within our beliefs. For an antifoundationalist, our knowing of the world is a *product* of our already-in-place beliefs. Our knowing cannot escape or transcend the constraints of our beliefs; our knowing is enabled by our beliefs and is limited and bound by them. Like Kant, this does not mean that antifoundationalism disavows itself of external reality and it certainly doesn't think that we are synthesizing reality or simply making it up (as some of Kant's followers mistakenly thought).[15] Rather antifoundationalism argues that the way we make sense of the world is bound and limited by constraints and our "knowing" of the world is a product—it is mediated—of them. Like Kant, antifoundationalism believes in external reality, but it acknowledges that there is no access to it apart from mediation. But unlike Kant, antifoundationalism is not concerned with a distinction between pure and empirical *a priori* concepts.

To briefly summarize, antifoundationalism is a mood that conceives of at least two things differently from foundationalism. First, it calls into question foundationalism's assumptions about where constraints reside. Constraints are local and particular, not universal and neutral. Second, and by a matter of consequence, antifoundationalism holds to an epistemology that argues that we know the world by way of the same local and particular constraints. Antifoundationalism is all for reasoning, fact-finding, presenting evidence, and making truth claims. It simply believes that what makes such activities possible are constraints that are local and particular, not universal and general.

If we take the claims of antifoundationalism seriously, then it means (among other things) that we must see the constraints that enable the interpretation of Scripture and the formation and articulation of doctrine as *particular* to the Church. All of the Church's life and practice—her interpretation of Scripture, her worship and proclamation, her formation and articulation of doctrine—are enabled by and find their meaning with, the one foundation of Jesus.

---

15. Magee, *Confessions of a Philosopher*, 149.

The Church and Her Doctrine

JESUS AS THE LONE CHRISTIAN FOUNDATION

One of the most popular hymns among Protestants in America is "The Church's One Foundation," written by Samuel J. Stone in 1866 as a response to false teaching:

> The church's one foundation is Jesus Christ Her Lord;
> she is his new creation by water and the Word:
> from heav'n he came and sought her to be his holy bride;
> with his own blood he bought her, and for her life he died

The Church's one foundation is Jesus Christ her Lord. This is one way of saying that the Church is founded by, bound to, and sustained by Jesus. This hymn is similar to the confession made by Peter in Matthew 16:13-20 (cf., Mark 8:27-38; Luke 9:18-27). After having fed thousands of people miraculously (twice), walked on water, and cast out a demon, Jesus takes a step back from the crowds that were following him and asks his disciples to assess what the crowds were saying about him. He asks, "Who do people say that the Son of Man is?" The disciples report that some are calling him John the Baptist, others say he is Elijah or even Jeremiah. Jesus then puts the question to his disciples, "But who do you say that I am?" This is the question that ultimately drives all of Christian reflection and is the most pressing question a human will ever face: *who do we say that Jesus is?* Is it as the crowds saw him, as a prophet or at the very least, a man of God? It is Peter's response—a response not derived by reason or quick thinking, but a response given to Peter by God the Father—that stands in stark contrast to the crowds: *Jesus is the Messiah, the Son of the living God*. However, it is Jesus' explanation of what this means later in the passage—he is the crucified Messiah and the Son of the Living God who will be raised from the dead on the third day by his Father—that fills out and deepens Peter's confession. It is this Jesus, the crucified and resurrected Messiah, and his on-going redemptive mission, that the Church confesses and not some other one. The Church and her doctrine need no other foundation for its validation and existence.

The foundation for the Church and her doctrine is Jesus, *and nothing else*. Every claim the Church makes, her worship, speech, doctrine, and practices are all founded by and bound to Jesus alone. Herman Sasse agrees: ""Jesus Christ is Lord." This is the original confession of the church. With it the Christian faith once entered world history. To understand the sense of this confession ever more deeply is the great, yes, basically the only task of all Christian theology. To repeat this confession, to speak it in ever new forms, to translate it into the language of all times and peoples, to protect it against misunderstandings and reinterpretations, and to understand its meaning for all areas of life—that is the task of all confession building within Christendom."[16]

It is upon this rock, upon this Jesus that the Church is built and it is because of him, that Peter's confession, "Jesus is the Messiah, the Son of the Living God," will never fail and the gates of hell will not prevail against it.

This is the same argument that I made earlier with Scripture: the crucifixion and resurrection of Jesus Christ is the *definitive and constitutive Christian event*. By his resurrection from the dead, Jesus was validated as the Son of God and his claims to be the true King of Israel (and by implication all of creation) and the fulfillment and rightful interpreter of the Old Testament (the Scriptures) were also validated. Because Jesus was validated in his claims, the witnesses he authorized (the apostles), their preaching about Jesus (the *kerygma*), and their written accounts about him (the New Testament), took on official status as deputized authorities for the community founded by Jesus: the New Israel reconstituted around Jesus' authority and rule. As we saw in chapter 3, it is because of Jesus' authority as the Son of God that Scripture is the authoritative standard and source by which the Church must judge and authenticate her preaching and teaching.

This same relationship is also true for the Church: it is because of Jesus' authority as the Son of God, that the Church not only exists, but has her identity and mission. Without Jesus there is no Scripture and there is no Church. Scripture, the Church and her doctrine needs no other—in fact, it has no other—foundation than Jesus. If Jesus is the definitive and constitutive Christian event then this necessarily means that he alone is the foundation for all of Christianity. This is an important move away from typical foundationalist accounts of doctrine.

Take for example, Pannenberg's assumptions about the proper foundations for doctrine and truth. While Pannenberg holds to typical Christian authorities, he is ultimately concerned with theology as a quest for universal truth in which theology's claims are put to the test of rational inquiry and must cohere with other fields of knowledge.[17] As Stanley Grenz explains about Pannenberg's project, "[T]ruth can only be personal when it can be claimed—at least in principle—to be true for all. On this basis, he concludes that dogmatics is universal in scope, encompassing all reality

---

16. Sasse, *We Confess*, 9.
17. Pannenberg, *Systematic Theology*, 1:1–63.

The Church and Her Doctrine

in its quest for coherence with all knowledge."[18] Even though Pannenberg recognizes the usual Christian authorities, it is ultimately some other foundation—i.e., the universal claim to truth—that becomes the basis for his account of doctrine and theology.

What makes an account of the Church and her doctrine properly *Christian* is the particular foundation of Jesus and the Word that derives from him. To put this within the parameters of this work, while a foundationalist account of doctrine may try and ground Scripture, Christian doctrine and its truth claims in so-called universal standards, norms, or experiences, an antifoundationalist account will look no further than the particular foundation of Jesus. As I have already said (and cannot say enough), antifoundationalism is not against foundations, it is simply against foundations that claim to be universal and free from a context. For my purposes—and to be a little bold—an antifoundationalist account of Christian doctrine is just another way of saying a *Christian* account of doctrine, because the account is predicated on Jesus alone. A Christian account of the Church and her doctrine need not and must not make appeals to any other source than Jesus and his Word for its validity, identity, and truthfulness. Appeals to something other than Jesus and Scripture are appeals to things that are considered more foundational and more authoritative than Jesus and his Word. As Lesslie Newbigin puts it, "To look outside of the gospel for a starting point for the demonstration of the reasonableness of the gospel is itself a contradiction of the gospel, for it implies that we look for the *logos* elsewhere than in Jesus."[19] What I am arguing for then, is not the supplanting of one mood with another—i.e., become an antifoundationalist instead of a foundationalist—so much as I am trying to supplant foundationalist accounts that ultimately appeal to some other *logos* than Jesus.

When it comes to accounting for the Church and her doctrine, like with Scripture, these things only make sense within the relationship to Jesus. The Church is not a stand-alone institution with its own ontology and purpose. The Church did not make itself nor does it guide its own course. The Church is unlike any other human institution in existence: it is the *divine-human* institution founded by Jesus and only has its existence and validity in relationship to him.

---

18. Grenz, *Reason for Hope*, 18.
19. Newbigin, *Proper Confidence*, 94.

THE CHURCH AS DIVINE-HUMAN INSTITUTION

Scripture confirms the dependent relationship of the Church to her Lord by its various descriptions of her throughout its pages. The Church is the people of God; the *ecclesia*; the body of Christ (Col 1:18); the Bride of Christ (Eph 5:22–33); reconstituted Israel around Jesus (Matt 21:43); a royal priesthood, a holy nation (1 Pet 2:9). Luther, in commenting on the term *ecclesia* (and its abuses and misunderstandings) offers this helpful description (and I think good Biblical summary) in "On the Councils and The Church,"

> *Ecclesia*, however, should mean the holy Christian people, not only of the days of the apostles, who are long since dead, but to the end of the world, so that there is always a holy Christian people on earth, in whom Christ lives, works, and rules, *per redemptionem*, "through grace and the remission of sin," and the Holy Spirit, *per vivificationem et sanctificationem*, "through daily purging of sin and renewal of life," so that we do not remain in sin but are enabled and obliged to lead a new life, abounding in all kinds of good works, as the Ten Commandments or the two tables of Moses' law command, and not in old, evil works. That is St. Paul's teaching.[20]

Luther's description works well with Peter's confession of Jesus in Matthew 16 in explaining what the Church is: it is the institution founded by and organized around Jesus. Or as Webster argues, the Church is founded as "an assembly around the self-bestowing presence of the risen Christ."[21] The institution founded by Jesus is defined by (among other things) his presence, his description of the world, his reading and appropriation of the Old Testament, and his interpretation of the events of his own life and future events as proclaimed by his authoritative deputies, the apostles. Therein, the community founded by Jesus and organized around his claims recognizes the authority of the Triune God and his authoritative Word as the only authorities for its life, doctrine, and practices. As Young argues, "Every group of people seeks self-definition in terms of distinctive characteristics that mark it off from others. Every community is in this sense exclusive, and the history of the church is no different from other human social groupings in this respect. A group coheres around a common interest, or esoteric rites and rules, creating boundaries."[22] For the Church, the

---

20 Luther, "On the Councils and the Church," 144.
21. Webster, *Holy Scripture*, 59.
22. Young, *Making of the Creeds*, 99.

"distinctive characteristic" is Jesus: everything else about the Church flows from this relationship. All of its interpretations, doctrines and practices are predicated and dependent upon Jesus for their meaning and existence.

In the same treatise "On the Councils and the Church," Luther points out seven distinctive marks of the Church[23] by which we can recognize the Church as the Church: possession of the Word of God as it is externally preached; the sacrament of baptism; the sacrament of the Lord's Supper; the exercising of discipline through the office of the keys; the calling and ordaining of ministers and other public offices; worship in terms of prayer, public praise and thanksgiving; the cross of suffering which the Church must bear like her savior.[24] These practices do not originate with the Church itself, they originate with Jesus. In fact, *they were modeled, instituted and commanded by him.* Luther states as much when he says, "Therefore the *ecclesia*, "the holy Christian people," does not have mere external words, sacraments, or offices, like God's ape Satan has, and in far greater numbers, but it has these as commanded, instituted, and ordained by God, so that he himself and not any angel will work through them with the Holy Spirit."[25]

This means that the Church was not founded by Jesus as her own separate and independent institution; the Church is the institution of the Triune God's *continued presence and action*. As Webster notes, "The church is, therefore, not constituted through human activities and undertakings, but by a reference to the revelatory divine Word [Jesus] and work by which alone it is evoked and maintained in life, for in accordance with its very *raison d'être*, the church is primordially defined as the *hearing* church."[26] The Church, while being a human community, is constituted, situated and finds its identity within the redemptive action (economy) of the Triune God. Far from being isolated from the Triune God, the Church's life and practices occur within his presence. Therefore the appropriate and only place for understanding Christian doctrine and practice is in the visible locus of God's continued action and presence, the Church. It is not in the world at large (though God is active in redeeming it) or the *Wissenschaft* of the university or in neutral concepts of "religion" (Lindbeck) where Christian doctrines

---

23. In other writings the list is both longer and shorter, but in general the list could be summarized to this: the preaching of the pure Gospel and the right administration of the sacraments.

24. Luther, "On the Councils and the Church," 148.

25. Ibid., 171.

26. Webster, *Holy Scripture*, 46 (emphasis in original).

emerge and have meaning, it is in the community of God's grace and mercy. The Church then, the *ecclesia*, as a politic, is a visible *divine-human community* and is characterized, both by the activity of God and as Luther rightly argued, by the practices given to her by her Lord. This leads to two points.

First, when we consider the Church in these terms, it is apparent that the Church only has its meaning and existence within the economy of salvation. It is only by God's use of the Church within his on-going work of redemption and therein with his continued presence, that she has her identity as the people of God. Second, this means (among other things) that the Church is not an idealized form that stands beyond the fray of human actions, but rather is comprised by human activity and by the continued presence, action, and rule of God. Jenson argues "The church is not an invisible entity; she is the, if anything, all too visible gathering of sinners around the loaf and cup. What is invisible is that this visible entity is in fact what she claims to be, the people of God.[27] While I might debate Jenson's negative assessment of the invisibility of the Church, he is correct on what he offers with the visible Church: it is, as Jesus understood it, full of sinners and saints, the sheep and the goats, the wheat and the tares, all mixed into one visible community called the people of God. As Jenson deftly notes, what is often invisible, what is hard to see at times is that it *actually is* God's people. The Church, despite the continued action and presence of God, is embroiled with the world (*simul iustus et peccator*) in ways that are indicative of her being "already" and "not yet." She is "already" set apart by her Lord, but she is "not yet" fully redeemed and is still dealing with besetting sin. Virtually any one familiar with the Church and her history knows that it has often looked anything but like the people of God, and yet she is still the Church.

No matter how the Church may look to a watching world and even to its members, she is a "hearing" community, a community that listens to her shepherd and is acted upon by him. At the same time she is also a "doing" community that is called upon to respond to her Lord's call. As Luther puts it, not only is the Church redeemed, vivified, and sanctified by her Lord (passive), the Lord does so in order that the Church might be enabled to follow him and do good works (active) (cf., Eph 2:10). Jesus redeems, makes alive, and sanctifies his people through his Spirit so that they will look like him and do the same sorts of things that he does, chief among these being the proclamation of the Gospel (preaching) and the making

---

27. Jenson, *Systematic Theology*, 2:174.

of disciples (teaching). This indicates that both the Triune God and the Church speak. Webster again: "The primary speech-act which takes place within the church and from which all other church speech-acts derive is Jesus Christ's own self-utterance. That self-utterance is mediated through the language of prophetic testimony to which Scripture bears witness and which then forms the basis and norm of the church's public speech."[28] It is as Torrance argues: "In the apostles as the receiving end of His revealing and reconciling activity, Jesus Christ laid the foundation of the Church which He incorporated into Himself as His own Body, and permitted the Word which he put into their mouth to take the form of proclamation answering to and extending His own in such a way that it became the controlled unfolding of His own revelation within the mind and language of the apostolic foundation."[29]

The primary speech-act that occurs within the Church is Jesus' own self-utterance through his apostles' preaching and the definitive written versions of their preaching and teaching (Scripture). But the Church also speaks, her speech being derivative from and ruled by this primary speech act. We have to confess, however that the Church, as a human community, does such activities imperfectly and many times fails in her attempts to model her speech on Jesus' own speech act. The Church needs the Gospel too. The Church then should not be understood to be solely divine or solely human; it is both. The Church is characterized by both the Spirit-led activity of God *and* the human community's response to the Spirit.

If you will recall in chapter 3, I briefly discussed John Behr's claim that understanding the authority of Scripture in terms of Scripture vs. Church, (i.e., text vs. reader) as if both Scripture and the Church are two independent authorities, is a confused notion. We can now fully see why. Both Scripture and the Church owe their existence and meaning to Jesus. Both are defined by his presence and have their existence with his use of them in the economy of salvation. Scripture and the Church should never be pitted against one another as if they are competing authorities, rather they should both be understood in terms of the roles given to them by their Lord.

Within this framework, we must say that the only proper institution for articulating and formulating doctrine is the Church. She does these activities in the Triune God's *presence* as a *derivative* speech act as measured by Scripture. But naming the Church as the lone institution for doctrine

---

28. Webster, *Holy Scripture*, 59.
29. Torrance, "Word of God and the Response of Man," 152.

only gets us so far. How can we account for how she actually goes about articulating and formulating doctrine? The question is similar to the question of interpretation I posed in chapter 3, i.e., how does the Church go about interpreting Scripture? Just because Scripture is the authoritative Word of God does not make it clear to whoever wants to read it. Likewise, just because the Church is the divine-human institution founded by Jesus does not mean that articulating doctrine just happens. The explanation for how such activities work is bound up with the notion of context.

THE CHURCH AND HER CONTEXT

Few Christian theologians would take me to task for calling the Church the people of God or a divine-human institution. Some may quibble over some of the particulars of my description, but in general, there would be agreement. Likewise, few would deny that the Church is a context or even the right context for doctrine, but calling the Church a context leads to confusion. The confusion lies in what typically is meant by the term "context."

Typically when people talk about "context" what they have in mind is a set of features (the features could be of a text, a play, a situation or event, or even the features of nature) that can be identified and interpreted by any observer that happens upon them. In this view, a context is something that is in the world and it trades on the same foundationalist assumptions we've seen with formalism and objectivism, i.e., meaning is inherent in the discernible structure of the text or object. This is similar to the view that Kant found popular in his day, i.e., that our minds conform to the objects that they observe. By this view, if we were to name the Church as a context, we ought to be able to point out structures and features that are easily discernable and therein be able to "read" the context. Of course, virtually anyone who grew up in the West can identify the structure of the Church, because she is a well-known institution with well-known practices and claims. But just because someone can recognize the Church as an institution, does not mean that person has discerned the Church's context. The two things are not the same, though they are often confused for one another.

Like Kant with his "Copernican Revolution," antifoundationalism turns the foundationalist notion of context upside down. For an antifoundationalist, a context is a structure of assumptions that have a hold on people and allow them to make a construction of the world that is itself, performed under contextualized conditions.[30] Instead of understanding

---

30. Fish, "With the Compliments of the Author," 52–53.

"context" as something *in the world*, antifoundationalists understand it as a *construction of the world*. However, using phrases like "construction of the world," has a tendency to be understood by foundationalists as "making up reality as we see fit." I mean nothing of the sort. Rather what is meant by "make a construction of the world," is to make an *interpretation of reality* according to an already-in-place structure of assumptions. Those who hold to the same structure of assumptions—the context—not only make sense of the world in the same way, holding to the same context provides a framework for discussion and debate over the relevant features of the context itself.[31]

For example, when a Christian looks at reality, he sees it as *creation*, in particular as the Triune God's creation, who brought it into existence, *ex nihilo*, by the power of his Word. This is opposed to an atheist who perhaps looks at the same reality and sees a closed universe that came into existence through accident or some other supposed natural phenomena. In both cases, reality is being interpreted; it is being "constructed," according to a structure of assumptions that give sense and meaning to reality for the respective interpreters. Both interpreters are making truth claims about the world and can provide reasons for their views. They will even point to features "in" reality (the geological record, vegetation, animal life, etc.) to support their claims. Nevertheless, for both interpreters what gives reality its particular shape, what allows them to make sense of the world and to reason about it, is their particular context, their structure of assumptions. Likewise, it is because both interpreters are gripped by different sets of assumptions that they see the world in conflicting ways. It is not necessarily the case that one interpreter is more reasonable than another (i.e., one is rational and one is irrational) or that one has a better claim on the so-called clear and obvious facts. It is rather that both interpreters are reasoning and interpreting according to an already-in-place structure of assumptions that enables them to make sense of the world.

By this way of thinking, a context must be thought of in terms of *a priori*, as having an already-in-place nature that is automatically assumed by those in the grip of its structure. We need only look at the sport of baseball to see that the game (along with the language that accompanies it) is neither inherent to the structure of reality (it is not intrinsic to nature) nor is it coherent without a prior understanding of its goals, purposes, and practices. A so-called neutral and rational observer cannot walk up to the

---

31. Ibid.

game, without prior knowledge of it, and hope to understand what is going on. "What is a home run and why is it called that? Why can you sometimes tag someone to get him "out" and other times you must "tag" the base? Why can't you run around in that big grassy area after you hit the ball and why do you have to hit the ball in the first place?" Americans may have a hard time believing my line of argument until I ask them to explain the game of cricket, which looks somewhat like baseball, but is a completely different *context*, with its own rules, purposes, and goals. Cricket is also a construction of the world and far from being clear to outsiders, the features of the game are muddled and incoherent to those who are not already gripped by its assumptions. The reason for this simple: baseball and cricket are two different kinds of interpretive practices with different structures of assumptions that allow those gripped by their respective contexts to make an interpretation of the world.

Having said this, isolated individuals do not hold a context; a context is held in community. If you will recall the question that initially drove Fish's thinking—and is the question that I have used as my *de facto* foundationalist example—is this: what is the source of interpretive authority, the text or the reader? For those who answered, "the text," there was no accounting for why various people *disagree* over a text's meaning. On the other hand, to those who answered, "the reader," there is no accounting for why so many people—even people of very different backgrounds, ethnicities, languages and even different time periods—can *agree* on the interpretation of a text. Fish's solution to the dilemma is his now famous notion of "interpretive community."

An interpretive community is not a group of individuals who share a point of view, but rather just the opposite: a point of view that shares individuals in the sense that its assumed "distinctions, categories of understanding, and stipulations of relevance and irrelevance were the content of the consciousness of community members who were therefore no longer individuals, but, insofar as they were embedded in the community's enterprise, community property." This community of interpreters is agreed on the same text, but this is not because of the text in and of itself, but rather because of their shared interpretive slant. "In this new vision both texts and readers lose the independence that would be necessary for either of them to claim the honor of being the source of interpretive authority; both are absorbed by the interpretive community which, because it is responsible for the texts those performances bring into the world."[32]

32. Fish, "Change," 141–42.

The Church and Her Doctrine

In other words, an interpretive community is a structure of assumptions—a context—that provides a point of view or a way of organizing experience for a *group of people*, not isolated individuals. The context provides distinctions, categories of understandings, and judgments on what is relevant and irrelevant, which in turn, forms the content, the knowledge of the members who are in its grip. People do not interpret texts (or anything else) in isolation, as if they were independent and autonomous islands; they interpret them in communities. The term "community" however, means more than just readers. What makes the act of interpretation possible is not the existence of independent texts or readers, but texts and readers who are part of the same structure of assumptions, i.e., the same community, and therefore share the same point of view. This means that both texts and readers are gripped by the same structure of assumptions (neither are independent entities) and in turn, both writing (texts) and interpreting (readers) occurs within the same constraints of the same context.

But it goes deeper than this: contexts in a sense, *own their members*. Membership in a particular community is not optional in the sense of having options on a menu that we can freely pick and choose from. We are not free to choose a context anymore than we can choose what beliefs to hold. It may be that an interpreter is completely unaware of his membership in a particular community (i.e., he is unconscious of the fact that he has a particular interpretive slant) and therefore is unaware he has a particular set of assumptions. Nevertheless, we all interpret according to a particular context, i.e., a particular interpretive community that carries its own point of view and its own structure of assumptions that enables interpreters (both texts and readers) to make sense of the world.

The temptation at this point is to understand the Church in just these terms and call it a context or an interpretive community, but this would be a mistake. A context is *a structure of assumptions* that allows for interpretation (and therein the organizing of experience) among its members to occur. The Church, as the divine-human institution founded by Jesus, is an institution that has a structure of assumptions, but she cannot be reduced to merely being a structure of assumptions. Part of the confusion (and inherent danger) of using terms like "interpretive community" is that what readily comes to mind is a concrete group of people that are easily demarcated from other people, e.g., "Lutherans," "Catholics," "Orthodox." To be sure, each of these groups has a structure of assumptions, but the groups themselves cannot be reduced to their interpretive slant, though it is an important part of their identity. To use the notion of context or interpretive community is simply to argue that the Church does not interpret texts (or anything else) without first having a structure of assumptions already in place. The concept is a helpful way for making sense of what happens when people both agree and disagree over the meaning of a text. This being said, the Church is not a context, rather it *has a context*, i.e., it has a structure of assumptions that enables proper interpretation to occur.

If the Church has a context, what exactly is it? The Church's context, its structure of assumptions for interpreting everything, is nothing less than the redemptive narrative of Jesus, the Son of the Living God, Messiah. It is his narrative about the creation and on-going redemption of the world by the Father, through the Son, in the power of the Holy Spirit that gives the appropriate and *particular* structure of assumptions for the Church. Phrases like "Jesus is Lord," or "you are the Christ, the Son of the Living God," are shorthand terms that assume this structure of assumptions. Included within this narrative is a whole matrix of beliefs about whom and what the true God is, who and what humanity is, what salvation is and why it is needed, among other things. For example when we read Paul's great Christological hymn in Colossians 1:15–20, we hear the retelling of the redemptive narrative of Jesus as both the Creator God and the Redeemer God:

> He is the image of the invisible God, the firstborn of all creation. For by him all things were created, in heaven and on earth, visible and invisible, whether thrones or dominions or rulers or authorities—all things were created through him and for him. And he is before all things, and in him all things hold together. And he is the head of the body, the church. He is the beginning, the firstborn from the dead, that in everything he might be preeminent. For in him all the fullness of God was pleased to dwell, and through him to reconcile to himself all things, whether on earth or in heaven, making peace by the blood of his cross.

Jesus is the Son of God, the Messiah, the Lord of all creation who, by his Word, created all things and by his same Word, holds all things together and who, in turn, making peace with his Father for us and our salvation by the blood of his cross. This is the context, the on-going redemptive narrative of Jesus Christ, that the Church assumes—in fact, she *intentionally* generates it—before she begins to read Scripture or formulate and articulate doctrine.

The notion that this redemptive narrative is the Church's context is nothing new. In chapter 3, I argued that from the very beginning, the Church assumed that in order to read Scripture as it was intended to be read, a reader needed to have the right disposition and rule for reading already in place. Irenaeus called this the canon of truth or the *regula fidei*, while Athanasius called it the *dianoia* or "mind" of Scripture. This is similar to Voelz's notion of the "implied reader": the person who holds to the structure of assumptions required by the text (Scripture) and who has been taught these assumptions by the community who has itself assumed this same role, i.e., the Church.[33] In order to read Scripture on its own terms, the reader must first assume the correct context, the correct structure of assumptions.

It is often argued by foundationalists, that the notion of context or interpretive community implies that it is merely readers who are gripped by a structure of assumptions, as if they have *decided* to read a text in a particular way that is congenial to them. Of course, sometimes this is true. But the Church did not create this context; *her Lord gave it to her*. Just as Peter did not devise his confession of Jesus by his own understanding (cf., Matt 16:17), nor did the Church devise her own narrative. This context was *given* to the Church by Jesus (just as Peter's confession was *given* to him) and was taught by his apostles and in turn was handed down from generation to generation up to the present. Scripture (text), the Church (readers), and her doctrine are produced, defined, and find their being in Jesus and therefore share the same context, i.e., the same on-going redemptive narrative about him.

Having said all this, the practice of interpretation must not be isolated to reading texts (though it obviously includes this), but must be understood as *a way of life*, a way of reflecting upon and taking in everything. Christian interpretation, as Holmer argues, is a practice in which Christians interpret all of life, "referring everything, our woes and weal, fears and joys, past and future, completely to God's love and care."[34] Another word for this is theology. "Theology is, then, an interpretation. But not as if it were willful, episodic, or subjective. Theology is that skein of thought and language in which Christians understand themselves, the Bible, God and their everyday world."[35] All Christians are involved in the practice of theology, and by

---

33. Voelz, *What Does This Mean?* 220
34. Holmer, *Grammar of Faith*, 19.
35. Ibid., 9–10.

virtue of being gripped by the same context must see the world from a *theological* disposition. We organize experience, make judgments on the world, act ethically, reason, make truth claims and give evidence for our claims, based on this Jesus and his redemptive narrative. Our interpretation, our making sense of the world, is bound and defined by Jesus and we do so as members of the same divine-human institution that is governed and ruled by Jesus' authoritative Word. If the context for the Church's interpretation of Scripture is this on-going redemptive narrative of Jesus and the matrix of beliefs that attend to it, it is within this particular context that the Church articulates and formulates her doctrine.

THE NATURE AND FUNCTION OF DOCTRINE

In the Introduction, I defined doctrine as those religious claims that have a legally binding quality to them and to which a person must assent in order to be considered part of the Church. Church doctrines are, as Lindbeck defines them, "communally authoritative teachings regarding beliefs and practices that are considered essential to the identity or welfare of the group in question."[36] For the sake of discussion, I identify Christian doctrines with the official doctrinal or confessional statements of the Church (or various Church bodies). Not only do they provide easy examples for discussion, they actually are used in just the way I describe them: as legally binding statements to which a Christian must assent. Good examples of this would be statements like the three ecumenical creeds (the Apostle's Creed, Nicene Creed, and Athanasian Creed), the Lutheran Augsburg Confession of 1530, the English Reformed Westminster Confession of Faith of 1646, the Chicago Statement on Inerrancy, and Gaudium et Spes or Lumen Gentium that came out of Vatican II in the 1960's.

There are obviously many more examples that could be listed here and while I find the identification of doctrine with official doctrinal statements to be helpful for discussion, doctrine need not be relegated to official statements alone. There are some doctrines—like the governing doctrine that Scripture is the sole authoritative text of the Church—that have no real official doctrinal statements. Some doctrines, like the Nicene Creed, may have an official status in many Church bodies, but in reality have long since ceased to be operational or indicative of the particular Church's identity.[37] Nevertheless, doctrines are not merely religious claims that a person ac-

---

36. Lindbeck, *Nature of Doctrine*, 74.
37. Ibid., 74–75.

cepts or rejects willy-nilly; doctrines are things to which a person either assents or dissents.

What I mean by the term "assent" is what Paul Griffiths means by it: "If you assent to a claim you take it to be true and to make a claim upon you; this is to say, roughly, that you believe it. Assenting to a claim in this sense is, by and large, an involuntary matter."[38] Usually when I assent to particular claims I will produce a set of reasons, habits, practices or perhaps a story or the recounting of an event to explain why I feel inclined to agree to particular claim. No matter what reasons or stories I may conjure up, "I find myself irresistibly moved to assent to the claim in question when it is proposed to me. I cannot deliberate and then decide whether to believe it or not. When I find myself assenting to some claim (believing it, taking it as true), then, my assent typically does not involve choice or deliberation. It is simply given to me."[39]

Griffith's concept of assent is similar to Fish's concept of beliefs and context, in that all three concepts argue for the notion of *a priori*, of the already-in-place nature of our thinking. We cannot help but *assent*—it is largely involuntary on our part—to particular claims because of the beliefs and the structure of assumptions that we already have in place. Conversely, we cannot help but *dissent* to other competing claims based on those same beliefs and assumptions.

Doctrines, however, are not the same thing as beliefs though the two are connected to one another. Doctrines are our attempts at articulating, reflecting upon, or codifying our beliefs. If a belief is *internal* to us, something that we think with that is not necessarily the focus of our attention; a doctrine is the *external* articulation or objectification of a belief or a set of beliefs. In the case of the Church, doctrine flows out of the context of the on-going redemptive narrative of Jesus and is both an attempt at articulating this narrative and conforming the Church's speech and actions to it, in particular as it is contained in Scripture. Doctrines are no more optional for us than are beliefs. In fact doctrines, like the beliefs and practices they attempt to articulate and regulate, involve *commitment* on the part of the people who hold them and are a deep expression of what they believe to be true about God, the world, and everything else.

If we compare this with Lindbeck's own regulative-only view of doctrine we can see what is at stake in the discussion: is doctrine capable of

---

38. Griffiths, *Problems of Religious Diversity*, 26.
39. Ibid.

expressing the deeply held beliefs of the Church as well as making a true description (a truth claim) of the Triune God, the world, and humanity? If we take Lindbeck's position seriously we can only say no: doctrine is nothing more and nothing less than the grammar that regulates the Church's talk about God. In contrast with this, I think doctrine has at least two functions worth discussing.[40] First, doctrine functions to articulate implicit beliefs that are held within the context of the on-going redemptive narrative of Jesus. This means that doctrine has a first-order function of articulating things like God, the world, humanity and so forth. Second, doctrine has a second-order or grammatical function in providing the rules and the boundaries for how the Church thinks, speaks, and acts.

One way of understanding the distinction of first and second-order functions of doctrine is to compare it to what Gerhard Forde argues is the proper distinction between proclamation and systematic theology. For Forde, proclamation is "explicit declaration of the good news, the gospel, the kerygma."[41] Proclamation is the Word of God or the Word from God, whereas systematic theology is the words about God, i.e., reflection and thinking upon what has been heard.[42] Forde understands the distinction between proclamation and systematic theology as a distinction between "primary" and "secondary" discourse. "Primary discourse is the direct declaration of the Word *of* God, that is, the Word *from* God, and the believing response in confession, prayer, and praise. Secondary discourse, words about God, is reflection on the primary discourse."[43] Proclamation as primary discourse is not about anything other than itself. It is speech directed from God to his people (and vice versa) and shows up in declarations like, "I baptize you in the name of the Father, the Son, and the Holy Spirit," or "I love you" and so forth. Secondary discourse is reflection on the meaning and implications of primary discourse and is exemplified by things like catechisms or seminary instruction.

---

40. Of course, doctrines have more uses beyond the two I mention. For example, Ellen Charry shows how important the pastoral function of doctrine has been since the time of the Church Fathers through the Reformation. My point is not to elucidate every function that doctrine may have, but rather to take issue with Lindbeck's account and show that doctrine has at least two important functions apart from foundationalist assumptions. Charry, *By the Renewing of Your Minds*.

41. Forde, *Theology Is For Proclamation*, 1.

42. Ibid., 3.

43. Ibid., 2.

Okamoto notes that the distinction between primary and secondary discourse is both helpful and unhelpful. It is helpful because it brings to the forefront the distinction between speech that engages hearers with God himself or that engages God himself by those who have heard him in contrast with speech *about* such engagements.[44] Throughout Church history, the perpetual problem has been the eclipsing of primary discourse by secondary discourse, in particular with the present-tense proclamation of the gospel, to the point that the gospel, for many Christians, only refers to a historical event in the distant past.[45] But the distinction Forde makes between primary and secondary discourse can also be unhelpful because it seems to be implying that secondary discourse is limited to only reflecting upon primary discourse.[46] Secondary discourse extends beyond the scope of primary discourse, but it is always rooted in primary discourse.

Kavanagh also makes use of the distinction between primary and secondary discourse and argues that "a liturgical act is the act of primary theology par excellence, the act from which other acts of secondary theology take their rise within that life of right worship we call the worshipping assembly, the community of faith, the Church."[47] By the term "liturgy," Kavanagh does not have in mind simply the ordering of a worship service, but rather the Triune God's engagement with his people that leads to a response of prayer, confession, praise, and thanksgiving. "A liturgical act *is* a theological act of the most all-encompassing, integral, and foundational kind. It is both precipitator and result of that adjustment to the change wrought in the worshipping assembly by its regular encounter in faith with its divine Source. This adjustment to God-wrought change is no less critical and reflective an act of theology than any other of the secondary sort." It is liturgy, "this constantly modulating, self-critical, and reflective adjustment to God-wrought change in the assembly's life of faith," which is the foundation for doing theology and interpreting Scripture.[48]

Kavanagh recognizes, along with Forde, that primary discourse gives rise to and enables secondary discourse and though the two should be distinguished, they are also necessarily correlated: one is impossible without the other. Without secondary discourse there will be no conscious

---

44. Okamoto, "Theology And The Life of the Church," 1.
45. Forde, *Theology Is For Proclamation*, 5–6.
46. Okamoto, "Theology And The Life of The Church," 1.
47. Kavanagh, *On Liturgical Theology*, 96 (emphasis in original).
48. Ibid., 89.

proclamation on the part of the Church. "Proclamation may perhaps happen instinctively. But this is more accidental than purposed. Systematic reflection is necessary to make the move to proclamation conscious and explicit. This is entailed in the contention that systematic theology is for proclamation. It ought to be the kind of reflection that fosters and drives back to the proclamation."[49] Secondary discourse serves the purpose of engaging with and helping to foster, primary discourse, in particular with the preaching of the gospel.

I highlight the distinction between primary and secondary discourse because it is similar for the distinction between first and second order uses of doctrine. In its first order use, doctrine functions to articulate the on-going redemptive narrative of Jesus. In this use, doctrine makes truth claims about the world as it regards the Triune God and his on going story of redemption through his Son Jesus in the power of the Holy Spirit. First order doctrines function along similar lines as primary discourse by saying directly what the story is, i.e., "we believe to be true, that there is one God, the Father Almighty, maker of heaven and earth, of all things, seen and unseen. And in one Lord, Jesus Christ the only Son of God, begotten from the Father before all ages, God from God, Light from Light, true God from true God, begotten, not made, of one Being with the Father, through whom all things were made." First order doctrines assume that the Triune God has spoken (and continues to speak) and that his on-going story of redemption is true and therein, it attempts to articulate, in a derivative fashion, the same redemptive narrative. This is perhaps best exemplified in creeds and confessions, as they are direct statements of the Church about what she confesses to be true. They are primary statements, direct discourse, on the part of the Church to the Triune God, to fellow members of the Church, and to the world.

But not all doctrines have a first order use because not all doctrines are trying to articulate what the Church believes in direct statements. Some doctrines function exclusively as second order doctrines, as the grammar or rules that regulate how the Church goes about reflecting on primary discourse and therein all of life. For example, the doctrine of Scripture is the *governing doctrine* that states what the source and standard by which the formation and development of doctrine (among other things) must be measured. Similarly, other doctrines will function with this second order use by setting the boundaries and parameters for how the Church must go

---

49. Forde, *Theology Is For Proclamation*, 4.

about expressing the story, e.g., Jesus is *homoousious* with the Father and when we speak about Jesus' divinity we must have this in mind. The second order use of doctrine is necessary for the Church's life because it provides the boundaries and rules for how the Church goes about reflecting upon and articulating the narrative of Jesus. This is precisely the point where Lindbeck misunderstood the grammatical function of doctrine.

For Lindbeck the *only* function doctrine has is the second order use. As I mentioned in chapter 2, Lindbeck is trying to explain the results of ecumenical dialogue and in turn offer a method for doctrinal reconciliation without capitulation. He bases his method on a historical claim—doctrine has only ever had a regulative function—which obviously cannot be sustained. Of course, doctrine has always had a regulative use, but historically the Church has made significant use of the first order function of doctrine too. By rejecting the first order use of doctrine, Lindbeck by implication rejects the notion that the Church has a true depiction of the world, which means that the redemptive narrative about Jesus cannot be considered anything other than "just" a story that the Church tells itself. At the very least, it certainly isn't the "true" story of the Triune God's redemption of the world. If my distinction holds between first and second order functions of doctrine (and I think it does), to talk about a second order use while denying a first order use is simply confused. The second order use of doctrine functions in light of the first order use, otherwise what is it providing a grammar for?

Because of Lindbeck's insistence on a regulative-only view of doctrine, he misses why the second order use is actually *beneficial* for the Church. Understanding doctrine according to its second order use is beneficial for training the Church in the various ways that its language and doctrine is used in the service of proclamation and witness.[50] As Okamoto argues, "theological reflection serves the primary discourse of the church when such reflection is understood as operating "grammatically," that is, as help and guidance for using language and leading lives in a faithful Christian manner."[51] As Wood explains, "Being helped in a language is something different from being offered a translation. A grammar is not a translation. . . . It is not a second language, superceding the primary idiom, but simply, a guide to the use of that primary idiom."[52] In other words, the purpose of

---

50. Ibid.
51. Ibid.
52. Wood, "Aim of Christian Theology," 27.

the regulative function of doctrine is to enable the Church to be more faithful to her Lord and to help her in proclaiming his story to the world (first order). It is not merely to be introspective, but to be introspective with the purpose of articulating and proclaiming the redemptive narrative of Jesus.

Holmer, in his discussion of the relationship of theology to the Christian life, articulates what I think is essentially the same relationship between doctrine and the Christian life: "If theology is like a grammar, and certainly it is, then it follows that learning theology is not an end to itself. I am not denying here that theology can be learned just as grammar and logic can; most particularly, it is perfectly proper to do so. But there is an additional difference about theology that, though it is like grammar in some respects, namely, in not being the aim and intent of belief and the substance in and of itself (i.e., in not being the end but the means), still it is the declaration of the essence of Christianity." The purpose of learning theology is not for the sake of merely learning to be theological; *the purpose is to become godly*.[53]

The point of doctrine, with its first and second order uses, is to both enable the Church to confess and proclaim her Lord in direct speech (first-order) and to enable the Church to be more *faithful* to her Lord in her speech and action (second-order). We don't learn doctrine for the sake of learning doctrine; we learn doctrine in order to be *godly*. Holmer again: "it is of little use to be logical about logic when the point is that we are supposed to have learned to become logical about whatever we think. This is how it is, then, with theology—namely, that we are to become Godly in all things, referring everything, our woes and weal, fears and joys, past and future, completely to God's love and care."[54]

When put into these terms we can see not only how pastoral and edifying doctrine should be, but also how misguided the cognitive-propositionalist and experiential-expressivist theories of doctrine are. Doctrine makes truth claims, but it is more than just a system of truth claims. Doctrine likewise expresses the deep emotion and commitment of our hearts, but again it is more than the expression of our emotions and dispositions. Doctrine is the Church's articulation of her belief and commitment to the Triune God and his on-going redemptive story as manifested in his Son Jesus in the power of the Holy Spirit (first order). But doctrine is also the Church's teaching, the handing down of this same story for the purpose of bringing people to faith in this God and in turn, *shaping* them to his story

53. Holmer, *Grammar of Faith*, 19.
54. Ibid.

(second order). When doctrine becomes merely about propositions, emotive expressions or regulating the Church's talk about God, when it ceases to articulate and foster commitment to Jesus, then it ceases to be Christian doctrine and becomes something else altogether.

All this is good as far as it goes, but what does it look like with actual doctrines? The remaining section of this chapter is an attempt to show how this view of doctrine works with a well-known and universally held creed in the Church, the Nicene Creed.

THE NICENE CREED AS AN EXAMPLE OF THE TWO FUNCTIONS OF DOCTRINE

The Niceno-Constantinopolitan Creed of 381 (or simply the Nicene Creed) provides an example of how both functions of doctrine work. Generally speaking, the Nicene Creed is an articulation of whom and what the Church believes the true God is: the Triune God of Father, Son, and Spirit. But in particular, the Nicene Creed is concerned with expressing what the Church believes about Jesus as both a divine and human being: he is of the same essence or reality with the Father (*homoousion to patri*), begotten not created (*poiethenta*), God from God, Light from Light, true God from God, yet incarnate and human (*enanthropesanta*). This creed has functioned for millennia as one of the definitive articulations of what the Church publically claims when she says Jesus is the Son of God, Messiah. The Church claims that this Jesus, the God-man, the Son of God, who was crucified and resurrected, who was preached by the apostles and is attested to in Scripture, is Lord.

This creed then works on a number of different levels. First, it works as primary discourse in that it is a statement of confession to God by the Church ("we confess that you, O Lord, are God"), but it also can be seen as a first order truth claim and therein as a political statement to the watching world: Jesus is the true Lord over all there is and by implication your god and perhaps your Caesar is not. Second, the creed functions as grammar for what the Church means when she says "Jesus." Jesus is the Son of the Father who shares equally in his divinity, who for us and our salvation, was crucified, etc. When the Church speaks of Jesus, she means *this* Jesus in just these terms and everyone who wants to be considered part of the Church must speak in just these ways.

So important is this creed that it is viewed as one of the key identity statements for Christians (we belong to *this* God) and therein, by the fourth century, it had taken on legal-status as the touchstone of orthodoxy. If then someone (think Arius) were to reject the creed it would be because that person's belief about the Triune God, in particular with Jesus, is different than what the Church claims to be true about Jesus and his redemptive story. The Nicene Creed and the person rejecting it would be talking about two different gods though they may be using all the same words; words like Jesus, salvation, and only begotten. The difference between assenting and dissenting to the Nicene Creed is not merely a difference between Church membership and excommunication, as the Church understands it, it is the difference between life and death because it is indicative of a serious commitment to the one true Lord.

The Nicene Creed then has a first order function of making explicit—by articulating what was held to be *already* part of the Church's worship and practice—an implicit belief about Jesus and his identity and ontology. It makes a *truth claim* not only about Jesus, but also by implication, about the world, i.e., this Jesus and his story is the defining story of the world. This claim is a publically contestable claim (it may debated, rejected, or accepted by those outside the Church) and entails both political (Jesus is the true Lord of all creation) and ontological claims (Jesus is God). The Creed also has a second order function of providing the rules, boundaries, and the grammar for how the Church thinks and speaks about her Lord, herself, and everything else. When we speak about Jesus we must speak about him in the terms set forth by the Creed: Jesus is of the same essence or reality with the Father (*homoousion to patri*), begotten not created (*poiethenta*), God from God, Light from Light, true God from God, yet incarnate and human (*enanthropesanta*).

We can further see these two functions with the role the Nicene Creed plays in the formation of the Definition of Chalcedon that came into existence over one hundred years after the original ecumenical council at Nicaea and some eighty years after the final version of the Nicene Creed that was approved by the Council of Constantinople in 381. The Definition of Chalcedon is concerned with articulating what the Church means when she says Jesus is both human and divine. It is clear from not only the history of the debate,[55] but from the Definition itself that certain theological positions— i.e., Eutychianism, Apollinarianism, and Nestorianism—were excluded as outside the bounds of what the Church means when it says Jesus is truly God and truly man. The Definition, like the Nicene Creed, reiterates what the Church believes about Jesus and his on-going story (first

---

55. Kelly, *Early Christian Creeds*.

The Church and Her Doctrine

order). But if you claim Jesus is Lord, then you must claim that he is fully God and fully man in just the way the Definition says he is (second order). The Definition then regulates how the Church thinks and talks about Jesus and there is no room for Eutychian, Apollinarian, or Nestorian articulations or categories in the Church's talk about the Triune God.

The Definition however, does not stand alone on its own authority. It too is subject to the same rules that it puts to other doctrinal statements that follow in its path. In the first part of the Definition, nothing essentially new is claimed and the language articulated by the Nicene Creed is largely copied verbatim. This is intentional and the second part shows why. The second part of the Definition, after defining how Jesus is both fully God and fully man (something the Nicene Creed does not do), makes an appeal to be within the parameters of what was handed down by Jesus, the prophets, and the symbol of the Fathers, i.e., the Nicene Creed. The council of Chalcedon recognized the authority of Jesus, the prophets, and the Nicene Creed and intentionally stayed within the parameters articulated by Nicaea and claimed to be teaching nothing that wasn't already taught by those authorities.

In due time, the Definition, alongside the Nicene Creed, came to be the legal measuring stick for judging whether a person or a tradition's Christology was considered orthodox, not just for the fifth century and the centuries that immediately followed it, but also up to the present time. For example, the Lutheran Formula of Concord (Ep VIII) rehashes much of the language of the Definition, some 1100 years after Chalcedon during the Reformation and it does so in order to show that Lutherans were well within the bounds of orthodox Christianity—as laid out by Scripture and the Fathers— and weren't saying anything that the Definition itself didn't say. In turn, both the Formula of Concord and the Definition are claimed by present-day Lutherans as orthodox summary statements of the faith that derive their meaning from Scripture, the Fathers, and the Reformers and they do so with the exact same purpose in mind: to show that what they believe is orthodox and well within what the Church believes about the Triune God.

Looking at the development of doctrine is helpful for demonstrating doctrine's first and second order functions. The Nicene Creed, the Definition, and the Formula of Concord all claim that that they are making explicit truth claims about Jesus and are doing so according to the grammar set forth by the creeds, within the Church's context as measured and ruled by Scripture. Obviously, when we look at doctrines like the Definition we can see how it added to the Church's public claims about Jesus—after all, where in the apostolic preaching can you find an explanation of how Christ is both human and divine?—but it added to it according to Scripture and within the grammar already set forth by the Nicene Creed. The Definition then, like the Nicene Creed and the Formula of Concord, can say with a straight face that it didn't actually add anything new to the tradition that wasn't already handed down from Jesus, Scripture and the Fathers; it merely articulated, within the grammar of orthodoxy, what was already implicitly believed from the beginning.

To what end? The purpose of doctrine, the reason for its existence is not merely to make truth claims or to regulate the Church's language, the purpose is akin to what Holmer says about theology: "The better and the clearer the theology, then, the more quickly the human heart will sing unbidden. For theology tells us what faith is; and the faith, when articulated with appropriateness and precision, is exceedingly good news."[56] Doctrine is intended to push us towards primary discourse, to liturgical acts of proclamation, praise, and confession. It is intended to shape the Church's speech and action to the Word of God for purpose that we might become *godly*.

The Nicene Creed is one such instance (albeit an important instance) of a doctrine intended to aid the Church in confessing her commitment and belief in Jesus, the Son of God who is both human and divine. But it also provides the grammar for the way the Church goes about thinking and talking about what this means. When we say Jesus is Lord, we are not talking about the Jesus of the gnostics or the Mormons; we are referring to the Jesus of Scripture, as preached by the apostles and handed down by the Fathers who is fully God and fully man. When we engage in evangelism, like Paul at the Areopagus, we preach this Jesus, the crucified and resurrected one. When we engage in apologetics, we do not appeal to some notion of truth that is neutral and beyond our context, we appeal to Jesus, the author and perfecter of our faith (Hebrews 12:2) as found in Scripture and confessed in Nicaea.

Doctrines however, do not in themselves bring forth godliness or faithful living. The Triune God alone does this. God alone makes faithful hearers and doers of his Word. As Okamoto argues, "The conviction that God's activity precedes, establishes, and shapes faithful theological reflection is embodied in the maxim *legem credendi lex statuat supplicandi*,

---

56. Holmer, *Grammar of Faith*, 19.

which might be rendered: "The law of worship *constitutes* or *founds* the law of belief.""[57] Kavanagh is helpful at this point:

> The law of belief does *not* constitute the law of worship. Thus the creeds and the reasoning which produced them are not the forces which produced baptism. Baptism gave rise to the trinitarian creeds. So too the eucharist produced, but was not produced by, a scriptural text, the eucharistic prayer, or all the various scholarly theories concerning the eucharistic real presence. Influenced by, yes. Constituted or produced by, no. Creeds, theories, texts, and prayers all emerged from that dialectical process and adjustment to change triggered by the assembly's regular baptismal and eucharistic encounters with the living God in its own faithful life, a life embracing saints and sinners alike.[58]

Doctrine does not bring people to faithfulness or godliness, doctrine is a tool in the hands of God for bringing people unto himself and shaping them as he sees fit.

SUMMARY

This chapter is admittedly ambitious in its scope and because of this, much has gone unsaid. My purpose has been to account for the Church and her doctrine apart from foundationalist assumptions. To that end, I began this chapter by presenting an antifoundationalist disposition towards questions of truth, fact, and interpretation. I did this in order to help explain in more detail how we can begin to think about things like Scripture, the Church, and her doctrine in terms other than foundationalist ones. If we take antifoundationalism seriously, then we must confess that the only foundation for Scripture, the Church, and her doctrine is Jesus, the Son of God Messiah.

As I argued in chapter 3 and again in this chapter, it is because of Jesus' authority that Scripture has it authority and role within the economy of salvation and the same must be said of the Church as well: she also finds her existence, identity and role within the economy of salvation. Neither Scripture nor the Church stand in isolation as independent authorities, both are derivative and dependent upon Jesus. The Church then is the divine-human institution, the rightful articulator and formulator of doctrine and she does

---

57. Okamoto, "Theology And The Life Of The Church," 3.
58. Kavanagh, *On Liturgical Theology*, 92–93.

so within the context given to her by her Lord, the on-going redemptive narrative of Jesus, as ruled and normed by Scripture. In this light of this, I argued that doctrine has at least two functions, a first order function of articulating the redemptive narrative of Jesus and a second order function of providing the grammar or rules for the Church's articulation of doctrine and her speech about God (among other things). Both functions go together and both are necessary for the Church's life. Ultimately however, doctrine's purpose is not simply to express truth claims or regulate the Church's talk about God, it is to aid the Church in her proclamation of the Gospel and in turn, to make her godly.

This chapter raises a number of questions for foundationalists, not least would be the question of conflicting Christian Scriptural interpretations and doctrines. Directly related to this question is the question of relativism, which is the fear that often accompanies foundationalist readings of accounts like mine. In the final chapter, I will take on these two objections and offer my arguments via a well-known conflict of interpretation: the debate between Lutherans and the Reformed over the Lord's Supper.

5

The Problem of Relativism and Other Lingering Questions

My account of doctrine is not novel in the sense of offering a new way of conceiving of doctrine or finding some unknown use of it. All I am advocating is making Jesus, the crucified and resurrected Son of God, the foundation for all Christian doctrine and theology. What is novel (at least in the modern discussion about doctrine) is my attempt to move the discussion past the categories provided by foundationalism. Even then, what I am advocating is old hat. All you need do is look at the publication dates of many of the authors who lend credence to my arguments and you will see that many of their works were published twenty to thirty years ago. Recently I explained my project to an old friend newly returned from studies in the United Kingdom and he merely shrugged and said, "So? What's new about what you're saying?" He's of course right. Most of my arguments would have been innovative twenty to thirty years ago, but by now many scholars have accepted an antifoundationalist disposition as the way things are.

Well, yes and no. As I demonstrated in chapter 2, many scholars want to embrace our situated, contextualized nature, but they can't really let go of foundationalism. Lindbeck, Vanhoozer, and Thiselton serve as examples of this in the debate over doctrine, but there are plenty of examples in all facets of theology, in particular among American theologians. Entrenched ways of thinking are hard to overcome and intellectual idols that appeal to our unconscious Western disposition towards questions of truth, fact, and interpretation are exceptionally difficult to move past. Hauerwas and Fish both serve as examples—the former with theology, the latter with literary criticism and legal interpretation—of just how hard it is to move readers past foundationalism and have spent significant amounts of time speaking against it with varying degrees of success. Nevertheless, I offer my account, not as a replacement method for doing theology—theology must always be bound to Jesus—but as a way of dissolving foundationalist categories in order for the Church to return to her proper Christological foundation for doctrine. By saying my account then is Christological, I simply mean that it claims no other foundation than Jesus, the Son of the Living God, the Messiah.

My account does, however, raise a number of questions for foundationalists that have yet to be answered. One such question is how to account for disagreement. If we reject the notion of some universal standard by which all claims must be judged or the similar notions of "determinate textual meaning" or "transcontextual reasonableness," how can we adjudicate between conflicting positions? Chapters 3 and 4 might have given the impression that Scriptural interpretation or doctrinal formation becomes clear and easy once we have the right rule for reading in place. Far from it. Recognizing both the authority of Scripture for all of the Church's doctrine as well as the proper Christological assumption for reading Scripture does not resolve the problem of interpretation, though it does provide the proper framework for debates to occur.

A second and related problem for foundationalists is the problem of relativism. For most foundationalists, my account reads virtually like Lindbeck's account in terms of matters of truth. That is, since I reject the notion of transcontextual reasonableness et al, by definition I have rejected the notion of truth and advocate relativism. Again, far from it. By rejecting the foundationalist account of truth and knowledge, I have not embraced relativism. Rather, I have simply been persuaded by a different account that thinks our knowledge of and claims about the world are enabled by constraints that are local and particular, not general and neutral. My account of doctrine simply argues that the lone foundation for Christian doctrine must be with Jesus alone, not some other foundation that is "out there." This is hardly relativism.

While there are many questions that can be raised about my account, these two questions—the questions of interpretive disagreement and relativism—are the most interesting to me and perhaps to my readers too. I will begin by accounting for why the One, Holy, Catholic, and Apostolic Church has such a hard time agreeing on the interpretation of Scripture

The Problem of Relativism and Other Lingering Questions

and doctrine. I will then move on to a specific example with the debate over the Lord's Supper between Lutherans and the Reformed and will provide an answer (not a solution) for why this debate occurs. In the final section, I will take up the problem of relativism.

ACCOUNTING FOR DISAGREEMENT

One of the questions I put to Vanhoozer in chapter 2 goes something like this: how is it possible for two people—who are both filled with the same Holy Spirit, who are both consciously trying to be in submission to Scripture, reading it faithfully while looking for the so-called "determinate textual meaning" of the text—to radically disagree over the meaning of the same passage of Scripture? Shouldn't Christians, even in different traditions, come to the same reading of the text if the meaning is "in" the text and if they both have the Holy Spirit? By making this statement I am assuming that the two readers are actually both part of the same Church, the *One, Holy, Catholic and Apostolic body of Christ*. But can I really make this assumption?

The Church, as I described her in chapter 4, has a number of marks that are shared across a wide array of Church bodies: the canon of Scripture as contained in the Old and New Testaments as the authoritative Word of God; the sacraments (at the very least baptism and the Lord's Supper); the ordaining of clergy; the preaching of the gospel; the exercising of discipline; the creeds (at least the Nicene Creed). These Church bodies also share in common the same structure of assumptions that Christianity is about the redemptive story of Jesus and the Church therein enjoys his continued presence.[1] Church unity is not manifested in interpretive agreement, but rather with the tacit agreement among her various members on the framework for discussing and debating the meaning of such things as Scripture, Jesus, the sacraments, redemption and so on.

This however, does not get us very far in explaining disagreement. Take for example, a well-known Christian phrase: "This is my body" (cf., Matt 26:26; Mark 14:22: Luke 22:19; 1 Cor 11:24). If we take Vanhoozer and other foundationalists seriously, these four short words ought to be easy to read and interpret for all Christians—after all, the sacrament of the Lord's Supper is universally recognized across the Christian spectrum as a practice handed down by Jesus—and yet, as anyone who is familiar with the

---

1. Frei, *Types of Christian Theology*, 8.

debate over the Lord's Supper knows, these four simple and unassuming words have occasioned severe and deep disagreement over their meaning. Why?

A first and obvious answer is sin. There is no aspect of our lives that sin has not touched in profound ways, including our interpretive abilities. Vanhoozer's view of this is worth reading again: "It may be that interpretive disagreement arises not because of some defect in the text, but rather because of a defect in us—all of us. What else is the doctrine of original sin but a statement of the universality of cognitive malfunction, a confession that our design plan has been flawed through illicit tampering? Not only do our cognitive functions not always function as they ought, but we interpret in an environment strewn with cognitive and moral pollution. Cognitive malfunction can be corporate as well as individual."[2] Vanhoozer is right. I find no defect in the Biblical text so much as I do in me (and the rest of humanity). To be a Christian is to confess the utter depravity of humanity, which of course touches not only our minds and bodies, but also everything around us, including the institution of the Church. Sin is so deep and debilitating that without the Holy Spirit, the Triune God remains veiled to those who read the Biblical text (cf., 2 Cor 4:3-4). This is not to say that someone without the Spirit cannot discern the story or understand something about God, but he will not be reading Scripture as it was intended to be read and therefore will not understand it correctly. This means that being a believer, i.e., someone who has received the Holy Spirit, is a *prerequisite* for reading the Bible as it was intended. The Holy Spirit is a necessary "component" for enabling the right reading of Scripture; he gives the right disposition—we become believers—but he does not guarantee right interpretations. Christians are *simul iustus et peccator* and their interpretations are certainly just as capable of being flawed or wrong as they are of being correct. Sin is a critical part of explaining why Christians sometimes fail to agree on the meaning of the text, but pointing to sin alone doesn't fully account for the divergence of interpretations. For that, we need to return to the notion of context.

Previously, I defined context as a structure of assumptions that have a hold on people and allow them to make an interpretation of the world. Instead of understanding "context" as something *in* the world, I understand it as an interpretation *of* the world. Those who hold the same structure of assumptions (the context) not only make sense of the world in the same

---

2. Vanhoozer, *Is There A Meaning in This Text?* 299.

The Problem of Relativism and Other Lingering Questions

way, holding to the same context allows for a *framework for discussion and debate to occur among those in the context as to the relevant features of the context*. This means that people don't hold to a structure of assumptions in isolation, they hold to it in community. This is what Fish intended by his term "interpretive community." But as I argued in the previous chapter, this term can be dangerous because it tempts us to see the Church herself as a structure of assumptions, as an interpretive community, but that's not right. The Church is an *institution* that fosters and generates a structure of assumptions, but she herself cannot be reduced to merely a structure of assumptions. The Church, as the divine-human institution founded by Jesus, has a particular context, a structure of assumptions that is no more and no less than *the on-going redemptive story of Jesus the Son of God*. It is this context, this on-going redemptive narrative that gives not only the right interpretive strategy for reading Scripture, but also the right framework for discussion and debate over its interpretation.

The reader may have mistakenly assumed with my initial description of the Church and her context that belonging to this context is a neat and tidy thing and Christians see the world clearly according to its assumptions. In the eschaton this will be true, but for now it is false. All people, including Christians, belong to many different contexts, some of which overlap and some of which vie for prominence over the other. Take for example, a few of the various contexts to which I belong: I am an American citizen, a southerner living in the Midwest, a musician, a Presbyterian pastor in a conservative evangelical denomination, a father, a husband, and a son (just to name a few). In each of these roles, I assume a structure of assumptions that allows me to make sense of my role and what is expected of me in it. Of course some of these roles overlap and inform one another: being a Christian has influenced how I understand my role as a father, but they need not do this. In fact, some contexts may even be in conflict, if not incommensurable, with one another. The Church's context *ought* to be the dominant context for Christians, so that in everything Jesus might be preeminent (Col 1:18), but this doesn't always happen. In fact, holding to the Church's context does not guarantee that some other context might not try to influence or shape it, if not outright dominate it. Yoder gives a good example of just how this works with the problem of Constantinianism.

"Constantinianism" is a problem symbolized by Constantine in the fourth century with his embracement of Christianity (*in hoc signo vinces*) that over the following generations would turn Christianity from a minority religion to not only the default religious position in the West (everyone is born a Christian whether they like it or not), but make it the stabilizing and unifying force for the Roman Empire. In Yoder's view, the shift that occurs with Constantine is an epochal change that does not end with the decline of the Roman Empire, but continues through the entirety of Western history all the way to our present-day modern American Democratic context. The problem, however, goes much deeper than society identifying itself as Christian. The real problem is that by aligning the church with the state—or more accurately, by confusing the two—the Church has misunderstood the fundamental eschatology of the New Testament and the identity and mission of her Lord. By the term "eschatology" is meant, "a hope that, defying present frustration, defines a present position in terms of the yet unseen goal that gives it meaning."[3] Biblical eschatology then is not merely an end-time apocalyptic (though it certainly includes this), it is a hope that the unseen future, in particular the full expression of the Kingdom of God, is so certain that it forces us to live our present everyday lives according to a particular ethic, as prescribed and lived out by Jesus. We can live this way now, because the Kingdom of God, though it will be fully realized in the future apocalypse, is already in existence and has been since Jesus inaugurated it in the first century. Constantinianism denies all this by advocating that the Church live as if the life, death, and resurrection of the Messiah had never occurred.[4] The denial is evidenced by the Church's replacement of Jesus and his on-going story of redemption as her *primary narrative* with the narrative of the State and its on-going project.[5] The practical implications being her refusal to engage in discipleship in the ways Jesus prescribed.

It is not difficult to find Christians (of various Church traditions) that hold deeply to an American mythology and in turn believe that this American narrative is the defining narrative of their lives. This American narrative, in turn, defines and shapes their Christian context, eclipsing Jesus and his narrative. These Christians do not see themselves as part of the on-going redemptive story of Jesus; they see themselves as part of the on-going drama of the State to which Jesus (and his Church) serves as chaplains.[6] It is easily seen with the expectations, hopes, and dissatisfaction that Christians

---

3. Yoder, *Royal Priesthood*, 145.

4. Carter, *The Politics of the Cross*, 156.

5. Cavanaugh even goes so far to say that Christianity in America has often blended, if not replaced, her Christian narrative, symbols, and rituals for those offered by the modern democratic state. See his *Migrations of the Holy*.

6. Clapp, *Peculiar People*, 18–32.

The Problem of Relativism and Other Lingering Questions

of both liberal and conservative leanings have when it comes to the election of public officials. It shows up when Christians assume that America is God's "special" country (a notion perpetuated by the Church in America for *hundreds* of years) or when they think public institutions need to be endorsed by Christianity by posting the Decalogue in local courthouses or demanding public prayer before "the big game."[7]

Constantinianism is just one instance of a particular context vying for dominance over the Church's context, even going so far as redefining the Church's context and putting her in the service of the State. The problem of Constantinianism is enabled by sin, in particular with the sin of unbelief, because the State's claims seem more relevant and abiding to the Church and her mission. The disagreement should be understood as conflict between rival narratives vying for interpretive primacy. Christians in American often fail to read Scripture correctly because they hold more tightly to some other context than the one generated by the Church, Constantinianism being just one example among many. But this doesn't account for all disagreement. Sometimes, the conflict is between rival narratives about Jesus. In this case the disagreement is over just what the context is. When this occurs, the conflict is about the context itself, i.e., it is a conflict over what counts as Jesus and his on-going redemptive story.

An easy example of this is the conflict between Christianity and Mormonism over the identity of Jesus as the Son of God. The Mormons, or as they officially call themselves, The Church of Jesus Christ of Latter-Day Saints, claim to be rightly Christian and to be the true Church. They use much of the same terminology as Protestants and Catholics and seem to employ it in the same manner, that is, until we consider their stated doctrine of Jesus and his divinity:

> Our first and foremost article of faith in The Church of Jesus Christ of Latter-day Saints is "We believe in God, the Eternal Father, and in His Son, Jesus Christ, and in the Holy Ghost." We believe these three divine persons constituting a single Godhead are united in purpose, in manner, in testimony, in mission. We believe Them to be filled with the same godly sense of mercy and love, justice and grace, patience, forgiveness, and redemption. I think it is accurate to say we believe They are one in every significant and eternal

---

7. For example, Roy Moore, the former Chief Justice of the Alabama Supreme Court, famously fought to put up the Decalogue in his courthouse and now runs The Foundation For Moral Law; an organization dedicated to undergirding American government and law with Christianity.

aspect imaginable *except* believing Them to be three persons combined in one substance, a Trinitarian notion never set forth in the scriptures because it is not true. Indeed no less a source than the stalwart *Harper's Bible Dictionary* records that "the formal doctrine of the Trinity as it was defined by the great church councils of the fourth and fifth centuries is *not* to be found in the [New Testament]." So any criticism that The Church of Jesus Christ of Latter-day Saints does not hold the contemporary Christian view of God, Jesus, and the Holy Ghost is *not* a comment about our commitment to Christ but rather a recognition (accurate, I might add) that our view of the Godhead breaks with post–New Testament Christian history and returns to the doctrine taught by Jesus Himself.[8]

This statement claims to worship the same god as was taught by the apostles, appeals to the authority of Scripture, and claims to be reading Scripture in a clear and literal fashion. The problem comes when Mormons claim that the post-New Testament Church broke with Jesus and struck out in new ways that Jesus did not teach, as is evidenced (so they claim) in the New Testament itself, i.e., claiming Jesus is equal in divinity, power, and glory with the Father. The Mormons, by articulating this view of Jesus, that he was divine but not equal or of the same *ousia* with the Father (cf., the Nicene Creed), recognize that they are perceived as outside the bounds of the Church and even go so far as to say, "But if one says we are not Christians because we do not hold a fourth or fifth-century view of the Godhead, then what of those first Christian Saints, many of whom were eyewitnesses of the living Christ, who did not hold such a view either?"[9]

As we saw in chapter 4, the Fathers at Nicaea and Chalcedon claimed to have taught nothing that Jesus, the prophets, and Scripture itself didn't teach, so the burden of the argument lies on the Mormons to show otherwise. In fact, they must show how their doctrine of Jesus is the one actually taught by Jesus and is the right redemptive narrative about him. Universally in the Church, Mormonism is excluded as a faithful expression of Jesus on just these grounds: they preach another gospel, another Jesus other than the Jesus as preached by the apostles and attested to in Scripture. But how can we determine this?

The conflict is not primarily about exegesis or the authority of Scripture (though these are both important topics for the conflict). Both Mormons

---

8. Holland, "Only True God and Jesus Christ Whom He Sent."
9. Ibid.

The Problem of Relativism and Other Lingering Questions

and the Church hold to the authority of Scripture and want to faithfully interpret it. In fact, the Mormons go so far as to argue, not unlike Arius and later with Athanasius' opponents in the fourth century, that their interpretation is the clear and literal one and if taken in foundationalist terms, *they may be right*: no where in the New Testament will we find an explicit explanation of Trinitarian doctrine as articulated by Nicaea and Chalcedon. To adequately account for the conflict we can't limit our explanation to exegesis or determinate textual meaning; we have to look at the interpretive assumptions of both parties. In other words, the conflict between Mormons and the Church is not primarily a conflict of exegesis because exegesis is always a product of interpretive assumptions. The conflict is between two different and rival *redemptive narratives*.

While my point is not to give an in-depth analysis of Mormon thought or their narrative, a small section from one of their modern authorities will be adequate to show what I mean:

> Jesus Christ possessed merits that no other child of Heavenly Father could possibly have. He was a God, Jehovah, before His birth in Bethlehem. His Father not only gave Him His spirit body, but Jesus was His Only Begotten Son in the flesh. Our Master lived a perfect, sinless life and therefore was free from the demands of justice. He was and is perfect in every attribute, including love, compassion, patience, obedience, forgiveness, and humility. His mercy pays our debt to justice when we repent and obey Him. Even with our best efforts to obey His teachings we will still fall short, yet because of His grace we will be saved "after all we can do."
>
> Although our memory of it is withheld, before we came to this earth we lived in the presence of God, our Eternal Father, and His Son, Jesus Christ. We shouted for joy when given the privilege of coming to this earth to receive a body and to move forward in God's plan for our happiness. We knew that we would be tested here. Our determination was to live obediently to be able to return to be with our Father forever. Part of that testing here is to have so many seemingly interesting things to do that we can forget the main purposes for being here. Satan works very hard so that the essential things won't happen.[10]

In these two paragraphs, we are able to see not only that Mormons hold to a very different narrative concerning the Godhead—Jesus is *both* the Yahweh

---

10. Scott, "Jesus Christ, Our Redeemer," 53–54.

of the Old Testament and the Son in the New Testament—we hear a very different story concerning humanity too. We don't have to dig very deep into the Mormon narrative to see that their context for reading the Bible is very different than the Church's, even though they are reading the same text and claiming similar sounding things, i.e., redemption comes through Jesus, the Son of God. It is the Mormon narrative about Jesus that is already in place that enables Mormons to read Scripture and articulate doctrine in the way that they do. Their interpretation of Scripture, articulation of doctrine, and therein their truth claims about the world are constrained by their version of the redemptive narrative, a narrative that is at serious odds with the Church's narrative.

It is easy enough to show how competing narratives about Jesus affect interpretation when the Church as a whole considers the Mormonism to be heretical. But what happens when two Christian traditions, both of which are considered part of the Church (i.e., neither are considered heretical), seemingly hold to the same story in largely the same way, and yet have serious disagreement? What then? Admittedly things are more complicated when it comes to internecine debates, in particular when all sides are largely in agreement on the context. The example I have in mind is an old one (that is still unresolved), and is centered on the four little words I mentioned earlier, "This is my body." The Lutheran and Reformed debate over the Lord's Supper provides a good example of how the Church's context fosters a framework for discussion and debate over what counts as the relevant features of that same context.

SERIOUS DOCTRINAL DISAGREEMENT: THE CASE OF THE LUTHERAN AND REFORMED DEBATE ON THE LORD'S SUPPER

During my doctoral studies, I was asked to present the Presbyterian (i.e., Reformed) doctrine on the Lord's Supper before a class of Lutheran divinity students. A few minutes into my presentation a student raised his hand and asked how I interpret the phrase, "this is my body." That is, he wanted to know to what "this" refers. I answered simply with, "the bread," i.e., during the Last Supper, Jesus connects the bread to his own body. The student in turn, asked me what I thought this means. I knew at this moment that we were starting down the path of disagreement, because the conversation was shifting to the meaning of the word "is." Nevertheless, I gave the standard

The Problem of Relativism and Other Lingering Questions

Presbyterian answer that compares Jesus' statement to similar ones of "I am the door" or "I am the vine" (cf. John 10:7–9; 15:5). The phrase, as Presbyterians read it, is metaphorical and Jesus is not saying that the bread in his hand at that moment is literally his body. Having given my answer, the student pounced upon my argument and promptly told me that grammatically, my interpretation could not possibly be correct, as the grammatical function of the phrase was clearly a trope. I answered simply with "OK." It was not a statement of acquiescence, but more so a statement of "And? What's your point?" Knowing the history of the debate and the Lutheran position, I wasn't buying his argument. His reason for mentioning a grammatical feature of the text is that he thought that the existence of a trope (about which I did not doubt its existence, but what the trope counted as evidence for) clearly and obviously supports the Lutheran position on the Lord's Supper and that by citing this bit of evidence, I really didn't have a leg to stand on. The Presbyterian position in his view is clearly wrong; the citing of grammar being the piece of evidence that sealed the deal for him. He's both right and wrong.

The student was right to think that the passage and its grammatical features clearly support the Lutheran view, but this is not because the text—let alone the grammar—is inherently clear, obvious, or *Lutheran*. What makes his interpretation obvious to him (he had the "literal reading") is that he had arrived at a view of Jesus *before* he read the text. He was operating with certain constraints about who and what Jesus is (many of which I agreed with, but not all) and the text—in particular the grammar—confirms his interpretation as the obvious and clear one to him and to other Lutherans. This, as experience and history shows (beginning with the Colloquy of Marburg of 1529 up to the present), will not be the case for those outside of the Lutheran tradition. The reason for this is simple: "Lutheran" is the name of an easily identifiable Christian tradition (with its own institutions) that interprets things like the Bible, Jesus, and the world according to a particular, "Lutheran," structure of assumptions. What constitutes interpretive agreement for Lutherans, is not the text itself (though it is authoritative for them), it is the structure of assumptions particular to being Lutheran that enables them to interpret the text and formulate doctrine.

As the conflict between Lutherans and Presbyterians demonstrates, not everyone belongs to the same tradition and therefore not all Christians read the text in the same way. What makes the conflict interesting (at least as I have personally encountered it) is that both Lutherans and Presbyterians are *agreed* on the authority of Scripture and the Church's context (i.e., Jesus and his on-going story of redemption.) Both traditions are agreed over how to interpret much of Scripture and are agreed on the centrality of Jesus for Christian doctrine and practice, in particular with the doctrine of justification. They are also agreed on the truth of the ecumenical creeds and the rejection of heretical groups like the Mormons. And yet, though the two traditions have so much in common (they even come out of the same century and claim Luther as the rightful father of the Reformation), they cannot come to an agreement over four little words.

So how should we understand the conflict? If both Presbyterians and Lutherans are agreed on the context, what really is at issue in the debate? If you will recall, I argued that holding to the same context allows for a framework for discussion and debate to occur among those in the context as to the relevant features of the context. In the case of Lutherans and Presbyterians, their debate is not over the context as a whole, but over a relevant feature of the context. Unlike with the Mormons, Presbyterians and Lutherans are agreed on the context in broad strokes, but where they disagree is over a feature, a detail of that story. In order to understand this we need to briefly look at representative official doctrinal statements of both traditions that are treated as legally binding statements to infer how both Lutherans and Presbyterians understand the story.

Looking at Luther's Large Catechism[11] provides ample source for inferring the Lutheran version of the story (but see also SD VII; CA VII; Ap XIII). Luther writes, "Here, too, we do not want to quarrel and dispute with those who despise and desecrate this sacrament. Instead, as in the case of baptism, we shall first learn what is of greatest importance, namely, that the chief thing is God's Word and ordinance and command." The sacrament of the Lord's Supper was not devised by the Church or any mere human, but rather "was instituted by Christ without anyone's counsel or deliberation." So what then did Jesus actually institute:

> Now, what is the Sacrament of the Altar? Answer: It is the true body and blood of the Lord Christ, in and under the bread wine, which we Christians are commanded by Christ's word to eat and drink. And just as we said of baptism that it is not mere water, so we say here, too, that the sacrament is bread and wine, but not mere bread and wine such as is served at the table. Rather, it is bread and wine set within God's Word and bound to it. It is the

---

11. All quotations that follow are taken from the LC.

The Problem of Relativism and Other Lingering Questions

Word, I say, that makes this a sacrament and distinguishes it from ordinary bread and wine, so that is called and truly is Christ's body and blood. For it is said, *"Accedat verbum ad elementum et fit sacramentum,"* that is, "When the Word is joined to the external element, it becomes a sacrament."

The Large Catechism begins its treatment of the Lord's Supper by locating the sacrament with the authority of Jesus as the Son of God. It is because Jesus is the Son of God, "the divine Majesty," that his Word is authoritative and so when he attaches his Word to this sacrament, it is rightly considered the Word of God too: "Now, this is not the word and ordinance of a prince or emperor, but of the divine Majesty at whose feet all creatures should kneel and confess that it is as he says, and they should accept it with all reverence, fear, and humility." The efficacy and existence of the sacrament is dependent upon the Son of God's Word and should not be separated from it:

> With this Word you can strengthen your conscience and declare: "Let a hundred thousand devils, with all the fanatics, come forward and say, 'How can bread and wine be Christ's body and blood?' etc. Still I know that all the spirits and scholars put together have less wisdom than the divine Majesty has in his littlest finger. Here is Christ's word: 'Take, eat, this is my body.' 'Drink of this, all of you, this is the New Testament in my blood,' etc. Here we shall take our stand and see who dares to instruct Christ and alter what he has spoken.
>
> For the Word by which it was constituted a sacrament is not rendered false because of an individual's unworthiness or unbelief. Christ does not say, "If you believe or if you are worthy, you have my body and blood," but rather, "Take, eat and drink, this is my body and blood." Likewise, when he says, "Do this" (namely, what I now do, what I institute, what I give you and bid you take), this is as much as to say, "No matter whether you are worthy or unworthy, you have here his body and blood by the power of these words that are connected to the bread and wine." Mark this and remember it well. For upon these words rest our whole argument, our protection and defense against all errors and deceptions that have ever arisen or may yet arise.

What stands behind Luther's articulation of the Supper is the redemptive narrative of Jesus: he is the Son of God sent by the Father to deal with the sins of his people for which he was rejected and crucified. Jesus was crucified "for us and our salvation," i.e., for the purpose of pouring the forgiveness of sins upon his people. The sacrament finds its purpose within this same redemptive purpose of Jesus:

> Now we come also to its power and benefit, for which purpose the sacrament was really instituted. For it is most necessary that we know what we should seek and obtain there. This is clear and easily understood form the words just quoted: "This is my body and blood, given and poured out for you for the forgiveness of sins." That is to say, in brief, that we go to the sacrament because there we receive a great treasure, through and in which we obtain the forgiveness of sins. Why? Because the words are there, and they impart it to us! For this reason he bids me eat and drink, that it may be mine and do me good as a sure pledge and sign indeed, as the very gift he has provided for me against my sins, death, and all evils.
>
> Here again our clever spirits contort themselves with their great learning and wisdom; they rant and rave, "How can bread and wine forgive sins or strengthen faith?" Yet they have heard and know that we don claim this of bread and wine—for in itself bread is bread—but of that bread and wine that are Christ's body and blood and that are accompanied by the Word. These and no other, we say, are the treasure through which such forgiveness is obtained. This treasure is conveyed and communicated to us in no other way than through the words "given and shed for you." Here you have both—that is Christ's body and blood and that they are yours as a treasure and gift. Christ's body cannot be an unfruitful, useless thing that does nothing and helps no one. Yet, however great the treasure may be in itself, it must be set within the Word and offered to us through the Word, otherwise we could never know of it or seek it.

Lutherans understand the sacrament not simply as a practice instituted by Jesus, but as having a particular role within the economy of salvation. For Lutherans, the Lord's Supper is, by virtue of Christ attaching his Word to it, the Word of God and as such, is a sign and seal of what it signifies: the forgiveness of sins through the death of Jesus on the cross. Forgiveness is given (it is poured out for us) by Jesus through this Word, not because there are any inherent "saving" properties in the bread or wine, but rather because the authoritative Word of the Son of God makes the bread and wine a Word that forgives sins. The Large Catechism brings this point out by placing the sacrament side by side with the proclamation of the Word:

The Problem of Relativism and Other Lingering Questions

> Although the work [of forgiveness] took place on the cross and forgiveness of sins has been acquired, yet it cannot come to us in any other way than through the Word. How should we know that this took place or was given to us if it were not proclaimed by preaching, by the oral Word? From what source do they know of forgiveness, and how can they grasp and appropriate it, except by steadfastly believing the Scriptures and the gospel? Now the whole gospel and the article of the Creed, "I believe in one holy Christian church . . . the forgiveness of sins," are embodied in this sacrament and offered to use through the Word. Why, then, should we allow such a treasure to be torn out of the sacrament?

In short, forgiveness is proclaimed through the preaching of the Word and it is offered to us through the sacramental Word.

With this brief look at the Lutheran doctrine of the Lord's Supper, we can summarize it in the following way:

1. Jesus is the Son of God and because he is the Son of God, his Word is authoritative.

2. Jesus has attached his Word to this sacrament and by implication the sacrament is the Word of God too. It is only a sacrament by virtue of the Word; otherwise it is merely bread and wine.

3. Because this sacrament is the Word of God, when Jesus says, "this is my body and blood broken and poured out for the forgiveness of sins," it means just what it signifies, that through this Word, Jesus forgives the sins of his people.

What enables the Lutheran doctrine on the Lord's Supper is how Lutherans understand the sacrament to fit within the wider redemptive narrative of Jesus. They understand the sacrament in light of Jesus' authority as the Son of God and understand his Word to operate in such a way that the sacrament is rightly understood as a necessary part of how redemption is applied. Without this sacrament, there is no forgiveness of sins, which means a crucial feature of the redemptive story is lost. This however, is not how Presbyterians understand the sacrament.

Presbyterians understand the same sacrament quite differently though they too assume the same redemptive narrative of Jesus. If we look at the Westminster Confession of Faith[12] as representative of the Reformed view,

---

12. All references are to chapter XXIX of the WCF, "Of the Lord's Supper."

we find a conflicting account not only of the sacrament, but its place within the economy of salvation.

> Our Lord Jesus, in the night wherein He was betrayed, instituted the sacrament of His body and blood, called the Lord's Supper, to be observed in His Church, unto the end of the world, for the perpetual remembrance of the sacrifice of Himself in His death; the sealing all benefits thereof unto true believers, their spiritual nourishment and growth in Him, their further engagement in and to all duties which they owe unto Him; and, to be a bond and pledge of their communion with Him, and with each other, as members of His mystical body.
>
> In this sacrament, Christ is not offered up to His Father; nor any real sacrifice made at all, for remission of sins of the quick or the dead; but only a commemoration of that one offering up of Himself, by Himself, upon the cross, once for all: and a spiritual oblation of all possible praise unto God, for the same: so that the popish sacrifice of the mass (as they call it) is most abominably injurious to Christ's one, only sacrifice, the only propitiation for all the sins of His elect.

Presbyterians connect the institution and validity of the sacrament to the authority of Jesus as Lord. It is a practice that he handed down to his disciples and to his Church that is to be continued until he comes again in power. In comparison to Lutherans, not much is directly stated about Jesus' authority (it is assumed from earlier in the confession) and no direct connection is made to his Word, outside of the words of institution. The sacrament gets its content and meaning from Jesus' death on the cross and his words of institution must be proclaimed in order to set the elements apart for a holy use.

For Presbyterians, the sacrament was instituted for a multifold purpose: 1) it is intended to be a continual reminder to the people of God of Christ's work on the cross; 2) to seal the benefits of Christ's death and resurrection to the believer; 3) to give spiritual nourishment and growth in Jesus for the believer in their following of him; 4) to be a bond and pledge for the Church and her communion with Jesus. Nowhere is the forgiveness of sins mentioned in connection with the sacrament and it is not implied by the phrase, "the sealing all benefits thereof unto true believers." What is sealed and signified in the sacrament is what has already been given to the believer, i.e., the forgiveness of sins. To this end, emphasis is placed on the one sacrifice of Jesus for the propitiation of the sins for the people of God,

"His elect" (the Large Catechism argues similarly). The forgiveness of sins is not applied by the sacrament; the forgiveness of sins is applied by grace through faith to the believer before she ever partakes of the sacrament.

This argument is made in contrast to what Presbyterians think is a faulty account of redemption, i.e., the medieval Catholic view that saw the mass as a re-sacrifice of Jesus. In fact, much of the Presbyterian understanding of the sacrament is articulated in contrast to the Catholic view of transubstantiation. All the same, Presbyterians do not understand this sacrament within the economy of salvation as Lutherans do because they do not see the forgiveness of sins as being applied by the sacrament. What then do Presbyterians think they are actually receiving?

> The outward elements in this sacrament, duly set apart to the uses ordained by Christ, have such relation to Him crucified, as that, truly, yet sacramentally only, they are sometimes called by the name of the things they represent, to wit, the body and blood of Christ; albeit, in substance and nature, they still remain truly and only bread and wine, as they were before.

> Worthy receivers, outwardly partaking of the visible elements, in this sacrament, do then also, inwardly by faith, really and indeed, yet not carnally and corporally but spiritually, receive and feed upon, Christ crucified, and all benefits of His death: the body and blood of Christ being then, not corporally or carnally, in, with, or under the bread and wine; yet, as really, but spiritually, present to the faith of believers in that ordinance, as the elements themselves are to their outward senses.

For Presbyterians, Jesus is truly present in the sacrament through his Holy Spirit—believers partake and feed upon the crucified body and blood of Jesus *spiritually*—but he does not, by his authoritative Word as the Son of God, make the elements his body and blood. He sets these elements apart for a "holy use" or for a "sacramental use," but nowhere is it argued that Jesus has bound himself to these elements (by his Word or otherwise) in such a way that he is corporally present by way of them. Jesus is corporally present to the believer through his Spirit. We can characterize the Presbyterian view of the sacrament this way:

1. Jesus is Lord and as Lord he instituted the Lord's Supper as a sacrament.
2. By his institution of the sacrament, Jesus set apart these elements of bread and wine for a holy or sacramental use, even so, they remain

bread and wine are not rightly thought of as the body and blood of Jesus.

3. Jesus uses this sacrament as a perpetual reminder of his propitiation and as spiritual nourishment for his people (those who have been saved by grace through faith). The sacrament serves as a sign and seal, as an affirmation and confirmation of what has already been given once and for all in his work on the cross.

Both Lutherans and Presbyterians are agreed on many of the main features of the Church's context, i.e., the salient plot points of the redemptive narrative in particular with the central place that Jesus' death and resurrection holds for understanding the story correctly. They are agreed on the one-time sacrificial death of Jesus (both would reject the Catholic insistence on the Supper as sacrifice) and are agreed on doctrinal matters like justification by faith. Where they disagree is over where and how redemption, "the forgiveness of sins," is applied. For Lutherans, the Lord's Supper is the crucial place where Jesus applies his forgiveness. This is why Lutherans spend so much time teaching on the sacrament (as is evidenced in the amount of space it occupies in their confessional documents) and why it takes such a prominent place in their liturgy. Not so for Presbyterians, they don't see any connection with the Supper to the actual application of the forgiveness of sins. The sacrament confirms and assures the believer of what has already been given to her by grace through faith: the forgiveness of sins, justification, and adoptions as sons and daughter into the Kingdom of God.[13] This is why when we look at the WCF, the statements on the sacrament are a fraction of what the LC articulates and even then, it is not treated until the twenty-ninth chapter (out of a total thirty-three) of the confession.

The conflict then is over where and how the Lord's Supper features in the over-all redemptive narrative. For Lutherans, it features critically in the story because Jesus attaches it to his Word of forgiveness and therefore without it, there is no forgiveness of sins. For Presbyterians, it is an important feature, but it does not figure as prominently in the story because for them, forgiveness is not applied by the sacrament. The debate over "this is my body," then cannot strictly be said to be a debate over exegesis or doctrinal articulation; these practices (exegesis and doctrinal articulation) are *enabled* by the way the redemptive story is understood by either tradition.

13. WCF, X–XVIII.

The Problem of Relativism and Other Lingering Questions

The debate then is over the story itself. It is not merely an issue of semantics or emphasis; both traditions think the other has gotten the story wrong and by doing so it has serious implications for Christian life and practice. Presbyterians think Lutherans have not been able to free themselves from Catholicism and Lutherans think Presbyterians don't have the Lord's Supper at all.

If we take the notion of context seriously, then we actually have a way of making sense of what's happening with interpretive and doctrinal disagreement. Seeing the debate in contextual terms does not mean, as so many foundationalists assume, that interpretation is according to whatever whim we happen to fancy (relativism). Rather, what it recognizes is that just because Lutherans and Presbyterians (like everybody else) are gripped by their understanding of the redemptive narrative does not mean they can interpret the text, "this is my body," (or any text for that matter) any way they choose. Lutherans are no more choosing to be Lutheran than I am choosing to be Presbyterian. Because Lutherans are constrained by their interpretive assumptions, they cannot help but *assent* to Lutheran doctrine and read Scripture as Lutherans. I would even go so far as to say, Lutherans *cannot* interpret the text in any other way without ceasing to be Lutheran.

This is not to say that one tradition cannot understand and articulate the doctrines of a different tradition, even one that they are in serious conflict with. After all, I have articulated the Lutheran position on the Lord's Supper, hopefully to the satisfaction of my Lutheran brothers and sisters. But the difference is that I don't accept the Lutheran position as true. Further, my Presbyterian tradition, even with my best abilities in play, constrains my interpretation of the Lutheran position. Presbyterians do not look at Lutheran exegesis or their doctrine on the Lord Supper from some detached position, but precisely the opposite: they interpret it *as Presbyterians and according to Presbyterian assumptions*. This isn't being biased or prejudicial in the pejorative sense of the terms: this is just what it is to be Presbyterian.

We are all gripped by multiple contexts and are therefore constrained in the way we interpret texts, objects, and all of reality. For Lutherans, being a Lutheran is just what it is to be Christian and they can't help but understand the redemptive narrative according to Lutheran categories. This explains in part, why Luther refused to call Zwingli a Christian after their debates over the Lord Supper: Luther's understanding of the redemptive narrative led him to think that Zwingli denied a crucial part of that narrative, i.e., the forgiveness of sins. But it is not just Lutherans who do this; *all Christian traditions do this*. Returning to my debate with the divinity student, hopefully by the end of the term he was able to articulate the Presbyterian position on the Lord Supper just as well as a member of the Presbyterian community, but he will not believe it be the true, obvious, and clear interpretation of Jesus' words. If he is truly a Lutheran, he can't help but interpret and reject other positions according to Lutheran categories.[14]

This gives us insight into just how difficult ecumenical discussion and agreement really is. What may be at issue in doctrinal debates between traditions is not merely an emphasis of some aspect of the story or an exegetical detail (though it may be), but a debate over the redemptive story itself. When this is the case, the conflict cannot merely be said to be a debate over how the story is signified (a la Lindbeck) or be glossed over with the acceptance that both parties have doctrines that seek to be faithful Christian utterances (relativism). No, the debate at this point cannot be overcome unless one side *capitulates* and if this happens, a significant change will have occurred. In my debate with the Lutheran student, if he were to have changed his position, he would have no longer rightly been called Lutheran. So much is bound up with the Lord's Supper for Lutherans that for the student to change his position would be, in essence, to reject the Lutheran view all the way down. Ecumenical debates are enabled by consensus on the broad strokes of the redemptive narrative, but at the same time conflicts are often over the details of that same story, and those details are often constitutive of a particular tradition's identity. Having said all this, the question of relativism is beginning to loom large. If things are as I argue, then how can we not say that everything is just relativistic? The Lutherans have their interpretation and the Presbyterians have theirs, how is this not relativism?

THE PROBLEM OF RELATIVISM

The question of relativism comes from a confusion predicated on two related assumptions. First, relativism is a concept that depends upon foundationalism for its existence. As the logic of foundationalism goes, if there are no universal foundations, then there are no foundations whatsoever and as a matter of consequence, truth goes out the window. The issue is

---

14. On the flip side, Lutherans are often annoyed and confounded by Catholic and Reformed descriptions of their position as consubstantiation. This happens precisely because the other two camps understand and interpret the Lutheran position according to categories that are distinctively not Lutheran.

The Problem of Relativism and Other Lingering Questions

fundamentally epistemological and is over whether some claim can be judged to be true or not. For foundationalists, their assumption—their "Cartesian anxiety"[15]—is that in order for something to be true (or false) there must be some norm or standard that can adjudicate between competing positions no matter the context or disputants; some measure that cannot be questioned, to which everyone must submit, and by which a decisive and clear ruling will be made. If there is no such measure, then how can we possibly ever know the truth? How can we ever determine who is right and who is wrong, what is true and what is false? The phrase "truth is relative" conjures up the notion that if there is no measure by which we can all agree, then some things may be true for you and other things are true for me, but they don't have to be true for both of us. What naturally follows (so it assumed by foundationalists) from this so-called abandonment of truth is nothing short of anarchy and the breakdown of society. Both foundationalism and antifoundationalism believe in truth. The conflict, as I have previously argued, is not whether there is such a thing as truth or not, it is over where constraints reside for determining the validity of truth claims. It just goes without saying, that some claims are true and some are false and some interpretations of the world are better than others. But the measure of whether a claim is true or false is with standards that are particular and local, not universal and objective.

A second assumption behind foundationalism's concern over relativism could be articulated this way: if there is no measure or standard that is context free for adjudicating claims then this means, as a matter of course, that we get to pick, *that we are free to choose,* whatever we want to be true, like a shopper in a mall. Antifoundationalists are no more at liberty to choose what is true or false than foundationalists, it is rather that we recognize that what is constraining our truth claims are local constraints, not universal ones. Relativism is only possible if I were to concede that there are no such things as constraints and that we are, at one time or another, free to interpret without constraints—*a position to which only a foundationalist could ascribe.* Of course, there are those who willfully try to create novel readings of texts, but this sort of relativism is not the *de facto* interpretive position after the demise of foundationalism. In fact, this sort of activity cannot be described as interpretation at all. When a person engages in the activity of interpretation she is trying to figure out the author's intended meaning. But to engage in self-consciously trying to find novel readings of

---

15 Bernstein, *Beyond Objectivism and Relativism.*

a text is not interpretation at all, it's rewriting or creating a new text. This of course happens frequently, but such activities do not serve as evidence that my account is relativistic.

Let's return to my example with the divinity student and the Lord's Supper. As a member of the Presbyterian community I am not persuaded by the student's appeals to grammar and cannot accept his interpretation of the text, even when his best evidence is presented to me because I am in the grip of my Presbyterian tradition. I have a set of interpretive strategies that happen to be different than Lutheran ones, at least when it comes to the Lord's Supper. In fact, my interpretation is rightly construed as also being literal, obvious, and correct (but not by Lutherans or any other group that does not hold to the same understanding of the redemptive narrative). This does not make the point that what we are left with is relativism. No one in the debate is interpreting according to whatever whim they fancy. The two traditions are constrained by a number of different assumptions they hold in common: the assumption that Jesus is Lord, the authority of Scripture as the rule and norm for doctrine, the creeds as authoritative doctrinal statements, and the shared Churchly context of the redemptive narrative of Jesus. All these things constrain the terms of the debate and the two traditions cannot step outside of these constraints, without ceasing to make Christian arguments. It is not the case then that there are no constraints on interpretation or that there is no norm or standard for judging interpretations or that the two groups are interpreting however they want. None of this is happening. What is in conflict is the understanding of the redemptive narrative, which is another way of saying that there is a disagreement over what the author's intended meaning is.

So how then are the conflicting positions on the Lord's Supper not relativistic? This is just another way of asking how we can determine who is actually right. If we no longer have universal standards and measures to which an appeal can be made (like a Scriptural text with determinate textual meaning) then how do we settle the debate? The foundationalist fear is that if we take antifoundationalism seriously, then people will interpret things according to their own particular Christian tradition and everything in turn will just become rhetoric. And they would be right. The point however, is not that everything since the overthrowing of the Enlightenment and its assumptions *just suddenly became rhetoric*—as if we have now somehow fallen from the pursuit of truth—it is that all interpretations are enabled by and are the result of particular view points and this is all they

The Problem of Relativism and Other Lingering Questions

have ever been, including those of the Enlightenment and its articulation of epistemology, truth, and interpretation.

One of the major problems facing foundationalist critiques of my account is the ability to demonstrate not only what a neutral and universal truth looks like, but also how to speak of it *in a neutral, unbiased, and universal way*. In order to do this they would need to be able to speak without recourse to their own personal positions, interpretations, and representations in place. What is needed then is a neutral language that is universal to all people, the definitive *Esperanto* that has yet to be devised. The problem of course, is that no neutral observation language exists and all attempts at creating one have failed.[16] The fact that we even use language—languages that have arisen out of particular contexts—points to the problem foundationalists face of even beginning to report on neutral facts that are perspective-free. "Whatever reports a particular language (natural or artificial) offers us will be the report on the world as it is seen from within some particular situation; there is no other aperspectival way to see and no language other than a situation-dependent language—an interested, rhetorical language—in which to report."[17] The notion of a person seeking after and reporting on truth that is uninflected, neutral, and devoid of a point of view is simply fantasy. Of course, a new twist on this is that some have claimed to be able to report an objective fact, from a subjective point of view (a la Vanhoozer and his "postfoundationalism"), but this just seems all the more confused. How would you know the fact is "objective" if you are reporting on it from a particular point of view? We can never get away from our structure of assumptions, which means we can never get away from rhetoric and arguing from a contextualized point of view. This means that all conflicts, like the conflict between Presbyterians and Lutherans over the Lord Supper, are really matters of force.

By the term "force" what I mean is a conflict of one structure of assumptions against another—or in the case of the debate on the Lord's Supper, one tradition against another—as one doctrine vies for prominence or authority over another. Force can literally mean "at gun point," but it can also mean—and these are the more typical varieties—acts of persuasion, the citing of evidence, thoughtful arguments, or two competing descriptions of the world. Returning to my debate over the Lord's Supper, the conflict resulted in the student trying to *force* me to change my position.

16. Kuhn, *Structure of Scientific Revolutions*, 126–27.
17. Fish, "Rhetoric," 488.

He cited evidence and authorities, he appealed to the grammar of the text, but it did not change his position from being an invested position (just like my Presbyterian position) that he was trying to "force" me to accept. We have no choice but to follow our interpretive assumptions because they themselves are enabling the way we see the world. It could be said then that force comprises our very identities, but force in this sense should not be understood as "mere" force, as in a mindless act of violence. Force is always connected with a point of view and is at work when we argue against other positions.

What we are left with is not relativism, but rather a situation where one point of view vies for prominence and authority over another. Another way of speaking about this is to say that all interpretations, all claims of fact and truth are inherently political. Such debates are political in the sense that they are not a principled ("principled" in the sense of ascension to a neutral position) debate, but rather the particular viewpoint of a group that is in conflict with the viewpoint of a different group. It is a battle where one interpretation seeks to dislodge or overturn a conflicting interpretation. In the case of Lutherans and Presbyterians, the two traditions cannot agree to change their position because they do not see the world in the same way. For either tradition to change its position would be for it to fundamentally change its identity and its way of conceiving of the world. This is not the same thing as simply losing a debate because an opposing position was more popular or because the force used to win was literally a gun. Even in such situations, the losing point of view will still be firmly in place, as the losing party in any election will tell you.

"Ok, fair enough," you say, "but still, how do we determine who is right and wrong in the debate between Lutherans and Presbyterians?" I am afraid my answer will not be very fulfilling for foundationalists. As there has been no undisputed winner for the last five hundred years, there will continue to be no winner until the eschaton comes in full and Jesus settles the debate. By saying as much, I do not concede Lutherans their position on the Lord's Supper, but I do rightly concede them their place in the Church. I have no issue with calling my Lutheran colleagues brothers, sister, mothers and fathers in the faith, even as I have serious disagreement with them over an important topic of doctrine. What gives unity to both Presbyterians and Lutherans is not doctrinal or interpretational uniformity (I don't even have that with fellow Presbyterians); it is the same Lord Jesus who has bestowed us both with the same Holy Spirit. While I will argue vigorously for the

The Problem of Relativism and Other Lingering Questions

Presbyterian position, I must wait until the second coming of Christ for either vindication or capitulation on my part. This is just what it is to be human, contextualized, and affected by sin.

Bibliography

Allen, Diogenes. *Philosophy for Understanding Theology*. Louisville: Westminster John Knox, 1985.
Barth, Karl. *Church Dogmatics*. 4 vols. Translated by G. W. Bromiley. London: T. & T. Clark, 2004.
Behr, John. *The Way to Nicaea*. Vol. 1, *Formation of Christian Theology*. Crestwood, NY: St. Vladimir's Seminary Press, 2001.
Berger, Peter L. *The Sacred Canopy: Elements of a Sociological Theory of Religion*. New York: Anchor, 1967.
Berger, Peter, and Thomas Luckman. *The Social Construction of Reality: A Treatise in The Sociology of Knowledge*. Garden City, NY: Doubleday, 1966.
Bernstein, Richard J. *Beyond Objectivism and Relativism: Science, Hermeneutics and Praxis*. Philadelphia: University of Pennsylvania Press, 1983.
Blond, Philip. "Theology Before Philosophy." In *Post-Secular Philosophy: Between Philosophy and Theology*, edited by Philip Blond, 1–66. London: Routledge, 1998.
Brown, Dan. *The DaVinci Code*. New York: Doubleday, 2003.
Calvin, John. *Institutes of the Christian Religion*. 2 vols. Translated by Ford Lewis Battles. Philadelphia: Westminster, n.d.
Cavanaugh, William T. *Migrations of the Holy: God, State, and the Political Meaning of the Church*. Grand Rapids: Eerdmans, 2011.
Charry, Ellen. *By the Renewing of Your Minds: The Pastoral Function of Christian Doctrine*. New York: Oxford University Press, 1997.
Christian, William A. *Doctrines of Religious Communities: A Philosophical Study*. New Haven, CT: Yale University Press, 1987.
Clapp, Rodney. *A Peculiar People: The Church as Culture in A Post-Christian Society*. Downers Grove, IL: InterVarsity, 1996.
Davidson, Donald. "A Nice Derangement of Epitaphs." In *Truth, Language, and History*, 89–107. Oxford: Clarendon, 2005.
Descartes, Rene. *Meditations on First Philosophy*. Translated by Elizabeth S. Haldane and G. R. T. Ross. Chicago: Encyclopaedia Britannica, 1955.
Dworkin, Ronald. "Law as Interpretation." *Critical Inquiry* 9 (1982) 179–200.
Edwards, James. *The Plain Sense of Things: The Fate of Religion in an Age of Normal Nihilism*. University Park, PA: Pennsylvania State University Press, 1997.
Ehrman, Bart. *Lost Christianities: Books that Did NOT Make It into the Canons*. Oxford: Oxford University Press, 2003.
Endo, Shusako. *Silence*. Translated by William Johnston. New York: Taplinger, 1980.
Fish, Stanley. *Doing What Comes Naturally: Change, Rhetoric, and the Practice of Theory in Literary and Legal Studies*. Durham, NC: Duke University Press, 1989.
———. *Is There a Text in This Class? The Authority of Interpretive Communities*. Cambridge: Harvard University Press, 1980.

Bibliography

———. *The Trouble With Principle*. Cambridge, MA: Harvard University Press, 1999.
———. *There's No Such Things As Free Speech and It's a Good Thing, Too*. Oxford: Oxford University Press, 1994.
Forde, Gerhard O. *Theology Is For Proclamation*. Minneapolis: Augsburg, 1990.
Fowl, Stephen E. *Engaging Scripture: A Model for Theological Interpretation*. Challenges in Contemporary Theology. Oxford: Blackwell, 1998.
Frei, Hans W. *Types of Christian Theology*. Edited by George Hunsinger et al. New Haven, CT: Yale University Press, 1992.
Gadamer, Hans-Georg. "Reflections on My Philosophical Journey." In *The Philosophy of Hans-Georg Gadamer*, edited by Lewis E. Hahn, 3–63. Chicago: Open Court, 1996.
———. *Truth and Method*. Translated by Joel Weinsheimer et al. New York: Crossroad, 1989.
Geertz, Clifford. *The Interpretation of Cultures*. New York: Basic, 1973.
Grenz, Stanley J. *Reason for Hope: The Systematic Theology of Wolfhart Pannenberg*. 2nd ed. Grand Rapids: Eerdmans, 2005.
Griffiths, Paul J. *Problems of Religious Diversity*. Oxford: Blackwell, 2001.
———. "The Properly Christian Response to Religious Plurality." *Anglican Theological Review* 79:1 (1997) 3–26.
Hammer, Olav, editor. *Alternative Christs*. Cambridge: Cambridge University Press, 2009.
Hauerwas, Stanley. *Unleashing the Scriptures: Freeing the Bible from Captivity to America*. Nashville: Abingdon, 1993.
Heidegger, Martin. *Being and Time*. Translated by John Macquarrie et al. New York: Harper & Row, 1962.
Hirsch, E. D. *Validity in Interpretation*. New Haven, CT: Yale University Press, 1967.
Hodge, Charles. *Systematic Theology*. 3 vols. Grand Rapids: Eerdmans, 1997.
Holmer, Paul. *The Grammar of Faith*. San Francisco: Harper & Row, 1978.
Hurtado, Larry W. *At The Origins of Christian Worship: The Context and Character of Earliest Christian Devotion*. Grand Rapids: Eerdmans, 2000.
Hütter, Reinhard. *Suffering Divine Things: Theology as Church Practice*. Translated by Doug Scott. Grand Rapids: Eerdmans, 2000.
Hyman, Gavin. *The Predicament of Postmodern Theology: Radical Orthodoxy or Nihilist Textualism?* Louisville: Westminster John Knox, 2001.
Irenaeus, Saint, Bishop of Lyon. *Against the Heresies*. Ancient Christian Writers 1. Edited by Walter J. Burghardt et al. Translated by Dominic J. Unger. New York: Paulist, 1992.
———. *On the Apostolic Preaching*. Translated by John Behr. Crestwood, NY: St. Vladimir's Seminary Press, 1997.
Jenson, Robert. *Systematic Theology*. 2 vols. New York: Oxford University Press, 1997–99.
Kant, Immanuel. *Critique of Pure Reason*. In *Kant's Critiques*, 6–383. Radford, VA: A. & D., 2008.
Kavanagh, Aidan. *On Liturgical Theology*. Collegeville, MN: Liturgical, 1992.
Kelly, J. N. D. *Early Christian Creeds*. 3rd ed. London: Longman, 1972.
Kelsey, David H. *The Uses of Scripture in Modern Theology*. Philadelphia: Fortress, 1975.
Knapp, Steven, and Walter Benn Michaels. "Against Theory." In *Against Theory: Literary Studies and the New Pragmatism*, edited by W. J. T. Mitchell, 11–30. Chicago: University of Chicago Press, 1982.
———. *Against Theory 2: Sentence Meaning, Hermeneutics*. Berkeley, CA: The Center For Hermeneutical Studies in Hellenistic and Modern Culture, 1986.

Kuhn, Thomas S. *The Essential Tension: Selected Studies in Scientific Tradition and Change.* Chicago: University of Chicago Press, 1979.
———. *The Structure of Scientific Revolutions.* 3rd ed. Chicago: University of Chicago Press, 1996.
Latour, Bruno. *We Have Never Been Modern.* Translated by Catherine Porter. New York: Harvester Wheatsheaf, 1993.
Lindbeck, George. *The Nature of Doctrine: Religion and Theology in a Postliberal Age.* Louisville: Westminster John Knox, 1984.
Lindsell, Harold. *The Battle for the Bible.* Grand Rapids: Zondervan, 1976.
Louth, Andrew. *Early Christian Writings: The Apostolic Fathers.* Rev. ed. London: Penguin, 1987.
Luther, Martin. "On the Councils and the Church, 1539." In *Luther's Works*, edited by Eric W. Gritsch, American Edition, vol. 41.3. Philadelphia: Fortress, 1966.
MacIntyre, Alasdair. *After Virtue: A Study in Moral Theory.* 2nd ed. Notre Dame, IN: University of Notre Dame Press, 1984.
Magee, Bryan. *Confessions of a Philosopher: A Personal Journey Through Western Philosophy, From Plato to Popper.* New York: The Modern Library, 1997.
McClendon, William James. *Systematic Theology.* 3 vols. Nashville: Abingdon, 1986.
McGrath, Alister E. *The Genesis of Doctrine: A Study in the Foundation of Doctrinal Criticism.* Grand Rapids: Eerdmans, 1990.
Milbank, John. *Theology and Social Theory: Beyond Secular Reason.* 1st ed. Oxford: Blackwell, 1990.
Milbank, John, et al. *Radical Orthodoxy: A New Theology.* London: Routlege, 1999.
Nafzger, Peter H. "These Are Written: Toward a Cruciform Theology of Scripture." PhD diss., Concordia Seminary, 2009.
Nagel, Thomas. *The View From Nowhere.* New York: Oxford University Press, 1986.
Newbigin, Lesslie. *Proper Confidence: Faith, Doubt and Certainty in Christian Discipleship.* Grand Rapids: Eerdmans, 1995.
Nietzsche, Fredrick. "The Twilight of The Idols." In *The Portable Nietzsche*, edited and translated by Walter Kaufman. New York: Penguin, 1976.
———. *The Will to Power.* Translated by Walter Kaufmann et al. New York: Random House, 1967.
Okamoto, Joel P. "Scriptures and their Uses." Unpublished lecture, Concordia Seminary, St. Louis, Missouri, 2010.
———. "The Emerging Church and the Postmodern World: Reflections on The Emerging Church Movement and It's Relationship To Postmodernity." Unpublished paper, Concordia Seminary, St. Louis, Missouri, 2008.
———. "Theology And The Life of the Church." Unpublished lecture, Concordia Seminary, St. Louis, 2010.
Pagels, Elaine. *The Gnostic Gospels.* New York: Random House, 1979.
Payton, James R. *Getting the Reformation Wrong: Correcting Some Misunderstandings.* Downers Grove, IL: InterVarsity, 2010.
Pannenberg, Wolfhart. *Systematic Theology.* 3 vols. Translated by Geoffrey W. Bromiley. Grand Rapids: Eerdmans, 1991.
Phillips, D. Z. "Lindbeck's Audience." *Modern Theology* 4 (1988) 133–54.
Pickstock, Catherine. "Duns Scotus: His Historical and Contemporary Significance." *Modern Theology* 21:4 (2005) 544–74.

Bibliography

Placher, William C. "Paul Ricoeur and Postliberal Theology: A Conflict of Interpretations?" *Modern Theology* 4:1 (1987) 35–52.

———. "Revisionist and Postliberal Theologies and the Public Character of Theology." *The Thomist* 49 (1985) 392–416.

———. *Unapologetic Theology: A Christian Voice in a Pluralistic Conversation*. Louisville: Westminster John Knox, 1989.

Polanyi, Michael. *Personal Knowledge: Towards a Post-Critical Philosophy*. Chicago: University of Chicago Press, 1962.

Rahner, Karl. *Theological Investigations*. 5 vols. Translated by Cornelius Ernst. London: Darton, Longman & Todd, 1961.

Rhees, Rush *Without Answers*. London: Routledge & Kegan Paul, 1969.

Rorty, Richard. *Consequences of Pragmatism*. Minneapolis: University of Minnesota Press, 1982.

———. *Contingency, Irony, and Solidarity*. Cambridge: Cambridge University Press, 1989.

———. *Objectivity, Relativism, and Truth*. Cambridge: Cambridge University Press, 1991.

Saarnivaara, Uuraas. "Written and Spoken Word." *Lutheran Quarterly* 2 (May 1950) 166–79.

Sasse, Hermann. *We Confess*. Translated by Norman Nagel. St. Louis: Concordia, 1999.

Scalia, Antonin. *A Matter of Interpretation: Federal Courts and The Law*. Princeton, NJ: Princeton University Press, 1998.

Schmemann, Alexander. *Liturgy and Tradition: Theological Reflections of Alexander Schmemann*. Edited by Thomas Fisch. Crestwood, NY: St. Vladimir's Seminary Press, 2003.

Schopenhaeur, Arthur. *The World as Will and Representation*. 2 vols. Translated by E. F. J. Payne. New York: Dover, 1966.

Scott, Richard G. "Jesus Christ, Our Redeemer." *Ensign* (May 1997) 53–59.

Smith, Christian. *The Bible Made Impossible: Why Biblicism Is Not a Truly Evangelical Reading of Scripture*. Grand Rapids: Brazos, 2011.

Smith, James K. A., *Desiring the Kingdom: Worship, Worldview, and Cultural Formation*. Grand Rapids: Baker, 2009.

Stout, Jeffrey. *The Flight From Authority: Religion, Morality, and the Quest for Autonomy*. Notre Dame, IN: University of Notre Dame Press, 1981.

The Lutheran World Federation and the Roman Catholic Church. *Joint Declaration on The Doctrine of Justification*. Grand Rapids: Eerdmans, 2000.

Thiemann, Ronald F. "Intratextuality and Speaking of God: A Response to George Lindbeck." *Theology Today* 43:3 (1986) 377–382.

Thiselton, Anthony C. *The Hermeneutics of Doctrine*. Grand Rapids: Eerdmans, 2007.

———. "Two Types of Postmodernity: 'Signs of the Times': Towards a Theology for the Year 2000 as a Grammar of Grace, Truth, and Eschatology in Contexts of So-Called Postmodernity." In *Thiselton on Hermeneutics: Collected Works with New Essays*, 581–606. Grand Rapids: Eerdmans, 2006.

Tompkins, Jane, editor. *Reader-Response Criticism: From Formalism to Post-Structuralism*. Baltimore: Johns Hopkins University Press, 1980.

Torrance, T. F. "The Word of God and the Response of Man." In *God and Rationality*. Oxford: Oxford University Press, 1971. Quoted in John Webster. *Holy Scripture: A Dogmatic Sketch*. Cambridge: Cambridge University Press, 2003.

Tracy, David. "Lindbeck's New Program for Theology." *The Thomist* 49 (1985) 460–72.

Vanhoozer, Kevin J. *The Drama of Doctrine: A Canonical-Linguistic Approach to Christian Theology*. Louisville: Westminster John Knox, 2005.

———. *Is There a Meaning in This Text? The Bible, The Reader, and the Morality of Literary Knowledge*. Grand Rapids: Zondervan, 1998.

Voelz, James W. *What Does This Mean? Principles of Biblical Interpretation in the Post-Modern World*. St. Louis: Concordia, 1997.

Webster, John. *Holy Scripture: A Dogmatic Sketch*. Cambridge: Cambridge University Press, 2003.

Wittgenstein, Ludwig. *The Blue and Brown Books*. New York: Harper, 1958.

———. *Philosophical Investigations*. Translated by G. E. M. Anscombe. New York: Macmillan, 1953.

Wright, N. T. *Jesus and the Victory of God*. Minneapolis: Fortress, 1996.

———. *The Last Word: Scripture and The Authority of God—Getting Beyond The Bible Wars*. New York: HarperCollins, 2005.

Wolterstorff, Nicolas. *Divine Discourse: Philosophical Reflections on The Claim That God Speaks*. Cambridge: Cambridge University Press, 1995.

———. *Reason Within The Bounds of Religion*. 2nd ed. Grand Rapids: Eerdmans, 1984.

Wood, Charles. "The Aim of Christian Theology." *Perkins Journal* 31:3 (1978) 22–29.

Yoder, John Howard. *The Politics of Jesus: Vicit Agnus Noster*. 2nd ed. Grand Rapids: Eerdmans, 1994.

———. *The Priestly Kingdom: Social Ethics as Gospel*. Notre Dame: University of Notre Dame Press, 1984.

———. *The Royal Priesthood: Essay Ecclesiastical and Ecumenical*. Edited by Michael G. Cartwright. Scottdale, PA: Herald, 1998.

Young, Frances. *Biblical Exegesis and the Formation of Christian Culture*. Peabody, MA: Hendrickson, 2002.

———. *The Making of the Creeds*. London: SCM, 1991.

Index

Allen, Diogenes, 34n38
antifoundationalism, xi, 42, 116–22, 130, 133, 169–70
antirepresentationalism, 61, 63
Athanasius, 108–9, 115, 135, 157
authorial intention, 24, 44–53, 70,

Barth, Karl, 84, 101
Behr, John, 86–87, 106–7, 129
beliefs, 21–22, 24–26, 34, 37, 52–54, 59, 61, 63, 68n60, 73–79, 117–22, 133–34, 136–38
Berger, Peter, 22, 121
Bernstein, Richard, 169
Bible (Scripture)
    authority, 65–70, 83–114
    inerrancy, 88, 90–92
    infallibility, 89
    inspiration, 88–89, 89n15, 91–93
Blond, Philip, 33n29, 33n32
Brown, Dan, 87n11

Calvin, John, 94
canon
    as collection of books in Bible, 86, 97, 100, 151
    dianoia (Athanasius, mind of Scripture), 108–11, 115, 135
    process of canonization, 94
    regula fidei (Irenaeus and rule for reading Scripture), 13, 73, 106–14, 115, 135
Cavanaugh, William, 154n5
Charry, Ellen, 138n40
Christian, William, 1, 7, 83–85
Christus est Dominus, 58–59

Church
    definition of, 126–30
    context for doctrine, 130–36, 153–55
Clapp, Rodney, 154
Constantiniasm, 32n28, 39, 153–55
context
    definition of, 130–34
    the Church's redemptive narrative, 134–36
contingency, 30, 38, 41–42, 74, 79
creeds and confessions
    function of, 3–7, 136, 140,
    Definition of Chalcedon, 144–46
    Lutheran Confessions, 160–63
    Nicene Creed, 136, 143–47, 151, 156
    Westminster Confession of Faith, 77, 84, 136, 163–67

Davidson, Donald, 22, 61, 63, 121
Dawkins, Richard, 22
deconstructionism, 19, 25
Descartes, Rene, 10, 17, 27, 33–39, 43, 61–62, 79
determinate textual meaning, 72, 80, 109, 111, 115, 122, 150–51, 157, 170
doctrine
    disagreement, 55, 72, 80, 150–73
    intrasystematic, 13, 57, 59
    intratextuality, 93
    nature of doctrine,
        first-order use, x, 14, 57–58, 60, 62, 64, 138–48

Index

doctrine, nature of doctrine (*cont.*)
   second-order use, 14, 55–57, 138, 142
   regulative/rule, 11, 13, 55, 57–58, 137, 141–42,
Dworkin, Ronald, 22

Edwards, James, 17–18, 21, 27–40, 33n31
Ehrman, Bart, 87n11
Endo, Shusako, 72n72
Enlightenment, 14, 19–20, 26, 82, 171
epistemology, 10, 33, 36, 38, 50, 54, 58, 67, 121–22, 169, 171

Fish, Stanley, x, 10–11, 22–26, 42, 52, 68, 70, 80, 118–21, 130, 132, 137, 149, 153, 171
Forde, Gerhard, 138–40
formalist, 23, 47, 65, 69–71, 73
foundationalism, x–xi, 10–11, 14–16, 17, 19–23, 26–30, 32–33, 38–40, 41–44, 51–54, 57, 61, 64–65, 67–68, 73, 79–82, 86–87, 116–18, 149–50, 168
Fowl, Stephen, 93, 106
Frei, Hans, 151

Gadamer, Hans-Georg, 74n75
Geertz, Clifford, 22, 121
God Delusion Debates, 22
Grenz, Stanley, 124–25
Griffiths, Paul, 1, 7, 18, 137

Hammer, Olav, 92n16
Hauerwas, Stanley, 111, 149
Heidegger, Martin, 21
Hirsch, E. D., 46–48, 51, 53, 70, 115
Holmer, Paul, 135, 142, 146
Hurtado, Larry, 6n15
Hütter, Reinhard, 66n54
Hyman, Gavin, 117–18

idealism (epistemological), 53, 61–62
interpretation, 6, 16, 19, 21–25, 37–38, 43–57, 64–88, 105–14, 115–18, 120, 124–27, 130–36, 149–53, 155, 157–60, 167–72
interpretive community, 53, 66, 132–33, 135, 153
Irenaeus, 6, 84–85, 106–09, 115, 135

Jenson, Robert, 128
Jesus, 1–7, 15–16, 29, 58, 66n56, 67–68, 72, 75–78, 90–97, 99–108, 110–16, 122–30, 133–38, 140–51, 153–66, 168, 170, 172

Kant, Immanuel, 11, 17, 28, 36–38, 61–62, 120–22, 130
Kavanaugh, Aidan, 139, 147
Kelly, J. N. D., 6, 144
Kelsey, David, 84, 93
Knapp and Michaels, x, 22, 42, 45–48, 50–51, 53, 64
Kuhn, Thomas, 22, 121, 171

Latour, Bruno, 27n14
Lennox, John, 22
liberalism, 19n4
liberal/conservative dichotomy, 9–10, 57, 155
Lindbeck, George, ix–xi, 2, 7–15, 26, 42, 54–62, 64–66, 68, 72–73, 76, 81, 93, 116, 127, 136–38, 141, 149, 168
Lindsell, Harold, 89
Lord's Supper, 16, 71, 127, 148, 151–52, 158–73
Louth, Andrew, 6
Luther, Martin, 59–60, 101, 103–4, 126–28

MacIntyre, Alasdair, 121
Magee, Bryan, 122

182

McClendon, William, 35n39
McGrath, Alister, 7
metaphysics (death of), 38–39, 63
Milbank, John, 33n32, 35
modernism, 117–18
mood, 10, 19, 21–22, 25–26, 81, 116–17, 122, 125
Moore, Roy, 155n7
Mormonism, 146, 155–58, 160

Nafzger, Peter, 88–89, 93, 101–4, 112
Nagel, Thomas, 36
Newbigin, Lesslie, 125
Nietzsche, Fredrick, 17, 22, 36–39, 63
nihilism, 38–40, 42–43

Okamoto, Joel, 66n56, 97, 100, 139, 141, 146–47

Pagels, Elaine, 87n11
Payton, James, 77n80
Pannenberg, Wolfhart, 2, 79, 124–25
Pelikan, Jaroslav, 1
Phillips, D. Z., 55
Pickstock, Catherine, 32n29
Placher, William, 7–8, 20, 81–82
Plato
    Idealism, 29, 31–33, 38–39
    Neo-Platonism, 32
    Platonism, 28, 33, 36
Polanyi, Michael, 22, 119n7, 121
postfoundationalism, 15, 68, 171
Postliberalism, 57, 66, 93
postmodernism, 6, 19, 66, 79–80, 93, 117–18

Radical Orthodoxy, 32n29, 33n32
Rahner, Karl, 74
realism, 53, 61–62, 64, 67–68,
relativism, x, 16, 25, 37, 39, 41–42, 52, 57, 61–62, 64–65, 79–82, 117, 149–73

representationalism, 38–39, 52, 61–64, 80
Rhees, Rush, 58–59
rhetoric, 170–71
Rorty, Richard, 22, 61–64, 80, 82, 121–22

Saarnivaara, Uuraas, 104
Sasse, Hermann, 123–24
Scalia, Antonin, 24
Schmemann, Alexander, 4
Schopenhauer, Arthur, 121
self-consciousness, 38–39, 52–56, 77, 169
Scott, Richard, 157
Smith, Christian, 71n68
Smith, James K. A., 5n12
Stout, Jeffrey, 22, 121

text vs. reader dichotomy, 23, 69–70, 76, 86–87, 96, 106, 129
textualist, 23, 68
textual meaning, 23–24, 44–52, 69, 71, 130, 151, 157
theory
    as a special project of foundationalism, 42–52
    antifoundationalist theory typology, 52–54
    theory hope and Lindbeck, 54–65
    theory fear and Vanhoozer, 65–73
    theory hermeneutics and Thiselton, 73–81
theory of religion,
    cultural-linguistic theory or religion, 8–14, 54–55, 57, 64–67
    canonical-linguistic theory of religion, 8, 65–67
    cognitive-propositionalist theory of religion, 9–12, 62, 142

Index

theory, theory of religion (*cont.*)
   experiential-expressivist
     theory of religion, 9–13,
     62, 65, 142
Thiemann, Ronald, 8
Thiselton, Anthony, x–xi, 5, 7–8, 42, 63, 73–81, 89, 110, 113, 116, 122, 149
Tompkins, Jane, 22
Torrance, T. F., 129
Tracy, David, 7–8
transcontextual reasonableness, 80–81, 150

Vanhoozer, Kevin, x–xi, 8, 42, 63, 65–73, 76–77, 80–81, 86, 88, 113, 116, 122, 149, 151–52, 171, 179
Voelz, James, 110–11, 135

wave poem (Knapp and Michaels), 48–50
Webster, John, 93n20, 94, 113, 126–27, 129
Western Religiousness
   definition of, 17–21, 27–29
   age of the gods, 29–30
   age of the forms, 30–33
   age of Cartesian ego-subjectivity, 33–35
   age of transvalued values, 35–40
Wissenschaft, 20, 127
Wittgenstein, Ludwig, 12, 22, 36n41, 61–62, 79, 82, 121
Wright, N. T., 95, 97–98, 100–101
Wolterstorff, Nicolas, 43–44, 95n24, 102
Wood, Charles, 141

Yoder, John Howard, 32n28, 153–54
Young, Frances, 3–5, 108–9, 126

www.ingramcontent.com/pod-product-compliance
Lightning Source LLC
Chambersburg PA
CBHW051742230426
43670CB00012B/2124